*FROM*
*CULTURE*
*TO*
*POWE*

# FROM CULTURE TO POWER

## The Sociology of English Canada

*Robert J. Brym*
*with Bonnie J. Fox*

Toronto  OXFORD UNIVERSITY PRESS  1989

Oxford University Press, 70 Wynford Drive, Don Mills, Ontario, M3C 1J9

Toronto  Oxford  New York  Delhi  Bombay  Calcutta  Madras  Karachi
Petaling Jaya  Singapore  Hong Kong  Tokyo  Nairobi  Dar es Salaam
Cape Town  Melbourne  Auckland

and associated companies in
Berlin  Ibadan

CANADIAN CATALOGUING IN PUBLICATION DATA

Brym, Robert J., 1951–
From culture to power

(Studies in Canadian sociology)
Bibliography: p.
Includes index.
ISBN 0-19-540689-3

1. Canada – Social conditions.  2. Sociology –
Canada.  I. Fox, Bonnie, 1948–  .  II. Title.
III. Series.

HM22.C3B79 1989        306'.0971        C88-095285-7

*For Rhonda, Shira, and Talia*
—R.B.

*For John*
—B.F.

# Contents

# Figures and Tables

# Acknowledgements

This book benefitted from the thoughtful criticism and advice of many people. Robert Brym is indebted to Hyacinth Irving, Rhonda Lenton, Seymour Martin Lipset, Dennis Magill, John Myles, Julia O'Connor, Rick Ogmundson, and Michael Shalev. Bonnie Fox thanks Karen Anderson, Elaine Brimley, William Carroll, Patricia Connelly, John Fox, Harriet Friedmann, Parvin Ghorayshi, Sedef Koc, Meg Luxton, Barbara Neis, and Ester Reiter for helpful comments and criticisms on Chapter 5. We are both especially grateful to Michael Ornstein, whose ideas have influenced our thinking on several key issues. We also thank Richard Teleky and Sally Livingston of Oxford University Press, who worked diligently to improve our typescript.

We acknowledge permission to reprint material from the following articles by Robert Brym: 'Social movements and third parties', in S. Berkowitz, ed., *Models and Myths in Canadian Sociology* (Toronto: Butterworths Canada, 1984) pp. 29-49; 'The Canadian capitalist class, 1965-1985', in R. Brym, ed., The *Structure of the Canadian Capitalist Class* (Toronto: Garamond, 1985), pp. 1-20; 'Anglo-Canadian sociology', *Current Sociology* (34,1: 1986), pp. 1-152; 'Foundations of sociological theory', in L. Tepperman and J. Curtis, eds, *Readings in Sociology: An Introduction* (Toronto: McGraw-Hill Ryerson, 1988), pp. 4-12; and 'Canada', in T. Bottomore and R. Brym, eds, *The Capitalist Class: An International Study* (New York: New York University Press, 1989) pp. 177-206.

# Introduction

This book is a study of the main controversies that have animated sociology in English Canada since the 1960s. Its focus is analytical, not descriptive. In the following pages one can certainly find hard data about Canada's economic development and underdevelopment, about inequalities that derive from class, gender, region, and ethnicity, and about the social bases of politics. But the book is no mere catalogue of facts. Rather, it is a critical evaluation of the radically different ways in which basic features of Canadian society have been interpreted by English-Canadian sociologists.

The present work originated as a long article commissioned by the editor of *Current Sociology*, the journal of the International Sociological Association (Brym 1986a). I have made it more current than the original by incorporating some research results published in the last three years and by adding a chapter by Bonnie J. Fox on the feminist treatment of social inequality and economic development. I have also tried to make the material accessible to a wider, undergraduate audience by simplifying some sections and by writing a very short introduction to the discipline of sociology itself.

I have delimited my subject in four ways. First, I do not deal with Québécois sociology. English-Canadian and Québécois sociologists form relatively distinct academic communities, each of which has produced substantial bodies of research. Although some overlapping ties exist, members of the two groups tend on the whole to speak different languages and live in separate parts of the country, join their own professional associations and write for different journals, attend separate conferences and adhere to unique intellectual traditions (Curtis, Connor, and Harp 1970; Hiller 1980; Nock 1974; Vallee and Whyte 1968). As a result, I feel that the two sociologies require separate treatment, and that the Quebec experience can be best handled by scholars who know it from the inside (Fournier and Houle 1980; Houle 1987; Maheu and Juteau 1989).

Second, I discuss some research that, in other countries, might not be considered sociological at all. One of the peculiarities of English-Canadian sociology is that it has borrowed rather heavily from other disciplines, especially political economy. I have therefore tried to ensure that my review accurately reflects that debt.

Third, I do not discuss the considerable body of purely micro-sociological research that has been conducted in English Canada. In my view, such work is Canadian only in an incidental sense and is properly thought of as contributing more to a substantive field—socialization, deviance, and the like—than to the study of a certain geographical area. I hope this does not suggest that I will thereby draw attention away from issues of universal concern and focus on matters of exclusively parochial interest. Area studies can contribute quite as much as other types of research to our knowledge of general social processes. But they do so by virtue of their (at least implicit) comparative, macrosociological orientation. Accordingly, sociological research that does not tell us something about how and why Canada is significantly different from, and significantly similar to, other societies has not been reviewed here.

Finally, I review research in only a few substantive fields of sociological inquiry. My choice of fields has been governed mainly by the results of several reports that show where English-Canadian sociologists concentrate their research and teaching efforts (Curtis, Connor, and Harp 1970: 121; Grayson and Magill 1981: 69; Whyte 1984-85: 122). The areas I highlight are among the chief foci of English-Canadian sociologists today. Because I do not have sufficiently detailed knowledge of feminist sociology, one of the major growth areas of English-Canadian sociology in the 1980s, I invited Bonnie Fox, who has done extensive research in the area, to write Chapter 5.

The book's main line of argument runs as follows. In the 1960s sociology became a respectable and institutionalized part of the English-Canadian intellectual landscape. During that decade such important figures in the history of Canadian sociology as John Porter, S.D. Clark, and Seymour Martin Lipset character-ized and explained the main features of Canadian society in remarkably similar terms by comparing Canada with the United States. In brief, they argued that certain historical experiences created a Canadian culture that emphasizes respect for autho-rity, the justification of inequality and lack of upward mobility, ethnic particularism, substantial state involvement in the economy at the expense of entrepreneurial initiative, and so forth (Chapter 1).

For a decade or so the research and speculation of these men engendered considerable debate. By the mid-1970s, however, a sufficient number of serious questions had been raised about their ideas to require a substantial theoretical reorientation and the formulation of radically new characterizations of Canadian society. Many of the generalizations accepted in the 1960s were shown to be empirically inaccurate. Moreover, an alternative framework for interpreting Canadian society became popular. The new paradigm focussed on how social structural features of Canadian society, such as the distribution of power, affect economic, political, and ethnic behaviour largely independently of the influence of culture (Chapters 2, 3, and 4).

From the mid-1970s on, feminist sociologists placed the new structural paradigm itself under increasingly critical scrutiny. Initially feminists argued that the main problem with mainstream sociology was its virtual exclusion of women as subjects of inquiry. For example, analyses of economic inequality and social mobility typically dealt with men in the paid labour force and ignored the important economic roles played by women—not only in the paid labour force, but also in the home. Later, however, feminists broadened their critique considerably. The opinion became widespread that once women were included in sociologists' research agendas, theories of inequality, economic development, politics, and so forth would have to be substantially overhauled (Eichler 1985). And indeed, the feminist critique has begun to alter our interpretation of Canadian society (Chapter 5).

The conceptual matrix of this book, then, is made up of three elements: the interpretations of the chief features of Canadian society that were proferred by the effective founders of English-Canadian sociology; the debates their work generated; and the alternative interpretations that have since been proposed. Before analyzing how these issues have been reflected in each of the substantive fields selected for discussion, it will prove useful to outline the development of sociology in Europe, the US, and English Canada. This I shall now do, in the briefest possible terms.

# 1

# The European and North American Backgrounds

## THE CLASSIC QUESTIONS OF EUROPEAN SOCIOLOGY

The three most important and enduring debates in the history of sociology concern the nature of the relationship between individual and society; the relative importance of economy versus culture in determining social behaviour; and the social bases of inequality. These issues invigorated social discourse in nineteenth-century Europe and, as we shall see, they continue to engage sociologists in English Canada and elsewhere.

The first debate originated at the time of the French Revolution. The revolutionaries were liberals, and they proclaimed liberty, equality before the law, and fraternity as their goals. They believed that the well-being of the French citizenry could be secured if traditional social constraints were eliminated so that people could be free to develop their natural talents. Implicit in this view was the idea that the social standing of the individual should not be fixed at birth; the revolutionaries argued that the individual should be able to rise (or fall) to a position in the social hierarchy that matched his or her talents.

In contrast, their conservative opponents saw the overthrow of the old government and the old ruling class as a grave threat to the well-being of the citizenry. In their view, if the individual were completely free society could not exist. The conservatives thus emphasized how established secular and religious authority, traditional forms of community, and rigid social hierarchy constrain human aspirations and actions, thereby preventing disorganization and anarchy. They also believed that society is not just an agglomeration of individuals, but a real corporate unit that stands over and above the wills of individuals.

## Individual and society in Durkheim

It was out of this conservative ideological animus that sociology first emerged (Nisbet 1943; 1952). Its influence can be clearly seen in the work of Emile Durkheim, who is generally regarded as one of the founding fathers of the discipline. Usually we assume that any act—prayer, marriage, war, revolution—is the outcome of an individual's (or many individuals') motives. Features of society, in turn, are usually viewed as the result of many individual passions and decisions. Durkheim, however, turned this conventional liberal-individualist wisdom on its head. He argued that individual passions and decisions are the result of certain features of society. And the study of how social forces influence individual behaviour is what sociology is all about (Durkheim 1966 [1895]).

Even an act like suicide, which appears to be highly individualistic, anti-social, and wholly determined by one's state of mind, is in fact a socially determined phenomenon, wrote Durkheim. He made his case in part by examining the association between rates of suicide and rates of psychological disorder for different groups. The notion that psychological disorder causes suicide is supported, he reasoned, only if suicide rates tend to be high where rates of psychological disorder are high, and low where rates of psychological disorder are low. But his analysis of European government statistics, hospital records, and other sources revealed nothing of the kind. For example, he discovered that there were slightly more women than men in insane asylums; but there were four male suicides for every female suicide. Jews had the highest rate of psychological disorder among the major religious groups in France; but they also had the lowest suicide rate. Psychological disorders occurred most frequently when a person reached maturity; but suicide rates increased steadily with age.

Clearly, suicide rates and rates of psychological disorder did not vary directly; in fact, they often appeared to vary inversely. Why? Durkheim argued that in modern societies suicide rates vary as a result of differences in the degree of 'social solidarity' in different categories of the population. Accordingly, he expected groups whose members interact more frequently and intensely to exhibit lower suicide rates. For example, Durkheim held that married adults are half as likely as unmarried adults to commit suicide because marriage creates social ties that bind the individual to society. Where these ties are absent, suicide is more likely. In general, he wrote, 'suicide varies with the degree of integration of the social groups of which the individual forms a part' (Durkheim 1951 [1897]: 209). Of course, this generalization tells us nothing about why any particular individual may take his or her life; but it does say something uniquely sociological about why the suicide rate varies from group to group.

## The phenomenological response

Many contemporary sociologists continue to argue that the proper focus of the discipline is the study of social pressures that constrain or influence individuals. Today, using sophisticated statistical techniques, researchers can measure the independent and combined effects of many social variables on many types of behaviour. For nearly a century, however, detractors from the Durkheimian view have been pointing to an important flaw in the theory. They argue that Durkheim paints an altogether too mechanical and deterministic view of the individual in society, depicting people as if they behaved like billiard balls, knocked about on predetermined trajectories, unable to choose to alter their destinations. But we know from our everyday experience that this is not the case. People do make choices—often difficult ones. Moreover, two people with similar social characteristics may react quite differently to similar social circumstances because, according to Durkheim's critics, they may interpret these circumstances differently. In the opinion of such 'phenomenological' sociologists, an adequate explanation of social phenomena requires that we understand the subjective meanings that people attach to social facts and the ways in which they actively create these social facts.

In order better to understand the phenomenological school of thought, let us return to the problem of suicide. If a police officer discovers a dead person at the wheel of a car that has run into a tree, it may be very difficult to establish with certainty whether the death was accidental or suicidal. Interviewing friends and relatives in order to find out the dead person's state of mind immediately before the crash may help to rule out the possibility of suicide. But, as this example illustrates, understanding the intention or motive of the actor is critical to explaining or labelling a social action. Suicide, then, is not just an objective social fact, but an inferred, and therefore subjective, social fact. A state of mind must be interpreted—usually by a coroner—before the dead body becomes a suicide statistic (Douglas 1967).

Some phenomenological sociologists tend to ignore the impact of objective, outside social forces on the lives of men and women, reducing the study of society to an analysis of subjective interactions in small settings: how person A perceives person B's actions, how person A responds to these actions, how B in turn perceives and responds, and so forth (Goffman 1959). Just as one-sidedly, strict Durkheimians ignore the subjective side of social life and draw attention only to objective, outside forces. But many modern sociologists endorse neither extreme. They think it makes more sense to combine the Durkheimian and phenomenological approaches and analyze how men and women interpret, create, and change their social existence within the limits imposed on them by powerful social constraints. This synthetic approach is found in the work of Karl Marx and, to an even greater degree, Max Weber, who, along with Durkheim, established the groundwork of modern sociology. Let us now turn to a brief examination of their work.

### Structure versus culture in Marx

Both Marx and Weber stressed the importance of analyzing subjective social actions and objective social constraints (Marx 1972 [1932]: 118; Weber 1947 [1922]: 103; Gerth and Mills 1946: 57-8). They also had compatible (though different) ideas about the nature of these constraints.

Marx, like Weber, recognized that the external determinants of behaviour consist of economic, political, and cultural forces. Marx tended to assign overwhelming causal priority to the economic realm. Weber did not deny the primacy of economic arrangements, but he rounded out Marx's analysis by showing how the political and cultural facts of life can act as important independent causes of many social phenomena.

In the middle of the nineteenth century Marx proposed a sweeping theory of the development of human societies. In this theory the locus of change is economic organization—more precisely, society's class structure and its technological base. He explained the rise and decline of capitalism as follows.

In European feudal society peasants tilled small plots of land that were owned not by the peasants themselves but by land-lords. Peasants were legally bound to the land, obliged to give their landlords a set proportion of their harvest and to continue working for them under any circumstances. In turn, landlords were expected to protect peasants against marauders and poor economic conditions.

By the late fifteenth century certain processes had been set in motion that eventually transformed feudal society into a modern capitalist system. Most important was the growth of ex-ploration and trade, which increased the demand for many goods and services in commerce, navigation, and industry. By the seventeenth and eighteenth centuries some urban dwellers—successful artisans and merchants—had accumula-ted sufficient capital to expand their production significantly. In order to maximize their profits, these capitalists required an abundant supply of workers who could be hired in periods of high demand and fired without obligation during slack times. It was therefore necessary to induce and coerce indentured peasants from the soil and transform them into legally free workers who would work for wages (Marx and Engels 1972 [1848]: 336 ff.).

In Marx's view, the relations between wage labourers and capitalists at first facilitated rapid technological innovation and economic growth. Capitalists were keen to reorganize the labour process and adopt new tools, machines, and production tech-niques. These changes allowed them to produce more efficient-ly, earn higher profits, and drive their competitors out of busi-ness. Efficiency also required that workers be concentrated in larger and larger industrial establishments, that wages be kept as low as possible, and that as little as possible be invested in im-proving working conditions.[1] Thus, according to Marx, workers and capitalists would stand face-to-face in factory and mine: a large and growing class of relatively impoverished workers opposing a small and shrinking class of increasingly wealthy owners.

Marx argued that in due course all workers would become aware of belonging to the same exploited class. This sense of 'class consciousness' would, he felt, encourage the growth of working-class organizations, such as trade unions and political parties. These organizations would be bent on overthrowing the capitalist system and establishing a classless society. According to Marx, this revolutionary change was bound to occur during one of the recurrent and worsening 'crises of overproduction' characteristic of the capitalist era. The productive capacity of the system would, he said, come to far outstrip the ability of the relatively impoverished workers to purchase goods and services. Hence, in order to sell goods and services, capitalists would be forced to lower their prices. Profits would then fall, the less efficient capitalists would go bankrupt, and massive unemployment of workers would result—thus deepening the economic crisis still further. The capitalist class system had originally encouraged economic growth, but eventually the crises of overproduction it generated would hinder such growth. At that time the capitalist class system would be destroyed and replaced by socialism.

As this thumbnail sketch shows, beliefs, symbols, and values —in short, culture—play a quite minor independent causal role in Marx's theory. He analyzed how, under most circumstances, ruling-class ideology forms a legitimizing cement in society and how, in rare circumstances, subordinate class consciousness can become an important force for change. But in his work it is always the material circumstances of existence that ultimately determine the role ideas play.

## Weber on capitalism and the world religions

Weber, like Marx, was interested in explaining the rise of modern capitalism. And, like Marx, he was prepared to recognize the 'fundamental importance of the economic factor' in his explanation (Weber 1958 [1904-5]: 26). But he was also bent on demonstrating the one-sidedness of any exclusively economic interpretation. After all, the economic conditions that Marx said were necessary for capitalist development existed in Catholic France during the reign of Louis XIV; yet the wealth generated in France by international trade and commerce tended to be consumed by war and the luxurious lifestyle of the aristocracy rather than invested in the growth of capitalist enterprise. For Weber, what prompted vigorous capitalist development in non-Catholic Europe and North America was a combination of propitious economic conditions such as those discussed by Marx and the spread of certain moral values by the Protestant reformers of the sixteenth century and their followers in the seventeenth.

For specifically religious reasons, followers of the Protestant theologian John Calvin stressed the need to engage in intense worldly activity, to demonstrate industry, punctuality, and frugality in one's everyday life. In the view of men like John Wesley and Benjamin Franklin, religious doubts could be reduced, and a state of grace assured, if one worked diligently and lived ascetically. This idea was taken up by Puritanism, Methodism, and other Protestant denominations; Weber called it the 'Protestant work ethic' (Weber 1958 [1904-5]: 183).

According to Weber, this ethic had wholly unexpected economic consequences: where it took root, and where economic conditions were favourable, early capitalist enterprise grew robustly. In other words, two independent developments—the Protestant work ethic (which derived from purely religious considerations) and the material conditions favouring capitalist growth (which derived from specifically economic circumstances) —interacted to invigorate capitalism.

Subsequent research has demonstrated that the association between the Protestant ethic and the strength of capitalist development is weaker than Weber thought (Samuelsson 1961 [1957]). In some places Catholicism has co-existed with vigorous capitalist growth and Protestantism with relative stagnation. Nonetheless, even if Weber was wrong about this particular case, his general view—that religious developments cannot be reduced to economic developments, and that religious ideas have economic consequences—is still widely regarded as a valid insight.

Just as some Marxist sociologists have adopted a strict economic determininsm, some Weberians have misinterpreted Weber's ideas in a way that supports a sort of cultural determinism. But the plain fact is that Weber assigned nearly the same relative weight to economic and cultural forces as did Marx; and there is nothing in Marx's work that is incompatible with Weber's insights into the relative autonomy of religious developments. Disputes between orthodox Marxists and orthodox Weberians over the relative weight of economic versus cultural causes of change may thus be as specious as the disagreement between rigid Durkheimians and phenomenologists.

## The bases of social inequality

Thus far I have singled out areas of similarity or compatibility in the thought of Marx and Weber. In Weber's 'long and intense debate with the ghost of Karl Marx' (Albert Salomon, quoted in Zeitlin 1987 [1968]): xi), however, there also emerged some ideas that are incompatible with those of Marx. Such ideas are especially obvious in Weber's work on social inequality.

Marx regarded ownership or non-ownership of property as the fundamental basis of inequality in capitalist society. In his view, there are two main classes under capitalism. Members of the capitalist class, or bourgeoisie, own means of production but they do not work them. Members of the working class, or proletariat, work but do not own means of production. In addition, Marx discussed some minor classes that are vestiges of pre-capitalist times. Most important, members of the petite bourgeoisie (e.g., farmers, owners of small family businesses) both own and work means of production. Marx also analyzed various divisions within the major classes. These class segments were distinguished from one another by their sources of income (e.g., financial and industrial capitalists) or skill level (e.g., skilled and unskilled manual workers).

In defining classes in this way Marx was not trying to account for gradations of rank in society. Instead, he sought to explain the massive historical change that results from the materially grounded opposition of interests between classes. In his view, the major classes were potentially self-conscious groups engaged in conflict that would eventually result in societal transformation.

Weber agreed that '"property" and "lack of property" are . . . the basic categories of all class situations' (Weber 1946 [1922]: 182), but his analysis of inequality differed from Marx's in three main ways. First, he was profoundly skeptical about Marx's interpretation of historical development. As a result he stressed that members of classes do not necessarily become class-conscious and act in concert. Second, Weber argued that property relations are just one aspect of a more general 'market situation' that determines class position. For example, expertise acquired through formal education is a scarce commodity on the labour market. Such expertise increases one's advantages or 'life-chances' and is therefore an important factor structuring the class system. On this basis, and in addition to the capitalist and manual working classes, Weber distinguished large and growing classes of technical/managerial personnel and white-collar workers who perform routine tasks.

Third, Weber was less concerned than Marx with the sources of conflict between discrete classes and more concerned with the structure of complex social hierarchies. For this reason he showed that the bases of social inequality are not exclusively economic. One non-economic source of inequality is the way honour (or esteem or prestige) is distributed in society. Weber referred to groups distinguished from one another in terms of prestige as status groups. For example, line of descent (including ethnic origin) may account for the level of esteem in which a status group is held, and esteem affects the life-chances of status group members. A second non-economic source of inequality is the political party. A party, in Weber's definition, is an association that seeks to gain control over an organization— ranging all the way from, say, a sports club to a state—for purposes of implementing specific policies. Parties may recruit members from specific classes or status groups, or both. In so doing, and to the degree that they achieve organizational control, parties bestow more advantages on their supporters than on non-supporters.

If parties and status groups are independent bases of social inequality, then, according to Weber, they are not wholly independent, especially in capitalist societies. There is an association between status group and party membership, on the one hand, and class position on the other. The structure of class inequality helps to shape status group and party membership; in fact, 'today the class situation is by far the predominant factor' (Weber 1946 [1922]: 190).

Much of modern sociology has been devoted to exploring the ramifications of Weber's refinement of Marx's stratification model.[2] What are the economic determinants of class that do not derive from ownership versus non-ownership of property? How does the concentration of ethnic and other status groups in particular class locations reinforce status-group cohesion? How do ethnic and other forms of status-group identification serve to reinforce patterns of inequality? To what degree do classes serve as recruitment bases for political parties? To what degree do different types of political parties enact policies that redistribute income? These are among the most popular questions asked by modern sociologists, and they are all indebted to Weber's elaboration of the Marxian schema.

Recent years have also witnessed an important addition to the stratification model sketched above. It is now generally acknowledged that gender is a basis of social inequality quite on a par with status groups, parties, and classes (see Figure 1.1).[3] Thus, in Canada and elsewhere, gender is as important a determinant of annual income as class (Ornstein 1983b) because women in the paid labour force tend to be segregated in low-pay, low-prestige jobs (Fox and Fox 1986; 1987). Even if one matches a group of Canadian men and a group of Canadian women in terms of education, occupation, amount of time worked each year, and years of job experience, one discovers that the women earn only 63 per cent of what the men earn (Goyder 1981: 328). Meanwhile, the great bulk of household labour continues to be performed by women, even if both spouses work; one study conducted in Vancouver found that when their wives entered the paid labour force husbands did on average only one hour more of housework per week (Meissner et al. 1975).

FIGURE 1.1

THE MAIN SOURCES OF SOCIAL INEQUALITY

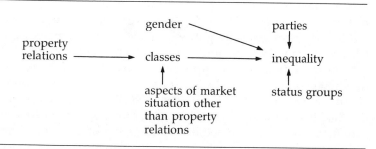

Classical theories teach us little about the causes of such gender inequality. That is, while Marx and Weber offered important insights into the reasons for the expansion and contraction of particular locations in the stratification system, they 'give no clues about why women are subordinate to men inside and outside the family and why it is not the other way around' (Hartmann 1984 [1978]: 174).

Gender inequality has been explained biologically, culturally, and social-structurally. Accumulated research indicates that while biological factors—especially women's childbearing function—may have encouraged some division of labour between the sexes in primitive societies, there is no biological reason why male and female jobs should have been rewarded differently, let alone why they continue to be rewarded differently today. Cultural theories, which locate the causes of gender inequality in the way people learn established practices, cannot account either for the origins of gender inequality or for the sources of variation in such inequality. Explanations that root gender inequality in social structure appear more promising. While the subordination of women is evident in all but the simplest foraging societies, it takes on different forms and degrees in different times and places. Unravelling the relationship between social structure, on the one hand, and the form and degree of gender inequality, on the other, is a complex task that lies at the cutting edge of contemporary research on social inequality.

## THE NORTH AMERICAN LEGACY

The three problems isolated above continue to engage lively minds in sociological debates that grow more sophisticated over time. In any given setting, however, some sides of the three debates have tended to dominate. This is certainly evident in the history of sociology in North America. We shall see that, compared to the European setting in which sociology originated, the US has provided an extraordinarily congenial environment for the entrenchment of presuppositions about the role of individual creativity in producing social structures. Assumptions about the external, coercive power of social facts to shape individual behaviour have fared less well. Moreover, when Americans have analyzed the social determination of economic and political behaviour, they have been inclined to focus on symbolic or cultural determinants above material or political/economic constraints.[4] That Canadian sociologists have at times been overwhelmingly influenced by the American orientation to sociology, at times not, will become clear in the following section, which concentrates on sociology's reception in English Canada.

## 1897-1960

There is some justification for viewing the period before 1960 as the prehistory of sociology in English Canada. Until 1961 there was not a single independent sociology department in the country aside from the McGill University department. The Canadian Sociology and Anthropology Association was formed only in 1965. The country's first English-language sociology journal, the *Canadian Review of Sociology and Anthropology*, began publication in 1964. Before 1965 no significant government or private agency for funding sociological research existed in Canada. Only about a dozen English-language books on Canada had been written by accredited sociologists prior to 1960. And by that year only a few sociology Ph.D.s had been awarded in the country, all by the Department of Political Economy at the University of Toronto.

Despite this minimal level of institutionalization and meagre research record, sociology was actually introduced in English Canada as early as the 1890s and 1900s—during the so-called 'progressive era'. And as in some other countries, where 'the social sciences, social criticism and social reform have proceeded hand in hand' (Bottomore 1967: 15), so too in Canada: sociological teaching and research were at first inspired by movements of social reform.

In English Canada the Protestant 'social gospel' movement played a major role in this respect (Campbell 1983: 7-52). The progressive era was a time of massive immigration and ethnic conflict, urbanization and rural depopulation, industrialization and working-class organization. Advocates of the social gospel reacted to the dislocations and hardships of the era by proposing that Christianity be concerned less with the hereafter and more with the quality of social relations on earth, with the promotion of democracy, equality, and progress. The social gospel was, in the words of one historian, a call for people 'to find the meaning of their lives in seeking to realize the Kingdom of God in the very fabric of society' (Allen 1973: 4).

This project required more than moralistic fervour: sound empirical descriptions of Canada's social problems were needed too. Consequently, sociology courses were organized in a few Baptist colleges (Acadia, Brandon, McMaster), and the Methodist and Presbyterian churches in particular sponsored sociological research (broadly defined) by those deemed qualified to undertake it (Ames 1972 [1897]; King 1973 [1918]; Irvine 1976 [1920]; Macdougall 1973 [1913]; Woodsworth 1972 [1909]).

It is hardly surprising that by today's standards this research was highly descriptive and overly prescriptive. What is rather more remarkable is that its typical intellectual style— highly empirical, focussing on social problems, ahistorical—had little impact on Canadian academic life except at McGill University. By contrast, the social gospel made a much greater impression on the content and growth rate of academic sociology in the United States. One commentator has even argued that 'to a large extent sociology in America may be seen as an outgrowth of the Social Gospel' (Morgan 1969: 42; 1970). The social gospel stimulated interest in a type of research that fitted in well with the unusually liberal ideological climate of American higher learning, its relative lack of regard for classical truths, and its emphasis on scientific subjects with practical applications. This helped to ensure that the movement's influence spread widely and penetrated deeply in the American academic world. Thus as early as 1900 a full third of universities and colleges in the US included sociology in their curricula and nearly 9 per cent had sociology departments.

In English Canada McGill University was one of the few universities (and the only major one) to experience this sort of influence (Magill 1980; Ostow 1984; 1985; Shore 1987; Willcox-Magill 1983). At the turn of the century Montreal was Canada's largest city and the undisputed centre of Canadian business. As a result McGill was the only Canadian university with a Board of Governors consisting largely of wealthy businessmen. McGill's Board members were keen to establish a university more interested in the development of a socially useful curriculum than in the preservation of traditional values. Especially in the years following the Second World War, when poverty, unemployment, and social unrest were widespread in Montreal, this general attitude created an unusually favourable environment in Canada for the growth of American-style sociology. In 1922 McGill hired Carl A. Dawson, a Prince Edward Islander, a

Baptist minister, and a student of Robert E. Park at the University of Chicago. From then until the 1960s virtually all sociology vacancies at McGill were filled by Chicago graduates, among the most notable of whom was Everett C. Hughes, the son of a Methodist minister.

In 1925 a separate department of sociology was established at McGill and in 1929 a $110,000 Rockefeller Foundation grant was awarded to several of the university's departments, including sociology, for the study of unemployment in Montreal. Thus originated the first major sociological research project in the country. Hughes and Dawson held that in order to understand unemployment, they had first to examine basic employment patterns, which were structured along ethnic lines. The series of MA theses (summarized in Younge 1944) and books (Reynolds 1935; Marsh 1940; Hughes 1943) that resulted from this work were concerned with the contours of Canada's system of social stratification; the class, gender, and age distribution of unemployment; ethnic-group assimilation; the ethnic division of labour; and the impact of industrialization and urbanization on ethnic-group relations. One of the two outstanding works of this period was Hughes's *French Canada in Transition*, which influenced a whole generation of anglophone and francophone sociologists. The second was Leonard Marsh's *Canadians In and Out of Work*, which laid the groundwork for his later *Report on Social Security for Canada* (Marsh 1943; Research Committee . . . 1977 [1935]; Horn 1980). Marsh was the Canadian equivalent of England's Lord Beveridge (who had in fact been his teacher at the London School of Economics); both were architects of their respective country's social-security systems.

Around the same time a second grant from the Carnegie Endowment was awarded to an interdisciplinary team of researchers from several central Canadian universities for the study of Canadian frontiers of settlement. While Hughes was concentrating on what he called the 'ethnic frontier' in Quebec, Dawson focussed his attention on immigration and settlement in western Canada. The three books that resulted from Dawson's work (Dawson 1936; Dawson and Murchie 1934; Dawson and Younge 1940) explored the community- and institution-building activities of new ethnic groups in the rural west, as well as the material (chiefly economic) forces that encouraged their assimilation.

In his research Dawson, like Hughes, applied the ecological

paradigm developed in Chicago by Park and his colleagues. And as a rule, McGill graduate students came to espouse the same theoretical orientation as their professors. Perhaps the only exception was S.D. Clark, who completed his MA at McGill in 1935. Before arriving there Clark had studied economic history and political science at the University of Toronto and the London School of Economics. His strong historical bent, coupled with the influence of the LSE, caused him to pick up a disdain for American-style sociology, which he once caricatured as 'doorbell ringing' (quoted in Hiller 1982: 45). For Clark, the ecological approach was too presentist, too static, and altogether too superficial a means of understanding how Canadian society developed its characteristic features (Berger 1976: 163). This attitude was reinforced when Clark took up Ph.D. studies at the University of Toronto and came under the guidance of that institution's premier economic historian, Harold Innis. And it held sway over much of English Canadian sociology from the late 1930s until the mid-1960s, during which time Clark became Toronto's, and Canada's, premier sociologist.

Before 1960 the University of Toronto had at least as much influence on the character of English Canadian sociology as did McGill. But the American-style sociology taught at McGill was shunned at Toronto; in general, social utilitarianism was devalued while the traditional role of the university as a guardian of established culture was widely respected. Because Toronto had the largest graduate school in the country, and was the only institution that granted Ph.D.s in sociology before the 1960s, the early fate of sociology in much of English Canada thus resembled the British, not the American, situation (Abrams 1968; Anderson 1968). That is to say, sociology, as an area of study distinguishable both intellectually and institutionally from cognate disciplines, grew slowly. Thus from 1939 until 1963 sociology was merely a division of the political economy department at Toronto. And the effective head of the division, S.D. Clark, did research during this period that was indebted more to Innis's 'staples theory' of economic development and the 'frontier thesis' of the American historian Frederick Jackson Turner than to the Chicago school.

Consider, for example, Clark's second book, *The Social Development of Canada* (Clark 1942). Innis had already interpreted Canadian economic development as a series of colonial responses to successive imperial demands for staple products such as fish, fur, wood, and minerals—responses that were conditioned by geographical and technological factors as well as the physical characteristics of the staples themselves (Innis 1956a [1930]). Turner had already written about the democratic spirit of new institutions formed on the frontiers of American settlement (Turner 1970). Clark brought together these two sets of concerns by examining the institutional consequences of staple exploitation in a number of Canadian settlement frontiers. His problem-definition thus borrowed from Innis and Turner, he had only to rely on the Chicago school for the idea that social disorganization 'naturally' gives way to social organization: he showed how old familial, religious, educational, and cultural institutions and norms of behaviour were disrupted when the exploitation of a new staple began, and how in due course a new social equilibrium came to be established as the institutional order adjusted to the new demands of the economy.

In this and other works of the period Clark rarely explicated the theoretical underpinnings of his research, and he hardly ever construed his work as a means of assessing the strengths and weaknesses of competing theories. One is therefore inclined to agree with Clark's biographer (Hiller 1982) and characterize his early research as sociologically informed social and economic history rather than historical sociology as the latter term is now understood. Furthermore, Clark initiated no new school of thought; with very few exceptions (Mann 1955), his students at Toronto were not much influenced by his brand of research (Hiller 1982: 159). In short, Clark's immediate impact on the growth of sociology *per se* in English Canada was minimal.

### 1960-1975

In 1960 the foundations of English Canadian sociology were thus weak—so much so that the rapid changes of that decade very nearly undermined the nascent sociological study of Canadian society. The Canadian government decided in the late 1950s that, for economic growth, a greater proportion of the population would have to receive a higher education. Moreover, the absolute number of potential university students took a big jump when the children of the post-Second World War baby boom reached university age. As a result the Canadian university system in general, and sociology departments in particular, experienced hothouse growth in the 1960s. While there were only 32 sociologists teaching in Canadian universities in 1956 (0.6 per cent of all faculty members), there were 917 by 1977 (2.9 per cent of the total) (Hiller 1982: 23).

Given that rate of expansion, and the fact that little had been done to promote sociology graduate training in Canada, it was inevitable that most of the new faculty recruits would come from outside the country, especially from the US. By 1971 only 34 per cent of the sociologists in English Canada were Canadian citizens (Grayson and Magill 1981: 8; see also Symons 1975). Had the *émigré* sociologists discovered a well-developed sociological tradition of Canadian studies upon their arrival they might have assimilated more quickly than they did. But in the absence of such a tradition many were slow to begin teaching about and researching their new environment. The majority simply imported American theories, data, and textbooks. This tendency is well illustrated by the results of one study on required course textbooks used in seventeen English Canadian sociology departments during the academic year 1972-73. Only 25 per cent of the required textbooks were written by Canadian authors, while in graduate courses the figure was a mere 9 per cent (Redekop 1976: 113).

The failure of many of the new recruits to adapt to their new surroundings was in some cases also a simple matter of metropolitan condescension. In addition, the view that Canada was somehow unworthy of serious study was frequently justified on methodological grounds—particularly by the argument that sociologists are in the business of trying to produce universally valid knowledge. In this view, the sociologist's job is to discover historically invariant laws of behaviour; therefore one ought to play down, not emphasize, the specificity of time and place in one's work. This was not necessarily to deny that the sociologist's choice of subject matter and theoretical orientation may be unconsciously influenced by his or her nationality (and/or class, ethnicity, or gender). But proponents of this view did argue that one commits a 'genetic fallacy' if one believes that the origins of an idea determine its truth-value: what makes knowledge scientific, they held, is the use of publicly scrutinizable methods of falsification, which ensure that wrong ideas are rejected and correct ideas accepted regardless of their origins in one group or another (Jarvie 1976).

This argument did not sit well with expatriate American radicals and the younger generation of Canadian-born sociologists. And their objections were not based on exclusively intellectual considerations. Nationalist and anti-American sentiment intensified in English Canada as a whole beginning in the mid-1960s, mainly because of the Vietnam war and the fact that American economic and cultural influence in Canada had reached a high point and was beginning to decline (Resnick 1975: 145-99). The repercussions on Canadian academic life were serious: for many scholars, the view of sociology as a universalizing science seemed little more than an ideological means of preventing Canadians from finding out what was going on in their own society. This attitude was exacerbated by the fact that the number of sociology Ph.D.s granted annually by Canadian universities rose steadily to a historical high of 58 in 1980 (von Zur-Muehlen 1982: 13) while the expansion of the university system slowed considerably and then ceased entirely in the 1970s. The fact that job prospects were not good for the first numerically substantial generation of Canadian-born sociologists provoked considerable resentment against the large contingent of tenured professors holding American citizenship and helped to fuel the students' demand for the 'patriation' of Canadian sociology.

A great deal more was involved in the debate over Canadianization, however, than a sublimated fight for scarce job opportunities or against American involvement in Vietnam. In the mid-1970s the Canadian Sociology and Anthropology Association, the Canadian Association of University Teachers, and the federal government began taking steps to ensure that qualified Canadian sociologists would be given preference in hiring. By 1978 a full 65 per cent of sociologists in English Canada were Canadian citizens (Grayson and Magill 1981: 8). In addition, a good deal of research using Canadian data began to be released at around the same time, as was evidenced by the inauguration of a second English-language professional journal, the *Canadian Journal of Sociology*, in 1975. From then on the Canadianization debate focussed less on the personnel issue and the advisability of using Canadian data in research and teaching (these questions now being taken more or less for granted), and more on

broad questions of method. Is it possible to produce a universally valid sociology? If not, exactly how should English Canadian
sociology differ from the dominant American model of the discipline? These were the burning questions of the mid-1970s
(Clark 1976: 120-44; Clement 1977c; Felt 1975; Hiller 1979a;
1979b; Jarvie 1976; Lamy 1976; Stolzman and Gamberg 1976).

The proponents of Canadianization made a number of very
useful arguments concerning what the sociology of Canadian
society ought to be about. Many of them, however, took positions that were more extreme than was required to make their
case. And they also tended to lump together three different
meanings of 'universal validity' that ought to have been kept
separate. Let me explain by first noting these three meanings
and then outlining the nationalists' criticisms of them.

First, universal validity suggests objectivity, or the idea that
sociological propositions ought to be falsifiable (but temporarily
unfalsified) by publicly scrutinizable methods of testing.
Second, universal validity suggests ahistoricism, or the notion
that sociologists ought to investigate phenomena that are invariant over time and place. Third, universal validity suggests
value freedom, or the view that sociologists ought to select
issues and formulate theories not according to the individual
researcher's national (or other) predilections, but according to
the norms and standards of the international community of
practising sociologists.

As far as the value-freedom issue was concerned, proponents
of Canadianization maintained that definitions of significant social phenomena, as well as the content of theories adduced to
explain those phenomena, vary over time and place. Among
others, Max Weber (1949: 6) could be cited in support of that
contention: he had argued that social research is necessarily shot
through with the values of the researcher, that the selection and
explanation of sociological problems depend upon culture-
specific definitions of what is significant and what is not. To this
insight was added the observation that members of different
subcultures (based on class, ethnicity, or gender) might also
define sociological problems and formulate sociological theories
differently. Hence value freedom, or the selection of problems
and the formulation of theories according to the dictates of some
universal consensus, is impossible, because no such universal
consensus exists.

The nationalists also stressed the need to develop a Canadian sociology that would borrow heavily from historical disciplines such as political economy, and from the discipline of history itself. They held that the properties of many important social phenomena do in fact vary widely over time and place. It follows that a society's unique patterns of social organization and development can be fully understood only by focussing attention on the historical peculiarities of that society. True, certain microsociological processes may not exhibit much historical variation (however, see Archibald 1978); but not so for most macrosociological phenomena. The sociology of Canadian society ought therefore to be concerned with developing a historical appreciation of the country's larger structural features.

Finally, the need to test theories rigorously and publicly was frequently minimized or ignored entirely by many supporters of a national sociology. They felt that if Canadian sociological research were interdisciplinary, historical, macrosociological, and based on problems and theories suggested by the national culture, then this in itself would add substantially to its validity or truth-value. Making a fetish out of techniques of testing was felt to detract from one's ability to do good and meaningful sociological research.

One of the two main problems with this viewpoint was that its often strident endorsement of historical approaches to the study of Canadian society left it open to the charge of parochialism. Clearly, an appreciation of historical development is a useful antidote to the static analyses typical of much American sociology. There is, however, a danger here as well: by stressing the historically unique features of Canadian society one might well perpetuate ignorance about other societies, about the common features of societies, and about the sources of variation between societies. This charge could have been avoided if the nationalists had more emphatically advocated socio-historical analysis as a means towards some more universalistic end, such as contributing to methods of comparative analysis or to the development of theories of whole societies. Instead, many nationalists repeated S.D. Clark's error, proclaiming the understanding of historically unique features of society to be an end in itself. And they ignored the fact that historically such proclamations have hardly aided the growth of sociology as an independent discipline in Canada.

The second main problem with the nationalist viewpoint, or at least its more extreme versions, lay in its minimizing of the need for rigorously testing theories. If taken seriously—and, unfortunately, it has been taken seriously entirely too often—such laxness towards empiricism makes it possible for subjective preferences and even dogmatically held beliefs to determine which theories are regarded as valid and which are not. Charges of relativism and dogmatism could have been avoided, however, by the recognition that there is no logical or practical reason why English Canadian sociology could not strive to be objective and value-laden at the same time. That is to say, there is no inconsistency between a rigorous empirical attitude, on the one hand, and, on the other, a desire to do research on culturally relevant problems with the aid of theories whose underlying values are indebted to that culture.

In sum, the Canadianization movement of the mid-1970s caused a valuable reorientation in English Canadian sociology. But it also provoked a reaction against mainstream American sociology that was strong enough to prevent many Canadian practitioners of the discipline from incorporating in their work some of the most useful elements in the American, and the international, sociological traditions.

## The interpretation of Canadian society in the 1960s

Thus far I have shown that the Canadianization movement of the 1970s raised important questions about the personnel, data, and methods of English Canadian sociology. I now want to emphasize that the movement also provoked some highly stimulating theoretical debates about the nature of Canadian society. In the 1960s there had crystallized among several of the most respected students of Canadian society an interpretation of the country's chief features that was heavily indebted to American social thought of the period. That interpretation soon became sociological orthodoxy; and the Canadianization movement was, among other things, an attempt to supplant that orthodoxy.

The conventional wisdom of the 1960s was produced by a group of prominent scholars including S.D. Clark, Seymour Martin Lipset, and John Porter (Clark 1968 [1962]: 207-42; Lipset 1963; 1967; 1968; 1976; 1985; Porter 1965; 1979: 89-101; see also

Horowitz 1968: 3-57; Naegele 1964 [1961]; Wrong 1955). An entire study in the sociology of knowledge could be written about the social linkages between, and common influences on, these men—their early acceptance of, and subsequent disillusionment with, socialist ideas, their more or less common generational experiences, their training or employment in the most prestigious universities in the US and Canada (Harvard and Toronto), their qualified acceptance in the 1960s of some of the key ideas of Louis Hartz and Talcott Parsons, the foremost American social thinkers of the era. But since my main concern is to evaluate their theoretical contributions, I will restrict myself to making only a few observations about the influence of American social thought in the 1950s and early 1960s on their analysis of Canadian society. I then want to conclude this chapter by providing a composite sketch of Canada as seen from the vantage point of their interpretative framework and, finally, examining in broad outline the criticisms that have been lodged against that framework. In Chapters 2 to 4 I shall present these criticisms in greater depth and discuss at some length the major alternative interpretations that were formulated in the 1970s.

The 1950s and early 1960s were, of course, years of remarkable economic growth and political conservatism in the US. The Cold War and the affluence of the times gave rise to the view that entire nation states, notably the US and the USSR, had replaced classes and other intranational groups as the main protagonists of social conflict. Consequently, the end of ideology, or the cessation of seriously disruptive politics within Western societies, was widely proclaimed. All movements of political protest, whether left- or right-wing, were categorized as forms of anti-democratic extremism emerging among dispossessed and socially unattached people in socially atomized mass societies. Liberal political systems and pluralist societies were hailed as bulwarks against instability. And the United States was held up as the most successful example of political and economic modernity; other, less developed countries were judged in terms of the US and, ideally, expected to emulate it (Bottomore 1975: 19-43; Frank 1969; Rogin 1967; Waxman 1968).

This interpretation of the nature of political and economic life in Western societies was accepted to varying degrees by most students of Canadian society. They seem to have been especially taken by those aspects of Hartz's and Parsons's writings that set out the American ideals and values against which other societies were supposed to be measured and evaluated.

Hartz characterized the US as a pre-eminently liberal society. In Europe, he wrote, liberalism was a bourgeois political movement of opposition to the old feudal order, but in the US, where there had never been a feudal order, liberalism was associated with no particular class. Instead it became the pervasive 'American way of life' from the seventeenth century on, and strict adherence to the liberal creed was expected from all citizens; as George Santayana once wrote, '[e]ven what is best in America is compulsory' (quoted in Hartz 1955: 57). Non-liberal ideas and movements could not possibly survive in such an environment, but respect for individualism, free enterprise, private property, equality before the law, and equality of opportunity supposedly flourished. Parsons's codification was considerably more opaque than Hartz's. But he too implied that truly modern societies, such as the United States, should be characterized first and foremost by their emphasis on certain values, such as rewarding people almost exclusively on the basis of their capabilities and applying laws and rules universalistically (Parsons 1951: 45-67; 101-12; 182-91).

Judged against this standard, Canada seemed to Clark, Lipset, Porter, and others a decidedly more conservative place. A variety of historical factors, dating back to the eighteenth and nineteenth centuries, were held to account for this difference. Among the most important were Canada's relatively 'hard' frontier, the threat of American designs on the northern half of the continent, the immigration to Canada of loyalist Americans opposed to the revolution of 1776, the predominance of relatively authoritarian religions in Canada, and the failure of Canadian movements of liberal reform to make much headway. Specifically:

1. The coastal fisheries, farmlands, and coal and iron fields of the United States were much more accessible and easily exploited than were Canada's resources. Canada's vastness, its less hospitable climate, the remoteness of its valuable minerals, and so forth, made it necessary for large-scale state-supported organizations to play a much bigger role in Canadian economic life than was the case south of the 49th parallel. In the US more

scope could be left for the initiative of the lone frontiersman and the individual entrepreneur; in Canada state-supported armies, police forces, ecclesiastical organizations, and corporate enterprises were needed to lay claim to the interior of the continent. These bodies exercised firm, centralized authority over the population.

2. The more pronounced Canadian tendency to respect authority, hierarchy, and the need for state control also involved a degree of opposition to the forces of liberal democracy. In S.D. Clark's words: '[T]he effort to maintain [centralized state control] in face of the continuous threat of the expanding revolutionary community to the south led to the development of a form of government directly opposed to the principles of political organization growing out of the frontier experience of Canadian peoples' (Clark 1968 [1962]:208). In this view a liberal-democratic spirit derived from the Canadian frontier experience quite as much as it did from the American, but in Canada liberal-democratic impulses had to be held in check for fear that any loosening of control over the population would permit American territorial expansion northward.

3. When the Revolution took place, a substantial number of Americans who remained loyal to the Crown fled to British North America. These were the least liberal of Americans, people who had tory sympathies. Their migration to the part of the continent that later became Canada firmly implanted a trace of conservatism in Canadian political culture and reinforced the non-liberal tendencies that were already set in motion by the environmental and political conditions mentioned above.

4. In the US the many Protestant sects that dominated religious life were generally non-conformist and anti-authoritarian, and they stressed the individual's responsibility before God. Most Canadians, by contrast, were Roman Catholic or Anglican. These hierarchical and relatively authoritarian churches inculcated a deep respect for authority wholly at odds with the dominant religious ethos in the US and in both countries these divergent influences spilled over into non-religious domains.

5. The failure of the American Revolution to advance northward either in 1776 or during the war of 1812, and the putting-

down of the liberal-democratic rebellions in Upper and Lower Canada in 1837, further buttressed the forces of conservativism in British North America. Canada's core values were thus set by the middle of the nineteenth century: while the political culture of the United States was purely liberal, that of Canada contained a significant admixture of toryism.

Lipset extended this argument by categorizing the central value systems of the main English-speaking democracies in terms borrowed mainly from Parsons. He argued that five continua define the core values of Canada, the US, England, and Australia, and that each country's position on these continua could be ranked on the basis of available evidence (see Table 1.1).

TABLE 1.1
VALUE RANKINGS OF THE ENGLISH-SPEAKING DEMOCRACIES

|  | US | Australia | Canada | Great Britain |
| --- | --- | --- | --- | --- |
| élitism-equalitarianism | 3 | 4 | 2 | 1 |
| ascription-achievement | 4 | 2.5 | 2.5 | 1 |
| particularism-universalism | 4 | 2 | 3 | 1 |
| diffuseness-specificity | 4 | 2.5 | 2.5 | 1 |
| collectivity-self orientation | 4 | 1 | 3 | 1 |

Note: The fifth pattern variable is not found in Lipset's original table, although he includes it in his discussion, from which I have inferred the ranking specified above.

SOURCE: Lipset 1963: 249, 270.

Among the generalizations from which Lipset derived Table 1.1 are the following. Canada is more élitist than the US in the sense that Canadians show more deference to authority and less opposition to class differences. Canadians are less entrepreneurial or achievement-oriented than Americans, one result of which is their lower level of economic development as measured by, say, per capita GNP. Canadians are less inclined than Americans to value actions that fulfil individual desires and more inclined to value actions that serve collective ends. Therefore the welfare state is better developed in Canada than in the US; and, for similar reasons, Canada, unlike the US, has a fairly important democratic-socialist political party. Canadians tend on the whole to show greater respect for particularistic differences, such as ethnic peculiarities, among people. Thus while Americans are more universalistic and assimilationist, Canadians tend to favour cultural pluralism, and ethnic groups in Canada tend as a result to be more cohesive than in the US.

This interpretation was very widely accepted in the 1960s. Lipset agreed with Naegele's view that Canada's values are 'in the middle between the United States and England' (Naegele 1964 [1961]: 501). Clark cited with approval Lipset's synthesis and wrote that '[i]n very broad, general terms, the temper of Canadian society can be described as more conservative, less dedicated to such cherished American values as democracy, equality and liberty' (Clark 1968 [1962]: 235). Porter was similarly laudatory; he wrote in 1967 that '[i]t would be difficult to disagree with Lipset['s]' synthesis of the ideas of Clark, Wrong, and Naegele (Porter 1979: 99). To be sure, in the 1970s and 1980s Lipset, Clark, and the others modified their original interpretations, introducing some non-cultural variables to explain Canadian-American differences (e.g., Lipset 1976), claiming that their arguments applied chiefly to the pre-Second World War period (e.g., Clark 1976), and admitting that in some respects they were plain wrong (e.g., Porter 1979: 139-62). But in the 1960s there was a more or less solid consensus of opinion among all the leading English-speaking sociologists of Canadian society about what the core values of Canada were, about how and when they were crystallized, and about the consequential nature of these values for behaviour, organization, and development.

Four main criticisms have been lodged against the cultural interpretation of Canadian society (see, for example, Brym 1984; Crawford and Curtis 1979; Davis 1971; Horowitz 1973; Shiry 1976; Truman 1971). Although these criticisms will be elaborated in the following chapters, they may be stated in general terms now. First, questions have been raised about the quality of evidence adduced to support the cultural argument. Frequently such evidence is impressionistic or unrepresentative. Moreover, even when systematically collected evidence is used to make a case, key concepts tend to be operationalized loosely, so that different and even contradictory inferences can easily be drawn from the same data. This tendency may be illustrated with reference to one survey of how Canadian and US educators and other adults perceive the tasks of education. According to the researcher who conducted the survey, 'Canadians appeared to believe, more emphatically than did Americans, that the public school should serve the individual; Americans believed, on the other hand, that it should serve society' (Downey 1968 [1961]: 214). This result obviously ran counter to Lipset's assertion about Canadians being more collectivity-oriented than Americans. As several scholars have pointed out (Crawford and Curtis 1979: 25; Romalis 1972: 223), however, Lipset excessively reinterpreted these findings. He claimed that they showed how Canadians valued schooling as a means of inculcating youth with tradition-al values and high culture; this, he said, supported his argument because it was evidence of Canadians' greater élitism (Lipset 1968). This example suggests that at least some of the contro-versy surrounding the cultural theory could be resolved if more evidence were systematically collected and if key terms were more rigorously defined and operationalized.

The second main criticism of the cultural interpretation as originally formulated is that, in two senses, it is an ahistorical theory. In the 1960s its proponents failed to specify the time period to which the theory was supposed to apply, and there-fore it appeared to be applicable to all phases of Canadian development. In addition, they paid scant attention to the process of social change; and when they did, they typically in-voked non-cultural factors as causal agents, thereby testifying to the relative unimportance of culture *per se* in effecting social change. These problems show up most glaringly in the work of Gad Horowitz (1968: 3-57; 1978). He argued that Canadian cul-ture congealed sometime around the middle of the nineteenth century and that it has continued—unaltered—to exercise a decisive impact on the structure of Canadian politics. Rather more flexibly, Clark and Lipset recognized by the mid-1970s that their earlier descriptions of Canadian culture might best apply to the pre-Second World War period; and this is by now widely judged to be the case (Curtis and Lambert 1980). Clark and Lipset mentioned in passing that a variety of processes, such as industrialization, urbanization, and law reform, have caused some convergence of certain Canadian and American values and patterns of behaviour. But these sources of change are left pretty much unexamined. And since they are structural causes, the very need to invoke them helps to weaken the general argument that culture is a decisive determinant of behaviour.

Third, the cultural theory tends to play down and in some cases wholly ignore the wide variations within Canada in virtually every aspect of social organization, behaviour, and development. Yet the economic and political diversity of Canada's regions has recently been the subject of much attention. It is now frequently argued and demonstrated that, with respect to many phenomena, what applies in one region can scarcely be held to apply in others. I have already noted that Hartz's 'fragment' thesis greatly influenced thinking about Canadian political in the 1960s. The comment of one highly respected historian on the thesis could easily apply to all variants of the cultural theory and summarizes currently prevailing opinion on the subject:

> The fragment thesis deals with the problem . . . by denying the importance of such variations in the society-building process. When this lunar perspective is applied to the history of the English-speaking colonies of British North America, significant detail recedes, angularities are softened and rounded, mountains are made low and rough places plain. Yet the more conscientiously the formula is applied, the more anomalies swim upwards into view. The view from space has a blurred symmetry. . . . (Wise 1974:2).

Fourth, proponents of the cultural theory did not seriously entertain plausible alternative explanations for political, economic, and other differences between the US and Canada, despite the fact that many alternatives are straightforward and obvious. In other words, virtually no attempt was made to weigh the importance of cultural versus other factors in explaining given phenomena. With few exceptions (e.g., Crawford and Curtis 1979; Guppy 1983), the surveys that have been conducted in order to assess the theory report only bivariate relations (see Table 1.2 for the results of some of the most frequently cited surveys). Usually no control variables are introduced to determine whether correlations between value differences, on the one hand, and differences in behaviour, on the other, may be attributed to factors other than culture. Yet even where value and behavioural differences are correlated one cannot assume, in the absence of appropriate controls, or at least of some systematic attempt to assess the significance of alternative explanations, that this demonstrates the causal significance of values. This shortcoming is particularly striking because, as we shall see in the following chapters, there is good reason to believe that values are frequently worse predictors of behaviour than are structural variables.

Most of the problems outlined above show up clearly in discussions of Canadian economic development and underdevelopment, to which we now turn.

TABLE 1.2
SELECTED SURVEY FINDINGS ON CANADIAN/AMERICAN VALUE DIFFERENCES

| source | sample | achievement/ ascription | universalism/ particularism | specificity/ diffuseness | equalitarianism/ elitism | self/collectivity orientation |
|---|---|---|---|---|---|---|
| Downey (1960) | regional | — | — | — | — | no |
| Pineo & Porter (1973) | national | — | — | — | yes | — |
| Arnold & Tigert (1974) | national | yes | — | — | — | no |
| Presthus (1974) | political élites | — | — | — | yes | yes |
| Rokeach (1974) | university undergraduates | yes | — | — | no | no |
| Truman (1977) | political activists & university undergraduates | — | — | — | — | no |
| Crawford & Curtis (1979) | mid-west small-town | yes | — | — | yes | no |
| Guppy (1983) | national | — | — | — | yes | — |

yes = finding in predicted direction    no = finding not in predicted direction    — = no finding reported

# 2

# Economic Development and Underdevelopment

## The entrepreneurial thesis

The drift towards a cultural interpretation of Canadian society in the 1960s is most readily apparent in S.D. Clark's writings on economic development. It is therefore instructive to trace the evolution of his ideas on the subject.

In his early work Clark was profoundly influenced by an older generation of Canadian political economists and economic historians who formulated what came to be known as the 'staples theory' of economic development. Harold Innis, Clark's teacher, was the most important representative of this school of thought (Berger 1976: 85-111; Innis 1956a [1930]; 1956b; McNally 1981; Schmidt 1981; Watkins 1967). Innis held that economic growth results from the spread of the market by means of trade. In new countries like Canada, this theory implies that shifts in metropolitan demand for raw materials (staples) have been ultimately responsible for patterns of development. But the effect of metropolitan demand on colonial development is not direct. Rather, it is mediated by the characteristics of the staples themselves. The physical attributes of staple products, the geographical settings within which staples are exploited, and the technology available for their exploitation are proximate influences on the shape of economic, political, and social institutions in new countries.

Innis was a geographical determinist who subsumed technology as part of what he called 'the geographic background'. 'Geography', he wrote, 'provides the grooves which determine the course and to a large extent the character of economic life. Population in terms of numbers and quality, and technology are largely determined by the geographic background . . .' (quoted in McNally 1981: 43-4). This emphasis is clearly evident in Innis's most important study, *The Fur Trade in Canada*, whose main theme he summarized with the famous dictum: 'The present Dominion emerged not in spite of geography but because of it' (Innis 1956a [1930]: 393). Innis showed that the geographical limits of the fur trade, which originated in early-sixteenth-century European demand for beaver pelts, are also the boundaries of modern Canada. These boundaries were set by the 'grooves of geography' (the Pre-Cambrian Shield and the river systems that extend into the continental interior). And they were traced in accordance with available technology (the natives' mastery of the canoe) and the characteristics of the staple itself (the rapid extinction of non-migratory fur-bearing animals). The political union of the British North American colonies, the construction of Canada's transcontinental railroads, and the settlement of the west in the late nineteenth and early twentieth centuries thus appear as logical culminations of a process that was set in motion much earlier.

These themes were not so much taken up as assumed in S.D. Clark's early work. Thus in a 1942 study he examined how new forms of staple exploitation disrupted social institutions and culture in Canada's main regions and the ways in which social institutions and culture eventually adapted to changed economic circumstances. Although he later softened his 'heavy emphasis on the economic factor' (Clark 1968 [1962]: xiii-xiv), he was well aware even in the 1940s of the reciprocal effects of religion on the organization of capitalism. For example, he noted on the one hand that religious revivals and new movements of sectarian religious protest have been closely related to 'the development of new staple or secondary industries in various parts of the country, while . . . the growth of conditions favourable to the church form of organization, have [sic] been closely related to the passing of the pioneer stage of capitalist expansion and the emergence of large-scale capitalist organization' (Clark 1968 [1962]: 149; see also Clark 1948). On the other hand, established religions were expensive, and the shift of support to new sectarian movements on the frontiers of settlement resulted in substantial economic savings. This freeing of capital gave impetus to the growth of economic enterprises in new staple-producing regions—an impetus that was lacking where established churches predominated. The various religious sects also facilitated the mobilization of capital and labour by helping to create a sense of community. And they converted 'economic and social misfits' into people imbued with 'a new standard of social conduct' and 'a new economic discipline', thus offering yet another example of how religion has influenced economic life in Canada (Clark 1968 [1962]: 153).

By the 1960s Clark's 'heavy emphasis on the economic factor' had given way to what may fairly be described as an emphasis on cultural causation. This is particularly evident in his essays on Canadian-American differences (Clark 1968 [1962]: 185-252), where many contemporary contrasts between the two countries were ascribed to the more conservative values that crystallized in Canada's past. The reasons for this reorientation are undoubtedly complex, but I believe that two factors—the institutionalization of sociology as a separate discipline in Canada and the effect of American social thought on Canadian sociology —were especially influential.

In 1963 Clark became chairman of the newly established department of sociology at the University of Toronto. Innis and others had long been sceptical of the discipline's potential and therefore saw little need for a separate department. Some intellectual distancing from political economy was thus required in order to legitimize sociology's independence. How better to accomplish this task than by minimizing the significance of economic factors in social causation and playing up the role of culture?

The tenor of American social thought in the 1950s and 1960s only served to confirm the reasonableness of this shift of focus. For anyone too young to have been a professional social scientist in the Cold War era, the virtual absence of any sense of social (let alone economic) structure during those years is surely the most startling feature of the American intellectual landscape. Parsons, Hartz, and other members of the American intellectual élite tended on the whole to ignore the degree to which concrete patterns of social relations organize opportunities, interests, and power so as to shape people's actions and beliefs. Instead, they directed attention to the analysis of people's values and the ways in which values are aggregated as culture.

In economic sociology a major upshot was the 'entrepreneurial thesis'. In Lipset's formulation the various economic prerequisites of industrialization are regarded as necessary but not sufficient conditions of development. A second requirement is that innovative businessmen imbued with an intense 'need for achievement' be present in significant numbers. Following Weber, Lipset stressed that some (particularly sectarian Protestant) cultures accentuate this need more than others; and he agreed that sustained economic growth can take place only if preceded by an increase in the need for achievement in society (McClelland 1963: 74-96). This was not to deny the importance of structural factors. ('Structural conditions make development possible; cultural factors determine whether the possibility becomes an actuality,' wrote Lipset [1967: 3].) But it was to ignore them: the structural prerequisites of development and underdevelopment were for the most part assumed, not analyzed.

By the 1960s Lipset, Clark, Porter, and others had incorporated this idea in an explanation of the economic gap between Canada and the US, and between more prosperous and less prosperous regions within Canada: certain historical and environmental factors, notably the 'hard' frontier of the nineteenth century, the 'defensive expansionism' of the Canadian state, and the supremacy of Catholicism in some parts of the country (especially Quebec), were, they submitted, the major sources of the relatively weaker Canadian need for achievement and the more modest growth of Canadian capitalism that resulted from it. These factors allegedly ensured that Canadians were more cautious, less prepared to take economic risks, and more reliant upon state intervention in the economy than were Americans. Canadians, and particularly Catholic Québécois, therefore had a lower standard of living than Americans (Clark 1968 [1962]: 147-66, 185-252; Lipset 1967: 11-12; 1985; Porter 1965: 99; see also Hardin 1974; Taylor 1964).

## Critique of the entrepreneurial thesis

In 1965 Canada's per capita GNP was 70 per cent of the US level; in 1983 it was 85 per cent. In 1984 the Canadian standard of living was 95 per cent of the American (Foster 1985; '1970s . . .' 1985; Tyree, Semyonov, and Hodge 1979: 416). At least in terms of the measures of economic well-being most widely used in the 1960s, it is therefore unclear that much needs explaining: there is now only a small GNP/standard of living gap between the US and Canada, and the size of that gap is shrinking.[1]

Nonetheless, most of the available survey data do support the proposition that Americans on the whole have a higher need for achievement than Canadians (see Table 1.2, column 1). This does not, however, corroborate the entrepreneurial thesis.

In the first place, there is no reason to believe that a high need for achievement is a necessary condition for economic development. Consider the argument, made by Clark, Lipset, Porter, and others, that hierarchical, relatively authoritarian religions inhibit economic development while sectarian Protestantism has the opposite effect. One does not have to delve very deeply into the Canadian literature to discover important cases where these posited relationships do not hold. For instance, the hundreds of thousands of former southern Italians living in Toronto and environs have been described by certain social scientists as people who in Italy displayed a traditional, non-entrepreneurial, 'morally backward' mentality and culture (Banfield 1958). Research indicates that Italians in Toronto are for the most part devout Catholics who attend church even more frequently than they did in Italy (Jansen 1978: 313-14). Their level of religiosity is without doubt higher than that of the now highly secularized Québécois. Yet despite this cultural background, and especially if one takes into account the relative recency of the bulk of the Italian immigration, the Italian community in metropolitan Toronto is an economic success story, now commanding, for example, a considerable part of southern Ontario's construction industry.

Readily available census and income data lend substance to the view that this is no isolated counterexample: in the ten provinces and two territories of Canada in 1981 the correlation between (a) *per capita* income and (b) the proportion of the population claiming to be Catholic was *not* statistically significant. If (b) is changed to proportion Catholic and Anglican there is still no statistically significant correlation (data from *1981 Census* . . . 1983: Table 1, 1-2; *National Income* . . . 1982: Table 35, 46-7).[2]

The population's religious composition and presumed need for achievement explain variations over time just as poorly as they explain cross-sectional variations. For example, the Maritime provinces were not remarkably poor by Canadian standards in the late nineteenth century. Now they are much worse off economically than Quebec or any other part of the country except Newfoundland. Some social scientists have concluded—on the basis of only impressionistic evidence—that Maritimers, too, lack entrepreneurial drive when compared to the rest of the population (George 1970; cf. Chamard, Catano, and Howell 1983). But if religion is taken as a proxy for the need for achievement, it is significant not only that the proportion of Catholics and Anglicans is below the national average in two of the three Maritime provinces, but also that their religious composition has barely changed over the course of the century—contrary to what the entrepreneurial thesis might predict. Similarly, during the Great Depression Alberta had proportionately fewer Catholics and Anglicans than any other province in the country, was among the most religiously sectarian, but was also among the poorest. Now it is one of the wealthiest provinces in Canada, although, as in the case of the Atlantic region, there has been next to no change in its religious composition.

One might justifiably claim that arguments based on such highly aggregated data may be ecologically fallacious: just because correlations hold at the provincial level they do not necessarily hold at the individual level. But individual-level studies of French Canadian/English Canadian value differences point to the same general conclusion. (These studies deserve special mention in any case, since the entrepreneurial thesis has most frequently been invoked to explain Quebec's lower level of economic development *vis-à-vis* Ontario.) The only field and survey research that seems to support the entrepreneurial thesis in the French Canadian/English Canadian case is based on small, unrepresentative samples (Jain, Normand and Kanungo 1979; Kanungo, Gorn and Dauderis 1976; Taylor 1964). On the other hand, the more representative surveys that have been carried out either offer no support for the entrepreneurial thesis or provide strong evidence against it. Thus Raymond Breton and Howard Roseborough interviewed about 1,100 white-collar and blue-collar employees in major Canadian cities and found 'little basis to argue that the observed difference in mobility behaviour between [English-Canadian, French-Canadian, and other] ethnic groups can be attributed to differences in values' (Breton and Roseborough 1968 [1961]: 690). In a later study of high school students Breton (1972) again found no difference in the predicted direction in the aspirations of anglophone and francophone students after controls had been introduced for socio-economic status and IQ. Two other researchers surveyed value differences among approximately 1,000 anglophone and francophone adults with diverse occupations and found no significant difference in achievement motivation between the two ethnic groups (Nightingale and Toulouse 1977). Douglas Baer and James Curtis (1984) recently published the most representative and sophisticated study of the subject to date. They analyzed the results of a survey conducted on a large (n = 3,173), nation-wide, multi-stage probability sample of adult English Canadians and French Canadians. Baer and Curtis found that the French Canadians actually scored significantly *higher* on achievement motivation than the English Canadians. Moreover, when they calculated the difference in strength of achievement motivation between older and younger members of both ethnic groups, they discovered that the magnitude of the difference was greater in the English Canadian case. In other words, the vestiges of past value differences that they found in their data were the opposite of those predicted by the entrepreneurial thesis. Baer and Curtis therefore agreed with a conclusion reached by Raymond Murphy (1981) in his study of Quebec teachers: French Canadians may emphasize the pursuit of economic success more than English Canadians because their less successful experiences in the workplace have forced them to regard economic security as more problematic. They recommended 'a moratorium on characterizations of contemporary French Canadians as less oriented to economic achievement and more family-oriented than their English Canadian counterparts' (Baer and Curtis 1984: 424).

All this suggests that no easy generalizations can usefully be made about culturally defined needs as necessary conditions for economic development in Canada. Doubts about the validity of the entrepreneurial thesis quickly arise from any systematic examination of representative data on the relationship between religion and economic growth. This conclusion, it must be added, is the same as that reached by many other social scientists who have conducted systematic research on the relationship between religion and economic action in places other than Canada (Samuelsson 1961 [1957]).

Proponents of the entrepreneurial thesis have also tended to ignore plausible alternative explanations. Consider, for instance, the following argument, which has been cited by Lipset (1985) in support of his view that Canadians are less aggressively entrepreneurial and achievement-oriented than Americans, and, as a consequence, less prosperous: Canadians have not been technologically innovative, and when they have invented new products and production processes they have often had to go abroad to market their goods. Rather than assume that this indicates a less intense Canadian need for achievement, one could reasonably interpret it as an outcome of the fact that a large proportion of the Canadian manufacturing sector is foreign-(largely American-) controlled, and therefore unusually small and lacking in opportunity for innovation. The mandate of branch plants in Canada rarely includes research and development, which are usually concentrated in the US as a matter of company policy. Thus there are very few opportunities for innovation in Canadian manufacturing (Craib 1981; House 1977; 1978; Levitt 1970; Myles 1978). Innovations there have been —but mainly in industries that are poorly developed in the US (such as the manufacture of public-transportation equipment) and that have not, as a result, come to dominate the Canadian market.

This example suggests that what adherents of the entrepreneurial thesis lack above all else is a better sense of the political and economic contexts that *constrain* economic behaviour, and the role of human action in sometimes *blocking* economic development. These matters have been emphasized in many recent discussions of the uneven pattern of economic development in Canada, and some of this literature is worth reviewing here for purposes of illustration. In the following digression I shall focus on how federal transportation policy has influenced economic growth in the Maritimes and the Prairies. Consideration of these cases highlights the importance of government policy, rather than values, in determining the pace and form of development.[3]

It is generally acknowledged that the regional pattern of economic development and underdevelopment in Canada was greatly influenced by the protective tariffs that were established by the federal government in 1879. The tariffs ensured that the Maritime and Prairie provinces carried more of the burden of higher commodity prices than did Ontario and Quebec since their *per capita* imports were much higher than those of the central provinces. Consumers in the Maritimes and in the

Prairies thus subsidized the growth of industry in central Canada by paying a disproportionately large part of the tariff bill (Fowke 1973 [1957]: 66-9; Saunders 1936-37).

True, between 1879 and the early 1920s the tariffs helped to set off a veritable explosion of manufacturing activity in the Maritimes (Acheson 1972; 1977). In the 1880s *per capita* growth in the value of manufacturing was higher in New Brunswick and Nova Scotia than in Ontario and Quebec. A disproportionately large share of many major manufacturing industries—steel mills, rolling mills, glass works, cotton mills, sugar refineries, rope factories—were soon concentrated in those two Maritime provinces. In some circles it was even believed that Nova Scotia might become the industrial heartland of the country, especially because it possessed the only known coal supply in the Dominion and could easily import iron ore from Newfoundland.

The tariff had these salutary effects only because low freight rates set by a regionally controlled railroad enabled Maritime producers to get their goods to central Canadian and even western markets at prices that were competitive with those of producers in southern Ontario and Quebec. By the early 1920s, however, the more numerous and powerful populations of central (and western) Canada managed to pressure the federal government to alter Canadian freight policies so as to undermine the Maritimers' ability to compete. Between 1917 and 1920 central Canadian freight rates were roughly doubled. At the same time Maritime freight rates were roughly tripled. This wholly vitiated the positive effects of the tariffs on Maritime industry: Maritime manufacturers could no longer get their goods to market at competitive prices. A rapid deindustrialization process set in as many Maritime manufacturers were forced out of business, and between 1919 and 1921 alone there was a 42 per cent loss in the number of Maritimers employed in manufacturing, most of it permanent (Forbes 1977; 1979).

Clearly, the ups and downs of the Maritime economy in the post-Confederation era, as well as its structural underdevelopment, had little to do with the distribution of mass values in the region. The same holds for the Prairies, where federal transportation policies effectively blocked industrialization. An 1897 agreement lowered rates for exporting grain from, and importing manufactured goods into, that region. Because it was cheap to export grain, specialization in agriculture was encouraged;

because it was cheap to import manufactured goods, the growth of manufacturing was discouraged. This situation persisted until 1925, by which time the protection offered by raising the rates for importing manufactured goods into the region did little to stimulate Prairie manufacturing: the central Canadians had by then established a very considerable competitive advantage, and the Prairies were henceforth 'destined' to remain a resource hinterland (Fowke 1973 [1957]: 68; Phillips 1982: 70-1; Regehr 1977).

Although any full analysis of Canadian regional development patterns would have to take into account the process of capital concentration and centralization (Acheson 1972; Frost 1982; Sacouman 1980; Veltmeyer 1979; 1980) and show the relationship between this process and the sorts of policy decisions summarized above (Clow 1984), this sketch establishes at least one important theoretical point: to make sense of economic development and underdevelopment in Canada, one must focus on the interplay between political and economic forces, on the one hand, and human action, on the other. That is precisely the focus of dependency theory, which became the dominant approach in the field in the 1970s, and to which we now turn.

DEPENDENCY THEORY AND BEYOND

## Canadian dependency

In the 1970s a changing political climate encouraged Canadian sociologists to begin thinking about the economy in a radically different way. This intellectual watershed is usually and, I think, justifiably ascribed mainly to the weakening role of the US in international affairs from the mid-1960s on (Gonick 1975: 208-39; Resnick 1977: 145-99). The US suffered defeat in Vietnam. The post-Second World War recovery of the Japanese and West German economies threatened the competitiveness of American manufacturers. Increasingly, wealth flowed from the US and other highly industrialized countries to the petroleum- and mineral-exporting nations as OPEC and other cartels secured enormous increases in the price of natural resources. The US government reacted to these and other symptoms of decline through a series of defensive measures. For example, in the early 1970s special duties were placed on imports in order to protect jobs in the US and the balance of payments deficit—a measure that was bound to be viewed unfavourably in Canada, the country's largest trading partner. Similarly, the American abandonment of the gold standard effectively exported inflation to Canada and other countries.

How did Canadians respond? Many became aware of some of the negative consequences of being so tightly bound, economically and politically, to the fortunes of the US. Also, the realization grew that new possibilities for economic growth were afforded by changing international circumstances, especially rising world market prices for Canada's abundant natural resources. Throughout the 1970s, and particularly with respect to energy, environmental, and maritime policies, a keen appreciation developed that American and Canadian interests were not necessarily the same.

On the whole, academics and university students responded more radically to the American decline and Canada's expanded opportunities than did other segments of Canadian society. Many intellectuals became left-wing nationalists. They popularized the idea that Canadian dependence on the United States —the existence of an unequal relationship between the two countries— allows the US to secure a wide range of economic advantages over Canada and cause a whole range of economic and other ills.

The term 'dependency' was borrowed from the work of André Gunder Frank (1969) and other contemporary radical Latin Americanists. Many left-nationalists argued, however, that the dependency approach to Canadian economic development and underdevelopment has unique indigenous roots as well. They pointed out that staples theory, the creation of the old Toronto school of political economy, also focussed on the effects of imperial/colonial or centre/periphery relations. In their view, the staples approach was submerged by the Americanization of Canadian social science in the 1960s, and the growing popularity of dependency theory in the 1970s was in part a simple matter of rediscovering a genuinely Canadian intellectual tradition (Drache 1976).

What were the dependency theorists' major arguments? First, they criticized the evolutionary typologies of American social science and argued that all societies do not necessarily pass through the same stages of growth. Second, they denied that some teleological necessity ensures that the highest stage of modernity is an American-like social system. Third, dependency theorists held that societies do not develop, stagnate, or decline as a result of their populations' attributes (e.g., the strength of their populations' need for achievement) but because of their position in a system of unequal or hierarchical relationships among nations.

Dependency theory has been developed in Canadian academic circles as follows (Britton and Gilmour 1978; Levitt 1970). One of the chief features of the relationship between Canada and the US is the control of substantial portions of the Canadian economy by American-based multinationals. In the manufacturing sector, for example, the level of foreign control is among the highest of any country in the world, and the great bulk of foreign investment is US-based. (In 1973, 56 per cent of the assets of the Canadian manufacturing sector were foreign-controlled; in that year only Nigeria had a higher level of foreign direct investment in manufacturing [Laxer 1983: 17].) This control facilitates the outflow of a great deal of capital from the country in the form of profits, dividends, interest payments, royalties, and management fees—capital that, in the absence of foreign control, would presumably be available for domestic investment and job creation. The magnitude of the problem is indicated by the fact that Canada has had growing deficits on the non-merchandise account of its international balance of payments throughout the post-Second World War period. In 1977, for example, the annual deficit amounted to over $7 billion. Nearly 75 per cent of that deficit is a result of capital transfers such as those just listed.

Not only does American direct investment cause a net capital drain, but (the adherents of dependency theory continue) the foreign capital that remains invested in Canada creates fewer jobs than would an equal amount of domestic capital investment. That is because foreign capital is invested in Canada for two main purposes: to provide a secure source of raw materials for manufacturing in the US and to produce manufactured goods for the Canadian market (Williams 1983). Plants established to produce only for the Canadian market are by definition prevented from trying to compete for international sales, from engaging in research and development, and in many cases from doing any more than assembling parts made outside the country. Thus foreign direct investment constrains growth in the manufacturing sector—which is one important reason why Canada imports substantially more manufactured goods than it exports ($11 billion more in 1977; $21 billion more in 1981). Moreover, massive American direct investment in the resource sector is an inefficient creator of jobs: generally speaking, a unit of investment in resource extraction creates fewer employment opportunities than a unit of investment in manufacturing, since resource extraction is generally more capital-intensive.

As a corollary it was further argued that 'Canada's dependency is a function not of geography and technology but of the nature of the country's capitalist class' (Laxer 1973: 28). This idea was first elaborated in a highly influential article by Tom Naylor (1972; see also Naylor 1975). According to him, the whole sweep of Canadian economic history is characterized by Canada's role as a supplier of raw materials to, and a purchaser of manufactured goods from, a progression of imperial centres: first France, then Great Britain, and finally the US. Naylor allowed that out of this trade there emerged a Canadian capitalist class specializing in the construction and operation of transportation facilities, as well as the provision of insurance, banking, and short-term credit services. But he further insisted that, historically, this class has had a vested interest in blocking the development of a vigorous and independent manufacturing sector in Canada. After all, he reasoned, using raw materials in Canada rather than shipping them abroad, and producing manufactured goods in Canada rather than bringing them in from elsewhere, would have undermined the trading and related activities upon which the Canadian capitalist class's prosperity was founded. The high import tariffs on manufactured goods established in 1879, and eagerly backed by members of Canada's mercantile bourgeoisie, served Naylor as an outstanding example of how Canada's capitalist class stunted independent industrial growth in the country. The tariff wall encouraged the rapid growth of foreign (mainly US) branch plants in Canada —plants designed to service only the local market and engage mainly in assembly and warehousing.

This argument, which came to be known as the 'merchants-against-industry thesis', was widely accepted until the mid-1970s. Consider, for instance, the important studies undertaken by Wallace Clement (1975; 1977). One of the tasks Clement set himself was to analyze the density and pattern of ties among dominant corporations in Canada—ties formed by individuals sitting simultaneously on more than one corporate board of directors. The senior executives and members of the boards of directors of the country's dominant corporations, or members of the corporate élite, actually comprise two main groups, according to Clement. First, the *indigenous* élite consists of people, for the most part Canadian-born, who head corporations engaged mainly in commercial and transportation-related activities. Their business is conducted chiefly inside, but also to a degree outside, Canada. (Typical are the large Canadian banks that have established branches throughout the Caribbean region.) Second, the *comprador* élite consists of people, some Canadian-born, others not, who merely operate or manage the Canadian branch plants of multinational corporations. The economic activities of these branch plants are also largely restricted to Canada itself, although in some cases they serve as intermediaries for American direct investment in third countries. (For example, the Ford Motor Co. in the US holds 85 per cent of the stock in the Ford Motor Co. of Canada, which in turn holds 100 per cent of stock in the Ford Motor Co. of Australia, New Zealand, and Singapore.) Most of the multinationals with branch plants in Canada have head offices in the US, and most of them are engaged in manufacturing and resource extraction.

Clement did not suggest that the cleavage between indigenous and comprador factions of the Canadian corporate élite implies conflict or rivalry between the two groups. Quite the contrary. The two groups play complementary roles in Canadian economic life, one basically financial, the other basically industrial and resource-related. Moreover, their boards of directors are highly interlocked, important financiers frequently serving on the boards of foreign-controlled companies engaged in manufacturing and resource extraction, and vice-versa. And they share a continentalist outlook on the nature of Canada/US relations, as is evidenced by their opposition to the growth of an indigenous Canadian manufacturing sector that could disrupt the existing pattern of economic relations between the two countries.

## Capitalist class cleavages

By the mid-1970s some Canadian researchers began offering some quite compelling criticisms of dependency theory. The merchants-against-industry-thesis was the first aspect of dependency theory to come under critical scrutiny. The thesis stands or falls partly on the degree to which indigenous manufacturers in Canada formed a relatively small, poor, and uninfluential segment of the capitalist class, constrained in its development during the latter part of the nineteenth and first part of the twentieth century by presumably more numerous, wealthy, and powerful commercial entrepreneurs. If, however, it can be shown that native industrialists were not so insignificant as the dependency theorists maintain, then a central element of the merchants-against-industry thesis is called into question.

Several historians of Canadian industrial growth have made precisely this point, and they have done so with a wealth of material attesting to the industrialization that began in the British North American colonies as early as the 1850s. There is no denying the predominance of staple production (especially lumber and wheat) in the pre-Confederation years. But Stanley Ryerson observed that in Upper Canada in the 1850s and 1860s there was 'a consolidation of the new elite of railroad and factory owners; the shaping of that ruling class of industrial capitalists who were to be the real (not merely the titular) "fathers" of Confederation' (Ryerson 1973 [1968]: 269; see also Kealey 1980; Ryerson 1976).

Certainly, by the 1880s and 1890s industrialization was well under way, and by the early decades of the twentieth century Canadian manufacturing was well developed even by international standards. Thus in 1913 Canada was the world's seventh largest manufacturing nation, outranked only by the US, Germany, the UK, France, Russia, and Italy. The great bulk of the products manufactured in Canada were not semi-processed, but fully finished goods such as farm implements, footwear, furniture, and so forth. With only 0.4 per cent of the world's population, Canada produced 2.3 per cent of all manufactured goods in the world that year (compared to Japan's 1.2 per cent and Sweden's 1.0 per cent) (Laxer 1983; 1985a; 1985b).

Nor was Canada's commercial sector particularly overdeveloped in the first decades of this century, at least in comparison with that of the US, Jack Richardson (1982: 29) computed ratios, for Canada and the US, of national income generated by commercial businesses to national income generated by industrial activity. He discovered that between 1920 and 1926 the Canadian ratio was about the same or lower than the American ratio, depending on the precise definitions of 'commercial' and 'industrial' activity used. Yet this is just the opposite of what one would expect to find if the merchants-against-industry thesis were valid.

In this light it seems unjustified to speak of a tiny and uninfluential manufacturing élite in late nineteenth- and early twentieth-century Canada. The current weakness of Canada's manufacturing sector is undeniable, but one may safely conclude that the twentieth century was well advanced before its frailty became obvious.

Why Naylor and Clement thought otherwise is partly a result of a definitional quirk. They alluded to Marx's distinction between industrial or productive capitalists who engage in 'the sphere of production' (i.e., manufacturing) and mercantile or non-productive capitalists who engage in the 'sphere of capital circulation' (i.e., banking, insurance, and the like). According to Marx, only the economic activity organized by productive capital directly adds value to raw materials. Moreover, industrial capital is characterized by a comparatively high ratio of fixed to circulating capital, which is to say that manufacturers tend to invest relatively more in plant and equipment than do mercantile capitalists, who prefer short-term liquid investments. That is why, in Marx's view, sustained and substantial economic development depends on the robustness of industry: only manufacturers organize the actual addition of value to raw materials by promoting the accumulation of long-term fixed investments.

The view that industry is generally the chief engine of economic development is, I think, unobjectionable. What is problematic is that Naylor and Clement classified entrepreneurs active in the railroad industry—one of the most important branches of the economy in late nineteenth-century Canada—not as industrialists but as financial or commercial capitalists engaged in trade. Yet 'railways had much the highest proportion of fixed to circulating capital of any nineteenth-century enterprise' in Canada; and Marx himself 'went out of his way in *Capital* to insist that the transportation industry was productive because it added value to commodities; for him, a railway was an industry, not a trade' (Macdonald 1975: 267, 268). In other words, if Naylor and Clement had characterized the railroad barons as industrial, rather than financial, capitalists they might not so readily have jumped to the conclusion that industrial capitalists were a minor force in Canadian economic life.

In addition, little evidence supports the view that there was a conflict of interest between domestic financial and domestic industrial capitalists. Financial capitalists in late nineteenth-century Canada had nothing against the formation of domestic manufacturing concerns. As Macdonald (1975) demonstrates, many financial capitalists promoted the growth of manufacturing and even became manufacturers themselves. Richardson (1982: 287-8) shows that this early tendency for merchants actually to become industrialists was clearly visible in the Brantford, Ontario, economic élite of the 1890s and in the Toronto economic élite of the 1920s. In Brantford 55 per cent of the 22 members of the economic élite were active in mercantile and industrial firms at the same time. In Toronto 53 per cent of the 164 most powerful men in the economic élite simultaneously held directorships in both types of corporations. If the economic interests of financial and industrial capitalists were opposed, one would not find such clear evidence of an identity of interest (and, indeed, of personnel) between these two groups.

Some analysts of the late twentieth-century Canadian capitalist class have taken this last point a step further. They hold that a *merger* of commercial and industrial interests has taken place in contemporary times. The most important researches that develop this theme are by William Carroll, John Fox, and Michael Ornstein (1982) and by William Carroll alone (1982; 1984; 1986).

Carroll, Fox, and Ornstein examined interlocking directorates among 100 of the largest financial, merchandising, and industrial firms in Canada in 1973. They discovered, first, that these firms were remarkably highly integrated by top corporate officials and managers serving simultaneously on more than one board of directors. Ninety-seven of the 100 firms were connected by single-director interlocks and 70 of the 100 by multiple-directorship ties. They also discovered no evidence to support the view that the largest Canadian firms were clustered in dis-

connected subgroups or cliques based on nationality of ownership or sphere of economic activity. Such cliques would presumably have been discovered if the cleavages within the capitalist
class posited by the dependency theorists did in fact exist. Finally, Carroll, Fox, and Ornstein found that non-financial corporations controlled by Canadians had few links to their foreign-
controlled counterparts; but both domestic and foreign-
controlled corporations were linked to large Canadian financial
institutions. In other words, banks lay at the centre of the
network of interlocking directorates, serving as the principal
points of articulation and integration for the corporate élite.[4]

Some of these interpretations were confirmed and elaborated
in Carroll's work. Carroll (1982) examined the boards of directors of the 100 largest Canadian industrial, financial, and
merchandising firms at five-year intervals between 1946 and
1976. He discovered the existence of dense ties between
Canadian-controlled financial firms and Canadian-controlled industrial firms, and markedly less dense ties between Canadian-
controlled financials and US-controlled industrials operating in
Canada. Moreover, the directorship ties among indigenous
Canadian financial and non-financial firms had become more
dense over time, while the ties between Canadian financials and
American-controlled industrials have become less dense. This is
just the opposite of what dependency theory predicts. In a
separate analysis (1984) of the 'inner group' of 298 key Canadian
corporate interlockers, Carroll found that dominant indigenous
interests predominated in this group, and that they represented
all major sectors of large-scale capital. These findings all contradict the predictions of dependency theory.

### Capitalist class boundaries

On the basis of available evidence, I conclude that the cleavages
in the Canadian capitalist class that the dependency theorists
purported to detect were greatly overdrawn. Does dependency
theory fare any better with regard to the question of the
boundaries of the capitalist class? Carroll (1982; 1986), for one,
thinks that the Canadian capitalist class is now autochthonous
and independent, not continental and dependent. Steve Moore
and Debi Wells (1975) came to much the same conclusion, and
Jorge Niosi (1978; 1981 [1980]; 1982; 1983; 1985 [1983]) has of-

fered a more qualified assessment. Let us consider the evidence upon which they base their conclusions.

Carroll (1982: 98) underscores the fact that the assets of top Canadian firms were overwhelmingly Canadian-controlled at the end of the Second World War and that they exhibited the same characteristic three decades later: in 1946 and in 1976 about 86 per cent of such assets were Canadian-controlled (about 56 per cent Canadian-controlled in the manufacturing sector alone) while roughly 11 per cent were US-controlled (approximately 33 per cent in the manufacturing sector). There was a period in the 1950s and 1960s when overall American control of assets in the largest Canadian firms nearly doubled, but that era began to fade into history after 1970. Similarly, Niosi (1981 [1980]: 32; 1983: 132) cites government statistics showing that, among all non-financial companies in Canada, the value of assets under foreign control as a percentage of all assets decreased from 36 per cent in 1970 to 26 per cent in 1981. In manufacturing alone the decline was from 58 per cent in 1970 to 41 per cent in 1983 (Urquhart 1984). Minimally, these figures support the view that Canadian capitalism has become more indigenous and less controlled by non-Canadians over the past two decades.

It is also worth noting that this independence has been reflected in the propensity of Canadian companies to increase their foreign investments: the boundaries of the capitalist class's activities are, in other words, less and less circumscribed by the country's political borders. The ratio of US direct investment in Canada to Canadian direct investment in the US declined from 6.7 in 1970 to 2.8 in 1985. The ratio of total foreign direct investment in Canada to total Canadian direct investment abroad fell from 4.6 in 1970 to 2.7 in 1979, and government forecasters expect it to fall to 1.0 by 1992. Significantly, in 1969 nearly 62 per cent of Canadian direct investment abroad was investment by Canadian-controlled companies; that figure had increased to 83 per cent by 1978. In absolute terms, Canada was the seventh largest overseas investor in the world by 1976 (after the US the UK, West Germany, Japan, Switzerland, and France). In relative terms, too, Canada's overseas investment record was impressive: in 1978 Canadian direct investment abroad amounted to $700 per capita—not much less than the American figure of $750. And by 1980 the annual rate of growth of Canadian investment abroad was 13.7 per cent, compared to 9.0 per cent for the

US ('Border exchanges' 1987; Moore and Wells 1975: 72; Niosi 1982: 24, 25; 1983: 132-3; 1985 [1983]; US Dept. of Commerce 1986: 780, 782).

On the basis of these figures some analysts are inclined to urge outright rejection of the view that the Canadian capitalist class is essentially dependent and largely constrained in its business dealings to Canadian soil. Carroll (1985; 1986) and others think of Canadian capitalists as having come of age, engaging in their own economic ventures overseas and no longer subordinate to American interests. In this view, the most powerful Canadian businessmen, both industrial and commercial, form part of an international class of finance capitalists, the members of which opportunistically co-operate and compete with other members of that class in their search for profits. Carroll goes on to observe that the internationalization of capitalism has recently involved the export of productive capital to less developed countries. The production process itself has thus become internationalized as modern methods of transportation and communication allow finance capitalists to take advantage of low labour costs and propitious political conditions in some parts of the Third World by setting up production facilities there. This innovation ensures that, in the long run, the penetration of foreign capital *facilitates* economic growth in less developed countries rather than, as the dependency theorists hold, blocking it.

Some of the evidence bearing on the relative merits of dependency theory (Stevenson 1980) versus more orthodox Marxist interpretations (Carroll 1985) is ambiguous as far as Third World countries are concerned. The same is true for the Canadian case. For, notwithstanding the facts cited above, Canadian-controlled multinationals are, as Niosi (1982; 1983: 133-4; 1985 [1983]) points out, still technologically dependent on research and development in the US, and they are restricted to supplying only a narrow range of products and services abroad (non-ferrous metals, banking, real estate, paper, farm machinery, distilling, synthetic rubber, footware, telecommunications equipment). Furthermore, the decline in foreign control of the Canadian economy witnessed over the past twenty years has largely been confined to extractive and mineral processing industries (especially oil and gas, potash, coal, asbestos, and metals). The Canadian manufacturing sector is, as the dependency theorists have stressed, still very weak. By international standards a very large proportion of manufacturing assets (and an even higher proportion of large enterprises in that sector [Rosenbluth 1970]) is still foreign-controlled. Because of the strict limits this places on its growth, the manufacturing sector continues to employ a smaller percentage of the labour force than is the case in highly industrialized countries (Black and Myles 1986). It does not even come close to supplying Canadians with all the manufactured goods they need. And much of the manufacturing that takes place in Canada actually involves the mere assembly of parts made elsewhere (Williams 1983). For these reasons Niosi concludes—quite sensibly—that the Canadian capitalist class cannot at present be characterized either as purely continentalist and dependent or as purely independent of foreign interests; either as tightly constrained to engage in business almost exclusively in Canada or as freely able to engage in wide-ranging business ventures abroad. The Canadian capitalist class possesses aspects of all these features simultaneously because of the domestic and international economic and political conditions within which it has evolved. I will mention some of these conditions in the next section.

### Domestic political economy, international context, and economic development

In the 1970s the characterization of the Canadian capitalist class as dependent represented an advance in social scientific thinking insofar as it drew attention to important structures and processes previously neglected in the study of the country's economic development. In particular, dependency theory highlighted the broader international context of economic development. It challenged the widespread assumption that the trajectory of a given country's growth or stagnation should be analyzed exclusively in terms of that country's internal conditions. At the same time, however, dependency theorists thought of the international context only in bilateral terms (Friedmann and Wayne 1977). In the Canadian case, for example, the nature of Canada/US ties was held to be responsible for both the character of Canada's development and the structure of its capitalist class in recent times.

As we have seen, the internationalists of the 1980s have challenged the validity of some key empirical implications of this theory. In the process they have sketched a more accurate picture of the structure of the Canadian capitalist class. We now know that banks lie at the centre of the network of interlocking directorates, that foreign control of the Canadian economy has waned, that Canadian multinationals have become important players in several economic spheres, and so forth.

Notwithstanding these important contributions, the internationalists, like the dependency theorists, have minimized the significance of internal economic and political processes in shaping Canadian capitalism. This point has been made especially effectively by Gordon Laxer (1983; 1985a; 1985b). Laxer has recently explored the ramifications of the following paradox. The late-industrializing countries that were able to overcome severe domestic capital shortages and generate robust independent manufacturing sectors were those with strong agrarian classes. In such countries as Japan and Sweden the agricultural sector traditionally encouraged expansionist military endeavours that caused the state to take an interventionist role in the economy and become directly involved in the manufacture of military wares. For security reasons, the state typically encouraged the domestically owned military manufacturing sector to become technologically independent. It employed many engineers and thus laid the foundation for later technological innovation. Out of the countryside there also issued a demand for cheap government, which lessened the problem of domestic capital shortage. Finally, politically influential agrarian elements fought for the breakup of old commercial banking systems, oriented towards short-term loans, and the creation of investment banks, oriented towards long-term loans, thus unintentionally making capital more readily available for industrial investment. In Canada, by contrast, farmers were politically weak and disunited, and this allowed the French-English conflict so completely to overshadow class-based politics at the turn of this century that the farmers had relatively little influence on public policy. As a result Canadian farmers could not have the unintended but beneficial effects on the growth of manufacturing that rural classes had elsewhere. In Canada military manufacturing was minimal. The state squandered enormous sums of money on the construction of unnecessary transcontinental railway lines. Investment banking developed very late. Consequently there was a shortage of domestic capital for investment in manufacturing.

This explanation of why Canada has a weak manufacturing sector neither minimizes the significance of the problem (as the internationalists do) nor locates its origins almost exclusively in external forces (as the dependency theorists do). By analyzing the Canadian case in comparative perspective and paying careful attention to domestic economic and political relations, Laxer has offered an innovative explanation of an issue that has galvanized the interest of Canadian social scientists for two decades. This is not to suggest that the Canadian capitalist class is best understood with exclusive reference to domestic political and economic processes. For example, the repatriation of Canadian capital and the greatly increased level of Canadian direct investment in the US that have occurred over the past twenty years can scarcely be understood apart from the weakening role of the US in the world economy (Carroll 1986: 186-212). Laxer's work does, however, offer a useful counterpoint to the internationalists' important contributions. It serves as a compelling reminder that the political economy of both international and domestic affairs ought to be examined in order to gain a well-rounded appreciation of the development and structure of Canadian capitalism.

# 3

# Politics

The sociological study of Canadian politics has evolved in much the same manner as Canadian economic sociology. American-influenced interpretations emphasizing the cultural sources of Canadian political behaviour predominated in the 1960s. In the 1970s this approach was widely rejected, partly on empirical grounds, and the structural (especially class) bases of Canadian politics became the chief subject of attention. This shift resulted in important explanatory advances. But the hurried and uncritical acceptance of certain alternative theories also gave rise to some explanatory problems. I will show that the subfields in which the most striking progress has been made are (a) the study of social movements and third parties, and (b) the analysis of voting behaviour. In this chapter's final section I will discuss studies of the Canadian state, in which less progress has been made.

SOCIAL MOVEMENTS AND THIRD PARTIES

## The cultural/institutional approach

While many types of Canadian social movements have been studied, most attention has been devoted to movements that have become institutionalized as political parties closely aligned with neither of the country's dominant political parties (Liberal and Progressive Conservative). This emphasis is *not* a result of Canada's having a relatively low level of non-institutionalized conflict. Thus cross-national studies have shown that the level of public violence in Canada between 1946 and 1970 was about the median for all countries and for industrialized countries considered alone (Torrance 1986: 57-65). Furthermore, in the 1970s Canada lost more working days *per capita* because of strikes than any other country in the world (Ward 1981): hardly evidence that Canada is a 'peaceable kingdom', as some commentators used to argue.

One of the main reasons that Canadian social scientists interested in social movements have focussed on the institutionalization of 'third parties' is that the Canadian party system looks peculiar when compared to its American and Western European counterparts. Since the 1920s Canada has had a tradition of weak third parties at the federal level, mainly on the left wing of the political spectrum. The CCF and the NDP are the main examples of such parties. In contrast, democratic socialist parties tend to be stronger throughout Western Europe and virtually non-existent in the US.

In a highly influential work written in the mid-1960s—during the high point of American influence on Canadian social scientific thinking—Gad Horowitz (1968) sought to explain, in cultural and institutional terms, the propensity of the Canadian political system to give rise to weak third parties. Horowitz modified somewhat a line of reasoning originally proposed by Louis Hartz (1964) and Kenneth McRae (1964). Hartz and McRae had argued that the United States was only one of several 'new societies' whose value systems were crystallized 'fragments' of older, European ideologies. Settlers in each of these societies typically carried with them certain cultural baggage. The Latin American countries and French Canada inherited a feudal political culture; the United States, English Canada, and South Africa a liberal political culture; and Australia a radical political culture. The central value system of each new society was alleged to have congealed soon after the arrival of its characteristic fragment culture from Europe. From this point of view, English Canada is similar to the US.

While Horowitz agreed that American political culture was forged out of liberalism pure and simple, he held that English Canadian political culture is an alloy, comprising, in addition to dominant liberal ideas, a strong element of toryism. This is significant because, in Horowitz's view, liberalism and toryism conceive of society and of people's relationships to society in very different ways. Toryism maintains that, ideally, society is a real corporate entity consisting of hierarchically ordered classes, and that people's positions in the class system are relatively fixed once they enter the class system at birth. Liberalism maintains that, ideally, society is just a nominal agglomeration of individuals whose social locations are not fixed but determined by equality of opportunity, which allows people to achieve as much or as little as their natural capacities allow.

Obviously, liberalism is the more radical and democratic set of ideas. It was in fact an important weapon in the fight of the thirteen American colonies against tory England—a fight that culminated in the American Revolution. Not that all Americans subscribed to liberalism, noted Horowitz: some remained loyal to England and fled to British North America in the late eighteenth century. Moreover, almost a million presumably non-liberal Britons immigrated to British North American between 1815 and 1850. Thus, although Canada's political culture is most heavily indebted to liberalism, some toryism was brought to Canada by the Loyalists and subsequent British immigrants.

What does all this have to do with the fact that Canada is more receptive than the US, but less receptive than Western Europe, to democratic-socialist parties? Simply that, according to Horowitz, democratic socialism can appear only where there is a history of liberalism *and* toryism. Democratic socialism is, after all, an amalgam and extension of the egalitarian impulse in liberalism and the corporatist view of society in toryism. Accordingly, democratic socialists insist that, if true equality is to be achieved, equality of opportunity must be augmented by a state-directed redistribution of the resources needed to take advantage of available opportunities. For example, poor adolescents who have to drop out of school in order to help support themselves might be able to take advantage of laws giving them the right to attend university if the state distributed wealth and income more evenly. A problem emerges, however, if, as in the US, the lack of a feudal tradition means that liberalism is the only available set of political ideas. In this case the democratic-socialist amalgam cannot develop, since there exists no source of corporatist belief. In contrast, if, as in the Western European countries, a feudal, corporatist value system forms the historical background of contemporary politics, then egalitarianism and corporatism are able to fuse into strong democratic-socialist ideologies and parties. Finally, if, as in Canada, liberalism co-exists with what Horowitz calls a mere 'tory touch', only a weak democratic-socialist ideology and party can emerge.

Seymour Martin Lipset (1976) added to Horowitz's argument by citing a number of historical events that supposedly rein-

forced the tory tendencies of Canadian political culture. Following S.D. Clark (1949) and others, Lipset noted that the failure of
the US to annex Canada in the war of 1812 represented a second
defeat for liberalism in British North America (the first being the
inability of the American Revolution to spread northward in
1776). The 1837 rebellions in Upper and Lower Canada—movements of liberal democracy—were put down, and this
entrenched still more deeply the values of toryism. For Lipset,
then, Canada's counter-revolutionary tradition is patent. Like
Horowitz, he concluded that the central value system of
Canada, insofar as it contains elements of both liberalism and
toryism, explains well the ideological content of at least the most
important third parties in the country's history.

It must be emphasized, however, that this argument is supposed to explain only the ideological content of third parties, not
the frequency with which they have been formed. Horowitz and
Lipset sought to account for the fact that the rate of third-party formation is higher in Canada than in the US by examining the different political-institutional contexts within which social movements are constrained to operate in the two countries. The American electoral system, they contend, makes it exceedingly difficult
for political protest movements to become institutionalized as
third parties, while Canada's facilitates third-party formation.

Two aspects of the Canadian and US electoral systems appear
to be particularly important in this regard. First, in Canada there
is only one elective political arena at the federal and provincial
levels—the legislatures—and seats in the legislatures are filled
on a constituency-by-constituency basis. In the US, aside from
contests for state legislatures and the federal Congress, separate
elections are also held for the executive branch of government,
for governorships and the presidency. These elections are state-
or nation-wide. Thus in a Canadian constituency in which
radicals are highly concentrated, a vote for a radical candidate is
more likely to 'pay' since he or she stands a reasonable chance of
winning and therefore influencing government policy in the
legislature. In voting for state governors or the President, however, Americans must take into account the political complexion
of a very large social unit that inevitably contains diverse interests, so that a vote for a third-party candidate is almost bound
to be perceived as wasted. In the US case, therefore, it is more
likely that the elector will vote for the presidential or gubernato-

rial candidate who offers the platform closest to the voter's interests *from among the potential winners*. In short, the separation of legislative from executive authority in the US militates against the success of third parties, while Canada's centralized parliamentary government is conducive to their success.

A second way in which electoral systems affect third-party strength has to do with the fact that the British parliamentary principle of party loyalty operates in Canada but not in the US. In both state legislatures and the US Congress representatives vote according to their individual views as these are shaped by the interests of the people who support and elect them; this in no way endangers the tenure of the administration. In Canada disputes within a party are resolved in caucus, and once the representatives leave caucus and enter the legislature they are obliged to vote as a bloc. If the representatives of a governing party fail to do so they may well cause the downfall of the government. In Canada interests that are not satisfied with the policies of the existing parties thus have little alternative to forming a third party. In the US diverse interests can be accommodated within existing parties without major difficulty.

## Criticisms of the cultural/institutional theory

Among the most serious criticisms that have been lodged against the cultural/institutional theory are the following: (a) the content of Canadian political culture is not what Horowitz and Lipset take it to be; (b) their theory does not make it clear when and why Canadian political culture congealed as it did; (c) variations within Canada in the rate of third-party formation and in the content of third-party ideologies cannot be explained by the theory.

Criticism (a) is based, in the first place, on Horowitz's and Lipset's willingness to accept what is sometimes called the 'tory myth' (Bell and Tepperman 1979: 43-64; Jones 1985). Historians now widely question whether the Loyalists who came to British North America in the wake of the American Revolution and who, according to Horowitz and Lipset, were responsible for injecting a substantial dose of toryism into Canadian political culture, were in fact tories. There had never been a strong tory tradition in the thirteen American colonies. Without an entrenched aristocracy, American colonial life could not inculcate the respect for organic collectivism that, according to Horowitz and Lipset, must be present for democratic socialism to develop at a later historical juncture. It thus makes little sense to talk about the transmission of tory ideas northward. The Loyalists were not so much tories as people who had been bound up in one way or another with the colonial administrative apparatus, and what they transmitted northward was less tory culture than a reinforcement of British political intervention in North American affairs. If the British connection has had an influence on political life in Canada—and there can be little doubt that it has—this has more often involved the shaping of Canadian political institutions and habits by British-connected ruling groups than it has the sympathetic and spontaneous evolution of tory values among Canadians.

Pushing the story ahead a couple of centuries, and examining relevant surveys conducted in the 1970s, one continues to find evidence that Canadian political culture is less indebted to toryism than Horowitz and Lipset would have us believe. For example, when a toryism-conservatism scale was applied to samples of American and Canadian university undergraduates and political activists it was found that the Americans scored as high or higher than the Canadians: precisely the opposite of what the Horowitz-Lipset thesis would lead us to expect (Truman 1977: 609). A second survey has shown that Progressive Conservative legislators in Ontario are no more collectivist in orientation than legislators in the Liberal or New Democratic parties (Winn and Twiss 1977: 205). Since Horowitz (1968: 19) claimed that the Progressive Conservative party is the 'primary carrier' of toryism in Canada, this finding directly contradicts his argument. A third survey of Canadian and American university students revealed 'no support . . . for Lipset's hypothesis' (Rokeach 1974: 164). Finally, in a survey conducted in one American and one Canadian town, it was found that Canadians under 61 years of age scored significantly lower on collectivity-orientation than Americans in the same age cohort, while for those 61 years of age and older the differences were negligible (Crawford and Curtis 1979). While these studies may not be representative of the entire population, they do at least establish that there is no compelling reason to believe that toryism exists in Canada to a degree that would have a bearing on Canadians' receptivity to democratic socialism.

The second major criticism of the cultural/institutional argument concerns the notion of congealment. It is a central thesis of Horowitz's book (but not of Lipset's work on the subject) that, at a certain historical moment, Canadian political culture took on a relatively fixed form. But when did this happen? And why? Horowitz equivocates in answering the first of these questions and is silent on the second.

Horowitz (1968: 15) originally admitted that it was very difficult to 'put one's finger on the point' when toryism and liberalism congealed. He suggested that congealment may have occurred at the time of the Loyalist migration, or when the million British immigrants came to Canada between 1815 and 1850, or indeed not until British trade unionists imbued with socialist ideals immigrated to Canada in the late nineteenth and early twentieth centuries. But this argument left Horowitz open to the charge of equivocation. How could it be true that Canada's political culture stopped developing and that it has always assimilated new ideas from immigrants (McNaught 1974: 419)? Nor did it clarify matters when Horowitz (1978: 387-8) subsequently asserted that Canadian political culture has *always* been sufficiently congealed around tory ideas to enable new democratic socialist ideas to 'fit' better in Canada than in the US; for Canadian political culture, like any historical product, must have had origins in time. In short, it seems undeniable that no once-and-for-all congealment has occurred, and that waves of immigrants—including non-British immigrants[1]—have been at least partly responsible for the continuous shaping of Canadian political culture.

This is not to deny that some elements of Canadian political culture have become dominant. But if one wants to know why, it seems necessary to set aside the concern that Horowitz and Lipset have expressed with mass cultural values and examine issues of power: how ruling groups of British origin, through their control over property, police, communications media, etc., have created a more or less general view of the world in their own image. But more of this later. For the moment let us move on to the third main criticism of the cultural/institutional theory.

Several scholars have pointed out that neither the supposedly strong trace of toryism in Canadian political culture, nor the adoption by Canada of the British parliamentary system of government, can explain variations *within* Canada in the rate of third-party formation or in the ideological content of third parties (Pinard 1971: 66; Truman 1971: 519). According to Horowitz and Lipset, where toryism approaches parity with liberalism as a cultural influence, democratic socialism will be strongest. Hence Canada has a stronger democratic-socialist tradition than the US. It follows that in those Canadian provinces where toryism is generally regarded as strongest— such as New Brunswick, which was founded by the Loyalists and has experienced so little in-migration that there have been few new ideological influences brought in via this route—one would also expect a strong democratic-socialist tradition. However, in its entire history only one federal third-party representative has been elected in New Brunswick. In the other Atlantic provinces, also widely considered bastions of toryism, there has been a similar low rate of third-party formation. Even Ontario, with its strong Loyalist and British heritage, has, with the exception of a brief period in the 1920s, failed to produce a strong contingent of third-party candidates, especially at the federal level. Federal and provincial third parties have received their greatest support in the ethnically heterogeneous Prairie provinces, in British Columbia, and, more recently, in Quebec. This, together with the fact that the Canadian parliamentary system exists in all provinces and therefore cannot, logically, be the explanation for interprovincial *variations* in support for third parties, leads inescapably to the conclusion that the cultural/institutional approach is of little value in explaining differences among the provinces in rates of political protest.

The same holds for variations over time. Protest movements and third parties in Canada have tended to grow in waves. Farmer and labour parties appeared almost everywhere from 1919 to 1925; right-wing populism and nationalism spread in Alberta and Quebec in the second half of the 1930s; democratic socialism in the form of the Co-operative Commonwealth Federation (CCF) made considerable progress in most parts of the country in the 1940s; nationalist movements on the right and, even more so, on the left, came to the fore in Quebec in the 1960s and 1970s; and the popularity of the New Democratic Party has grown in the 1980s. Again, constants (congealed values, the parliamentary system) cannot explain a variable (changes over time in the rate of third-party formation and support).

Mention of this diversity of ideologies prompts recognition of yet another weakness of the cultural/institutional thesis. It is one-sided in that it concentrates mainly on non-nationalistic, democratic socialist parties. Yet right-wing populism, in the form of the Social Credit party of Alberta, or left-wing national-ism, in the form of the Parti québécois, or right-of-centre nation-alism, in the form of the Union nationale, were or are important and established facts of Canadian political life. A theory that comes close to equating third parties with only the left-wing, non-nationalist variety leaves a great deal outside its explana-tory ambit.

This shortcoming—and most of the others noted above—stems ultimately from the undue emphasis that Horowitz and Lipset place on mass values as causes of political behaviour. Re-cent research demonstrates that mass values have, at best, a weak and diffuse effect on the number, strength, and policy orientations of political parties in Canada. For example, one study of politics in Atlantic Canada showed that in the 1960s electors were more dissatisfied with political life than electors elsewhere in the country, yet they did not form any new parties to reflect their interests (Brym 1979). A national sample survey conducted in the mid-1970s demonstrated that ideological dif-ferences between the provinces of English Canada were small and the reverse of what party support suggested. On average, Atlantic Canadians were the most left-wing, Ontarians were in the centre, and Westerners were most right-wing (Ornstein 1986). Research on Quebec politics in the 1960s revealed that the 'lower classes often supported conservative organizations or parties, but only because they were not presented with strong alternatives more consonant with their interests and sentiments' (Pinard 1973: 268). A number of national sample surveys con-ducted in the 1960s and 1970s indicated that the major Canadian political parties were generally perceived as too much 'for the middle class', even by middle-class voters themselves, and did not reflect the class issues that concerned the electorate (Lambert and Hunter 1979; Ogmundson 1976; Ornstein, Steven-son and Williams 1980). Several comparative policy studies have demonstrated that, although electors may believe parties differ from one another on major policy issues, the identity of the party in power, at both federal and provincial levels, actually has had no consistent effect on government actions (Cameron 1986; Winn and McMenemy 1976). After reviewing some of the rele-

vant literature, one researcher was forced by the weight of evidence to conclude that 'citizen attitudes, and the structures
through which they are expressed, either do not have the influence on policy outcomes which they are thought to have, or
they have an impact which is independent of any political in-
tentions by the public expressing them' (Shiry 1976: 43).

It seems, then, that mass values are far less important determinants of the number and policies of Canadian political parties
than adherents of the cultural/institutional thesis are prepared
to recognize. As an alternative, many scholars have sought to locate the chief causes of third-party formation in concrete
patterns of social, economic, and political relations.

## The structural approach

The intellectual roots of this structural orientation to the
problem of third-party formation in Canada extend back to the
1950s, when the late C.B. Macpherson (1962 [1953]) published
*Democracy in Alberta*. His subject was the meteoric rise to power
of the Social Credit party in the 1935 Alberta provincial election.
Macpherson stressed two factors that encouraged the success of
Social Credit: the nature of Alberta's class structure and the
relationship between its economy and eastern Canadian economic forces. He described the class structure as essentially *petit
bourgeois*, by which he meant that the largest class in the
province consisted of farmers who owned comparatively small
amounts of property. And he described the economic system as
quasi-colonial, by which he meant that control over its major
features was, especially through national tariff and transportation policies, exercised by capitalist interests in the East. The relative homogeneity of the class structure ensured that most
people in the province faced the same kinds of economic
problems, had the same interests, and were aware of them.
Because small property owners constituted the largest class,
political protest was populist: unlike the propertyless workers
who turned to socialism, the farmers supported capitalism, and
unlike the large property owners who typically supported liberalism, they pitted the 'little man' against the evils of a plutocratic
system. Finally, the quasi-colonial nature of the economy established a highly visible enemy in the east who could be perceived as the major source of the population's disadvantaged

position. In other words, there was a high degree of social cohesion *within* the major disadvantaged class and a high degree of segmentation *between* that class and external powers. Together, these elements facilitated the emergence of the Social Credit party.

Macpherson undoubtedly overemphasized the homogeneity of Alberta's class structure and failed to account for the emergence of different types of populist ideology in different Prairie provinces (Brym 1980; Richards and Pratt 1979). But his work did stimulate Maurice Pinard (1971) to generalize Macpherson's theory to the point where it could cover most cases of third-party formation in Canada. Examining in depth the rise of the Quebec Social Credit party in the 1962 federal election, Pinard argued that cleavage between a quasi-colonial economy and a dominant metropolitan economy is not the only form of social segmentation that is conducive to the rise of third parties. In fact, virtually any significant cleavage—between social classes, between ethnic groups, etc.—will suffice. Moreover, class homogeneity and solidarity among potential partisans of a third party are not the only forms of social cohesion that facilitate protest. Strong social attachments among members of any disadvantaged group—through voluntary organizations, face-to-face contact in small communities, common work contexts, and so forth—will have much the same effect. Finally (and this was a valuable addition to, rather than a generalization from, Macpherson's work), a system of one-party dominance facilitates the rise of third parties. This last point requires elaboration.

When Pinard wrote of one-party dominance he was referring to a situation in which one of the two establishment parties receives less than a third of the vote for some considerable period of time, or where it suddenly loses popular support as a consequence of, say, the revelation of flagrant corruption among party officials. In either case, only one of the establishment parties has a chance of forming the government. When seriously aggrieved segments of the population face a choice between a dominant establishment party and a very weak establishment party, they will be inclined to vote for neither. The dominant party is too closely identified with the sources of the population's grievances and the other establishment party is not seen as a realistic alternative since it is so weak. A third, alternative party is then likely to emerge.

Pinard offered some compelling evidence to support his thesis. For example, in 88 per cent of 33 provincial elections where the main opposition party was strong and received more than a third of the vote, third parties received 20 per cent of the vote or less. In 59 per cent of 22 provincial elections where the main opposition party was chronically weak and received less than a third of the vote, more than 20 per cent of the ballots were cast for the third party. And in 90 per cent of 10 provincial elections where the main opposition party was suddenly weakened, third parties received more than 20 per cent of the vote.

In a subsequent article Pinard (1973) made it clear that one-party dominance is in fact only one variant of a more general set of conditions that are conducive to the rise of new parties: the non-representation of social groups through the party system. That is to say, a strong two-party or even multi-party system can fail as completely as a system of one-party dominance to provide channels of expression and representation for aggrieved groups, and so may give rise to new parties. This may occur, for example, in times of crisis when establishment parties form a coalition, thereby preventing large groups that oppose the government from gaining representation. Or (and here Pinard endorsed an aspect of the cultural/institutional theory), representative failure may occur more frequently when a party system is organized along British parliamentary lines and consequently inhibits the accommodation of diverse interests within existing parties. Thus an unpolished summary of Pinard's argument is that Canadian third parties have tended to emerge where members of disadvantaged groups are (a) bound together in dense social networks, (b) highly socially polarized from advantaged groups, and (c) relatively unrepresented by existing parties.

Recently these social-structural and political conditions of third-party formation have been further elaborated (Brym 1979; 1980; 1984; 1986b; 1986c; Brym and Neis 1978; Brym, Gillespie, and Lenton 1989). Regarding social structure it has been noted that segmentation between, and solidarity within, potential conflict groups are not the only social-structural conditions that facilitate third-party formation or, more generally, political protest. Specifically, protest activity increases with declines in the ratio of authorities' to potential partisans' power. The power of a class or other group, it is held, depends on three factors. In descending order of importance, these are: (a) the group's access to material resources (property, money, jobs), normative resources (communications media, educational institutions), and coercive resources (police, armed forces); (b) the density of social ties within the group; and (c) the size of the group's membership and support base. The more powerful the potential partisans of a social movement or a third party are, relative to their opponents, the greater is the likelihood that a social movement or a third party will form and gain support. Conversely, the greater the relative power of the opponents of a social movement or a third party, the less the likelihood of a social movement's or a third party's emerging and gaining support—even if potential partisans are seriously aggrieved. For example, in economically depressed Atlantic Canada third parties tended not to be formed in the pre-Second World War period, despite widespread deprivation and dissatisfaction with government, because power was so highly concentrated in the hands of ruling circles. The only exceptions occurred in those few areas where atypically high levels of capital investment created relatively solidary and prosperous classes of blue-collar workers, farmers, and fishers at a time when the establishment parties were temporarily disunited.

With respect to political structure, it has been suggested that electoral systems and other features of the state that may inhibit interests from gaining representation in existing parties are themselves linked to historical variations in the social-structural determinants of power listed above. The state, after all, is the principal institutional means by which raw power is transformed into actual rule. In proportion to their relative power, classes and other groups are able to use the state to confer the right to pass laws, dispense patronage, design school curricula, and take a variety of other influential actions. These actions become institutionalized in the form of state structures, which then shape political life to a considerable degree independently of any short-term variations in the distribution of power in society. State structures continue to exercise this impact until the social-structural determinants of power are substantially redistributed.

The full significance of these points will become clear only in the following sections of this chapter. As we shall see, they tie together areas of the field that were formerly treated in isolation and thus provide the groundwork for a more unified Canadian political sociology.

VOTING

It seems plausible that one consequence of the existence of a separate democratic-socialist party in Canada is that a higher proportion of workers gets mobilized by, identifies with, and votes for a particular party than is the case in the US. But research conducted in the 1960s by Robert Alford, an American sociologist, showed that the 'class vote' in Canada was actually lower than the class vote in the US (Alford 1963; 1967; see also Clark 1963). (This brand of research further shows that in most Western liberal democracies one's class position is always an important, and frequently the most important, determinant of whether one supports a left-wing, a right-wing, or a centrist party; but Canada and the US, along with Ireland, have the lowest class vote in the Western world.) Some subsequent American-inspired survey research, conducted for the most part by political scientists, seems to confirm that class is a very weak predictor of voting behaviour in Canada. These surveys have been interpreted to show that only place of residence, religion, and ethnicity generally have some independent and statistically significant effect on whether or not one votes for a left-wing party. Moreover, place of residence, religion, and ethnicity are moderately correlated among themselves. For example, French Canadians tend to live in Quebec and to be of Catholic origin. It has thus become commonplace to attribute the low class vote in Canada to these mutually reinforcing, non-class, regionally based cleavages. As the authors of the standard work on Canadian voting behaviour put it:

> Patterns of settlement by various ethnic and religious groups in different regions with persistent disparities in levels of economic well-being and types of economic activity have produced a societal cleavage structure which may be among the most strongly reinforcing of any contemporary Western democracy. (Clarke *et al*. 1980: 73)

Moreover, Canada's constituency-based electoral system presumably exaggerates these regionally based differences because, everything else being equal, parties whose support is geographically dispersed win fewer seats than parties with geographically concentrated support (Cairns 1968). Similarly, the constitutionally defined division of powers between federal and provincial levels of government increases regional conflict and thereby perpetuates the salience of regional communities and interests (Cairns 1977; Simeon 1977). In short, while British politics is commonly regarded as pure class politics, 'Canadian politics is regional politics' (Simeon and Elkins 1974: 397; cf. Schwartz 1974).

Beginning in the 1970s this interpretation of Canadian voting was criticized, mainly by Canadian sociologists, for four reasons: (a) the position of the various Canadian political parties on class issues was measured inadequately in the earlier voting studies; (b) the class position of individuals was also measured in a problematic manner; (c) the earlier studies incorrectly assumed that voting patterns indicate class consciousness alone (in fact, voting patterns also reflect the structure of voting opportunities); (d) there are exceptions to the voting patterns identified by the American-inspired voting studies (analyzing these exceptions allows one to specify more precisely the conditions that account for variations in the class vote). Let us consider each of these points.

## Parties, class issues, and class positions

In Alford's original work two parties were classified as leftist (the New Democratic Party, formerly the CCF, and the Liberals) while two parties were classified as rightist (the Progressive Conservative and Social Credit parties). But in an analysis of national sample survey and other data dating largely from the 1960s, Rick Ogmundson (1975a; cf. Zipp 1978) demonstrated that this classification does not correspond to voters' perceptions of the parties' stands on class issues, the parties' bases of electoral support, the social origins of the parties' members of Parliament, or the major sources of party financing. Ogmundson instead proposed that no single left-right scale could adequately illustrate party differences. Rather, separate social and economic left-right scales are needed. On the economic scale the NDP and the Social Credit party are on the left in terms of voter perceptions and the other measures of party position listed above. These minor parties tend to be more supportive than the major parties of policies that redistribute income and social services to the benefit of the less advantaged. On the other hand, the NDP and the Liberals occupy the left position on the social scale. They are less traditionalist than the Progressive Conservative and Social Credit parties.[2]

The upshot is that in recent voting studies Alford's categorization of Canadian political parties has been abandoned (see, for example, Myles 1979; Zipp and Smith 1982). In some cases the NDP and the Social Credit party are classified as leftist; in others the NDP is classified as the only leftist party in the country and Social Credit is ignored entirely. This is justified on the grounds that federal Social Credit support was always weak and concentrated in Quebec and Alberta, while Social Credit support has recently declined to the point where it has failed to elect any members of Parliament. In either case the recategorization of leftist and rightist parties increases the measure of class voting in Canada.

The measure of class voting also increases if one refines the statistical techniques employed by Alford (Myles 1979) and if one abandons the simple manual/non-manual distinction he used to measure individuals' class positions. Evidence indicates that the major cleavage in political attitudes in advanced capitalist societies does not run between manual and non-manual workers, but between lower-level white-collar and blue-collar workers, on the one hand, and, on the other, people occupying higher positions in the stratification system (Hamilton and Wright 1975). Furthermore, it has been demonstrated that some occupations do not fall unambiguously into manual or non-manual categories, and that the results of Alford's analysis depend heavily on how these ambiguous occupations are assigned. Switching only one occupation from one category to the other can significantly alter Alford's results (Korpi 1972). Research on voting in Winnipeg in the 1945 federal election showed that using income, education, and occupation as measures of class instead of the manual/non-manual distinction increases the level of apparent class voting (Wiseman and Taylor 1974). And two analyses of a national sample survey conducted after the 1974 federal election demonstrated that the use of neo-Marxist class categories results in a somewhat stronger measured class vote at the federal level than is found in the older literature (Hunter 1982; Zipp and Smith 1982; see, however, Ornstein, Stevenson, and Williams 1980 for less encouraging results).

The fact remains, however, that even with all these refinements in conceptualization and measurement, the most that can be said about the class vote in Canada is that it is no lower than the class vote in the US. The level of class voting in both countries still appears to be below that of other industrialized countries. In John Myles's (1979: 1236) words, 'future research should address the North American exception . . . . [T]he Canadian exception is a pseudofact which can be laid to rest.'

## Voting, class consciousness, and political opportunity

The view that the level of class voting, however measured, tells us something exclusively about the level of class consciousness in Canada also appears naïve in the light of subsequent research and theorizing. In the first place, cross-national studies of social class self-identification show that the level of working-class consciousness in Canada is probably not very much lower than that in most Western European countries (Rinehart and Okraku 1974; but see Goyder and Pineo 1979 for some important methodological qualifications). Second, one may readily call into question the assumption that attitudes and ideologies determine voting preferences, and that voting preferences determine the number and policies of political parties. As was noted in the preceding section, more than half a dozen attitudinal and policy studies show that there is a major disjuncture between mass attitudes, on the one hand, and the number and policies of parties, on the other. This has led some students of Canadian voting behaviour to suggest that the structure of voting opportunities—the range of political choice available to the electorate—is at least as important a determinant of who votes for which party as mass attitudes are.

Ogmundson's analysis of national sample survey data collected in the 1960s is particularly important in this connection (Ogmundson 1975b; 1975c; Ogmundson and Ng 1982). Ogmundson introduced the idea of the subjective class vote, that is, the degree to which people in a given class believe they are voting for a party that reflects their class interests—independently of whether the party actually does so. He discovered that the subjective class vote in Canada was significantly higher than the objective class vote. In other words, the class vote increased markedly if parties were classified according to voters' *perceptions* of the degree to which the parties were 'for the middle class' or 'for the working class', rather than according to some other (objective) criterion of the parties' positions on class issues. Using comparable data from the UK, and measuring individuals' class positions by income, Ogmundson and Ng (1982) actually discovered a negligible difference between subjective class voting in Canada (sometimes called the outstanding case of pure non-class politics) and the UK (sometimes called the outstanding case of pure class politics).

*Intended* class voting, and voter interest in class issues, is thus considerable in Canada. As one national sample survey conducted in the late 1970s showed, socio-economic status and neo-Marxist measures of class account for more of the variation on broad questions of political ideology than does region of residence. These questions include support for labour, political protest, minority rights, restrictions on foreign control of the Canadian economy, income redistribution, and expanded social-welfare services. Moreover, left-wing attitudes towards these issues are significantly and independently associated with occupying a lower position in the stratification system (Ornstein, Stevenson, and Williams 1980; Johnston and Ornstein 1982).

Nevertheless, the *objective* class vote *is* comparatively low, and it seems reasonable to conclude that this is at least partly the result of the relative unavailability of an outlet for existing class sentiment. John Zipp and Joel Smith (1982) have recently examined an important empirical consequence of this argument. They hypothesized that class ought to be most strongly related to voting for the NDP where that party has a fair chance of winning (conservatively, where it won more than 25 per cent of the vote in the preceding election). In constituencies where the NDP stands little chance of winning, however, class ought to be associated with *non*-voting. Members of the working class are more likely to abstain from voting altogether if no party serving their class interests is likely to win. Using a 1974 national sample survey, and employing neo-Marxist class categories, Zipp and Smith found precisely this sort of interaction effect among class, the presence of a viable NDP candidate, and voting. They concluded that

Canada is not the bastion of pure non-class politics. The purported weakness of the influence of class on politics and the seemingly low levels of class voting found previously in Canada [cannot be attributed just to] a presumed disinterest in class issues and an absence of class consciousness among Canadians. . . . Our results indicate that the reason does not lie totally with individual Canadian citizens, for class is related more strongly to voting where the citizen is presented with a viable outlet for the expression of class sentiments (Zipp and Smith 1982: 753).

### FIGURE 3.1

### TWO MODELS OF VOTING BEHAVIOUR

*A. The Pluralist Model*

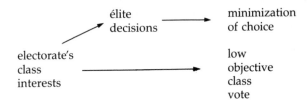

*B. Ogmundson's Alternative Model*

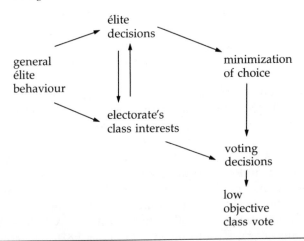

SOURCE: Adapted from Ogmundson 1980: 52; Schreiber 1980: 43.

The pluralist voting model and the alternative model that Ogmundson and others have proposed are illustrated in Figure 3.1. The pluralists view electoral interest as the fundamental reason why upper classes and political élites do not politicize class issues more and why citizens do not vote along class lines more. The alternative model also recognizes that electoral interest is of some importance in shaping upper-class and political-élite decisions and preventing a higher level of class voting. But considerable independent causal weight is also assigned to upper-class and political-élite interests. In this view, apart from anything the voters may themselves want, upper classes and political élites are able to minimize party choice along class lines.

## Class power and variations in the class vote

Studying variations in the class vote illustrates how voting patterns are shaped by the interplay between subordinate and superordinate class power. Among Canadian provinces the level of class voting is higher in British Columbia, Ontario, Manitoba, and Saskatchewan than in the other provinces. A number of constituencies have been shown to have quite a high class vote, the city of Winnipeg having come under especially careful scrutiny in this regard (see, for example, Clarke *et al.* 1980: 85; Kornberg, Mishler, and Clarke 1982: 117; Stevenson 1977a; 1977b; Wilson 1974; Wiseman and Taylor 1974). If Ogmundson, Zipp and Smith, and others are correct, then such differences ought to be related to variations in the capacity of upper classes and political élites to limit political choice and minimize class voting.

Two recent studies suggest that this may well be the case. In the first (Brym 1986b), two measures of workers' and farmers' relative power in each province were proposed: the proportion of the population belonging to trade unions and co-operatives (an index of how well organized these classes are), and *per capita* income (an index of subordinate class access to money, one important material resource). These measures were used to predict statistically the proportion of electors in each province who voted NDP in the 1980 federal election. Excluding Alberta and Quebec (for reasons given below) nearly 80 per cent of the inter-provincial variation in the NDP vote was explained with an equation that statistically was highly significant.

This study established the existence of relationships between the distribution of class power and the level of support for the NDP at the provincial level. It did not establish that these relationships corresponded to individual-level behaviour (e.g., that relatively well-to-do, unionized members of the working class were most likely to vote NDP). In a second study (Brym, Gillespie, and Lenton 1989), 1968 voting and other data were analyzed for this purpose. The researchers found that two measures of class resources at the level of the province—percentage of union members and percentage of co-operative members—continued to affect an individual's decision whether to vote NDP after controlling for the individual's occupation, union membership, and income. This result indicates that the findings of the earlier analysis were not merely an outcome of using provincial-level correlations. Moreover, support for the power-resources theory was also found at the individual level in the form of an interaction between union membership and income. The effect of union membership on voting NDP increased with the income of the voter. Finally, the effects of residence in Alberta and Quebec were replicated. Union membership and income had little effect on voting NDP in these provinces.

These findings suggest the plausibility of a class explanation of variations in level of class voting. With the exceptions noted, one can reasonably accurately predict the level of NDP support in 1968 and in 1980 from measures of the relative power of the subordinate classes in the province. In general, it seems that the greater the relative power of subordinate classes, the higher the level of NDP support (and the greater the degree to which the party system consequently reflects the interests of subordinate classes).

What accounts for the unexpectedly low level of NDP support in Alberta and Quebec (Brym 1986c)? The NDP has traditionally stood for a strong central government and tightly circumscribed provincial autonomy. Centralism, however, remains an attitude that is unlikely to win many supporters in the two provinces that have been the most ardent advocates of provincial rights and the most fertile ground for the growth of separatist movements in recent decades.[3]

Many scholars have linked the strength of autonomism and separatism in Quebec and Alberta to a feature of their class structures: the unusual power of local capitalist and 'new middle' classes (Cuneo and Curtis 1974; Guindon 1964; Hamilton and Pinard 1976; McRoberts and Posgate 1980 [1976]; Ornstein, Stevenson and Williams 1978; Pinard and Hamilton 1977; Pratt and Stevenson 1981; Richards and Pratt 1979). In Alberta the post-Second World War oil boom created an unusually large and prosperous class of entrepreneurs engaged in the real-estate, oil, and gas businesses, as well as a large and prosperous new middle class of technicians and professionals. In Quebec the Quiet Revolution of the 1960s greatly expanded job opportunities for university-educated Québécois in the government bureaucracy, Crown corporations, and the system of higher education. In both cases these powerful classes have encouraged provincial governments to stimulate provincial development by intervening directly in the local economy. One index of their success is that between 1959 and 1982 the assets of provincial Crown corporations have grown faster in Quebec and Alberta than in all other provinces. These classes have also pushed for more provincial autonomy, it being in their best interest to do so: business-people who can profit most if they are free from federal government interference, and members of the new middle class, who—as a result of the invigoration of the local economy—are employed either in the provincial government bureaucracy or private industry, stand to benefit most from the decentralization of authority.

Decentralizing sentiment in Alberta and Quebec has been reflected at the federal level by substantial voter alienation, which has taken the form of an unusually high level of non-voting and support for absurdist parties, notably the Rhinoceros Party in Quebec. More important, voters in Alberta and Quebec have tended to support federal parties that favour provincial autonomy to the greatest degree: hence the fate of the federal Liberal party in Quebec—and therefore in Canada as a whole—in the 1984 election. The Liberals lost heavily to the Conservatives, who co-operated with Parti québécois members to ensure the election of a federal government that was sympathetic to Quebec autonomism and prepared to enshrine constitutionally Quebec's special place in Confederation. The 1987 Meech Lake accord was the outcome of that unofficial coalition.

Recent developments have altered somewhat the political landscape just sketched. In the past few years the popularity of autonomism and separatism in Alberta and Quebec has declined, and levels of NDP support in these provinces has approached the national average. But if Alberta and Quebec are no longer so out of the ordinary, traditionally they have stood out as exceptions that prove the rule. In the other provinces there has been for decades a more or less clear relationship between the relative power of wage labourers and farmers, on the one hand, and the degree of NDP support, on the other. But until recently this relationship has been obscured in Alberta and Quebec because members of certain other classes have been sufficiently powerful to generate a high level of autonomist and separatist feeling that runs counter to traditional NDP ideology.

The main implication of this analysis is that low levels of class voting do not result exclusively or even largely from low levels of class awareness and insensitivity to class issues. Undeniably, regional and ethnic issues dominate Canadian electoral politics. For the most part, elections and parties in Canada thus help to create a unified sense of purpose between classes—a 'national interest'. Relatively low levels of class voting, however, appear to be associated with unusually highly skewed power distributions, which allow political élites to present citizens with comparatively few opportunities for expressing their class interests.

This generalization also holds cross-nationally. For most of the major capitalist democracies, the relative power of the working class is associated with the popularity of working-class parties (Brym 1986c). That is, in countries with strong working classes Parliament is the main locus of conflict over the distribution of rewards in society. In contrast, working-class parties in countries such as Canada, Italy, and the US have secured little if any Cabinet representation since the Second World War. In countries of the latter type there takes place what might be called a displacement of political class conflict: distributional questions tend to be debated more in the workplace than in Parliament.[4] Thus Canada, Italy, and the US lost more time *per capita* because of strikes than other Western countries in the 1970s. And it has been demonstrated that for the major advanced capitalist countries, including Canada, there is a very strong association between (a) the pre-Second World War/post-Second World War difference in mean strike volume and (b) the pre-Second World War/post-Second World War difference in democratic socialist and communist cabinet representation (Hibbs 1978; Korpi and Shalev 1980).[5] In other words, in advanced capitalist societies with relatively strong upper classes and relatively weak working classes there tends to be a low level of socialist representation in the political élite, which in turn encourages a high volume of strike activity. In such circumstances class conflict is displaced, but concern over class issues on the part of the working class does not necessarily disappear; members of the working class may be pragmatically resigned to the capitalist economic system and the capitalist state, but they do not necessarily believe in the legitimacy of capitalism (Brym 1979; Mann 1970; Vanneman and Pampel 1977).

A second important implication of my argument is that a new variable should be added to Lipset's interpretation of voting behaviour. Lipset tends to think of (a) the type of electoral system in a polity, as an independent variable that influences (b) the number and types of parties in existence, and, therefore, (c) the broad outlines of voting behaviour. In contrast, I have suggested that (d), the distribution of power in society, has a profound impact on (a), (b), and (c).[6] Electoral systems (as well as other state institutions) are, I submit, resolutions of past conflict between classes and other groups. The form, timing, and outcome of such conflict depends on how power was distributed between major social collectivities (classes, ethnic and religious groups, etc.) at the time important constitutional decisions were worked out. Once in place, electoral systems do influence the party system and voting behaviour in profound ways. But so do shifts in the distribution of power caused by urbanization, industrialization, and immigration. In the Canadian case such power shifts have given rise to social movements and third parties. And it is not inconceivable that under some circumstances they may result in substantial electoral-system reform. It therefore seems to me that the implication of much work in contemporary Canadian political sociology is that variations in a wide range of political phenomena may be profitably analyzed from the point of view of power relations. Analysis of power relations helps to explain the level of class voting, the rate of social-movement formation, the volume and shape of strike activity, the strength of democratic-socialist and other third parties, the degree to which electoral systems shield ruling parties from challenge, and, as we shall see, the degree of welfare-state development as well.

THE ROLE OF THE STATE

*Theories of the capitalist state*

I have argued that an emphasis on the distribution of power is beginning to emerge as the basis of political analysis in Canadian sociology, replacing the earlier American-influenced focus on cultural and institutional causation. This is, however, more true in some subfields than others. The study of social movements, third parties, and voting behaviour has experienced a marked shift in this direction. Analysis of the state has not.

This is not because the mainstream American theory of the state—pluralism—is especially well entrenched in Canada. Indeed, the opposite may be the case: it is significant that in John Porter's pathbreaking and enormously influential *The Vertical Mosaic* (1965), which introduced Canadian sociologists to the question of the relationship between state and society, no reference is made to any of the works of key American pluralists. As a result, when the sociological study of the state in Canada became a major area of interest, in the 1970s, it was open to the influence of some of the more popular currents of European Marxism. Specifically, the 'instrumentalist' theory of the state, most closely associated with the work of Ralph Miliband (1973 [1969]), predominated until the mid-1970s. Subsequently, Nicos Poulantzas's (1975 [1968]) 'structuralist' approach gained widespread acceptance. I will argue below that this development has had the unfortunate consequence of drawing attention away from the issues concerning power that have invigorated other subfields of political sociology in Canada. But first some background.

In the mid-1960s Porter sought to establish that élite members—the chief power-holders in economic, political, media, bureaucratic, and intellectual institutions—tend to be recruited from well-to-do families of British and Protestant origin in numbers far greater than the proportion of such families in the population. Moreover, he argued that members of the different élites come to share certain values and attitudes as they interact with one another. This cohesion enables them to achieve 'the over-all co-ordination that is necessary for the continuity of the society' (Porter 1965: 523). Cohesion is attained informally by élite members' attending private schools together, intermarrying, and forming strong friendship ties. In addition, a number of formal mechanisms reinforce cohesion. For example, various commissions and advisory boards are set up by governments, and members of the economic élite are usually the preferred appointees. Similarly, funding for the establishment political parties comes almost exclusively from wealthy corporate patrons. A 'confraternity of power' is thereby established among the various élite groups.

In Porter's opinion, the existence of this confraternity does not, however, mean that Canada's élites form a ruling class: '[T]he élite groups remain separated and never become merged into one effective power group' (Porter 1965: 215). He emphasized that harmony among élites has limits, as is indicated by the fact that various élites come into conflict over a wide range of issues.

A decade later Clement, Porter's student, acknowledged the existence of such conflict. But he underscored its limits, not the limits of élite harmony. Clement concluded that Canada's major institutional élites do indeed form a cohesive group that represents the country's capitalist class, and that this cohesion makes the élites a ruling class. The members of this class are presumably united around the goals of protecting private property, preventing the spread of public sovereignty over economic resources, and preserving continentalism as the dominant Canadian way of life. Yet Clement based his argument largely on the same type of data that Porter had used to come to the opposite conclusion—data showing the relatively similar class, ethnic, religious, and even family origins of members of different élites; and the effective operation of formal and informal mechanisms that bind together corporate and political élites in particular (Clement 1975: 353, 359; cf. Olsen 1980). Even among those scholars inclined to accord the state greater independence of, or autonomy from, the corporate élite, it was common in the mid-1970s to remark on 'a particularly striking characteristic of the Canadian state—its very close personal ties to the bourgeoisie. Whatever the merits of Poulantzas's contention that the most efficient state is that with the least direct ties to the dominant class, it is a rather academic point as applied to Canada' (Panitch 1977a: 11).

This line of reasoning was greatly indebted to Miliband's (1973 [1969]) early work. Miliband portrayed the various institutions that the state comprises—the government, legislature, judicial system, military, police, and public bureaucracy—as operating more to the advantage of the capitalist class than of other classes. He claimed that this bias exists because the capitalist class directly controls state institutions. For example, top officials in all state institutions throughout the Western world are recruited substantially from the upper reaches of the capitalist class itself. Therefore, said Miliband, they reflect that class's interests. Similarly, state officials tend to rely on members of the capitalist class for advice in policy formulation and, in the case of political parties, for material support in election campaigns. Because of these and other mechanisms, the state allegedly serves as an *instrument* of the capitalist class's will; hence the school's name.

On the whole, the best available Canadian evidence fails to support this theory. In the first place, there are important political and ideological cleavages between corporate leaders and state officials. Thus the Liberal Party has been in power for most of the post-Second World War era, yet it has rarely been overwhelmingly supported by the corporate élite, which appears to be mainly Tory. Accordingly, survey results show that members of the state élite are significantly less right-wing than corporate leaders (Ornstein 1985; 1986). Second, a systematic analysis of people who held both corporate and state positions at some time between 1946 and 1977 demonstrates that the level of interlocking between corporations and the state was not nearly high enough to suggest direct corporate domination of the state (Fox and Ornstein 1986). Third, critics of instrumentalism have argued that there is insufficient cohesion and unity of purpose within the capitalist class itself to allow direct rule. In this view, many important political conflicts in Canada reflect, at least in part, cleavages within the capitalist class—between, say, its different ethnic or national segments (notably Québécois versus English Canadian) or between its different regional components (such as western versus Ontarian) (Sales 1985; Stevenson 1982). In sum, inter- and intra-élite divisions attest to the disunity of the capitalist class and its inability to rule the state directly and with the stability that would promote its overall best interests.

In the light of these perceived shortcomings, many Canadian scholars accepted the ideas of Nicos Poulantzas (1975 [1968]) as an alternative to instrumentalism. Poulantzas's theory of the relationship between the capitalist class and the state is usually referred to as 'structuralism'—a term derived from his insistence that it is the environing system of socio-economic relations that is responsible for the state's serving the long-run interests of the capitalist class as a whole. This system (or structure) allegedly places certain restrictions on the state's freedom of operation. For example, state officials are unlikely to take actions that offend capitalist interests too profoundly for fear of provoking an 'investment strike' (i.e., encouraging the flow of capital out of the country). It is restrictions like these, not direct ties between the state and the capitalist class, that, according to Poulantzas, make the state act with its characteristic bias. In order to ensure the persistence of capitalist economic relations, state officials may even find it necessary to take actions opposed by one or more powerful segments of the capitalist class. In this sense the state must not be closely tied to, but rather 'relatively autonomous' of, the capitalist class; only thus can it perform its functions efficiently.

The work of Tom Traves (1979) illustrates how this theory has been applied to Canada.[7] Traves sought to explain how the Canadian state came to play a more interventionist and regulatory role in the country's economic life during the period 1917-31. He argued that a variety of competing claims were placed on the state—for and against tariff protection, for and against direct financial assistance, and so forth—by different segments of the capitalist class and by industrial workers and farmers as well. The governments of the day did not heed only the demands of the most powerful subgroups in the capitalist class, nor only the demands of the capitalist class as a whole. Rather, they tried to mediate conflicts by working out compromises and maintaining 'a delicate balance of power between contending classes and interest groups' (Traves 1979: 156).

One might well ask how this analysis differs from the pluralist interpretations favoured by political analysts in the 1950s and 1960s, and now widely held in disrepute. Pluralists too thought of the state as performing certain 'brokerage functions' and acting as a mediator of conflict between competing classes and other interest groups. But there is one critical difference between structuralism and pluralism. In the structuralist view government supposedly assumes 'the burden of perpetuating capitalism itself. In this sense it is not a value-free broker, but rather the protector and promoter of a specific set of rules and social relationships founded upon capitalist property relationships' (Traves 1979: 158).

This may seem like functionalist reasoning, and indeed it is. Structuralists like Traves think that, fundamentally, it is the 'needs' of the socio-economic system that compel state officials to adopt policies that appear to satisfy all interests but actually have the effect of perpetuating existing class relations, and therefore of benefiting capitalists more than others.

Such reasoning, however, introduces a number of serious conceptual and empirical problems, some of which have been raised with reference to functionalist reasoning in general. In the first place, imputing needs to socio-economic systems makes it seem as if these systems have human attributes, including the ability to engage in goal-directed behaviour. Of course, people have needs and goals, and powerful people are often able to convince, pay, or force others to act in ways that serve the needs and goals of the powerful. But socio-economic systems do not have needs and goals other than those that people, including entire classes of people, impose on them. A capitalist system's 'need' to perpetuate capitalist class relations is no more than a desire on the part of people who benefit from those relations to see things continue pretty much as they are. The teleological and anthropomorphic tendencies of structuralism obscure this fact.

Second, structuralist logic is circular. According to the structuralists, government policies are functional for the capitalist system; that is, they have certain salutary consequences for existing class relations. How does one know that a given policy is functional? By virtue of the fact that it was adopted: in the structuralist schema all existing state policies are functional. In other words, policies are enacted because they are functional, and they are functional because they are enacted. One is bound to admit that this reasoning provides little clarification regarding the evolution of particular state policies.

Third, structuralists interpret the introduction of unemployment insurance, public health care, laws recognizing the right of workers to form unions, to strike, and to engage in collective bargaining, and all other reforms associated with the growth of the welfare state as 'fundamentally' irrelevant to the long-term well-being of employees, since such reforms merely 'legitimize' the existing social order (e.g., Cuneo 1980: 38). What this argument wholly ignores, however, is that reformist changes may have a cumulative effect on the distribution of income and, more generally, advantages in society. Thus there is considerably less economic inequality in Sweden than in Canada, largely because Sweden has a better developed welfare system that provides universal public day-care and other benefits unknown in Canada. Such a system may indeed increase the longevity of capitalism. But one must remember that this more mature capitalism is not the same capitalism that existed in Dickens's England; and that, as Marx and Engels used to argue, it is at least possible that in the most advanced capitalist societies socialism may evolve gradually through electoral politics (Brym 1986b; Korpi 1983; Korpi and Shalev 1980; O'Connor and Brym 1988).

That these reforms are hard-won suggests a fourth and final criticism of the structuralist viewpoint. By claiming that state policies are automatic responses to the needs of the capitalist system, structuralism plays down the fact that workers and farmers had to fight, in many cases bitterly, in order to have these policies implemented. Structuralists also imply that workers and farmers were gullible or irrational to do so, since 'fundamentally' they were only contributing to a legitimizing myth that enabled the process of capital accumulation to continue. It is ironic that some Marxists should minimize the significance of class (and other group) conflict and assume a patronizing attitude towards working people, who, after all, may frequently elect to engage in reformist action because that strategy assures them of more certain benefits and fewer likely costs than other possible strategies.

## From relative autonomy to level of intervention

If one strips away these untenable functionalist assumptions, the idea that the state is relatively autonomous of the capitalist class nevertheless amounts to a very useful insight. It overcomes the major weaknesses of instrumentalism and enables one to portray more accurately the relationship between capitalist classes and states.[8]

The state's relative autonomy derives partly from the mundane fact that state officials want to keep their jobs. State officials thus have an occupational interest in not offending any class or group to such a degree that their re-election or reappointment is jeopardized. Remaining somewhat removed from the will of the capitalist class is thus a matter of survival for the political élite.

A second and more profound source of relative autonomy is the frequently overlooked fact that state policies and institutions are no more than long-lasting legal resolutions of historically specific conflicts among classes and other groups. In other words, states are socio-legal structures that reflect the distribution of resources, organization, and support—in short, of power—among classes and other groups at given points in time. These structures, once created, usually pattern political life for many years—specifically, until power is massively redistributed, at which time newly manifest conflicts may change them.

Electoral systems have already been mentioned in this connection. They are forged out of conflicts over how effectively different categories of the population will be represented in the state. There seems to be an association between the relative historical strength of the working class in the advanced capitalist countries and the openness of electoral systems to working-class representation (Brym 1986c). Significantly, however, electoral systems, once in place, are reformed only infrequently and gradually: despite the massive changes undergone by class structures in the advanced capitalist countries in the twentieth century, there have been no major changes in their electoral systems since the 1920s, and in many cases even earlier (Lipset and Rokkan 1967). The enormous influence of electoral rules on how well different classes and other groups will be represented is thus relatively autonomous of current class and other group pressures. Analogous arguments can be made for other state institutions and policies.

The view that state institutions and policies reflect contemporary and historical class and other group conflicts suggests that state autonomy is not a fixed quantity but a variable. That is, states may be more or less autonomous of the capitalist class, and there is an association between degree of autonomy and the distribution of power between superordinate and subordinate classes: the lower the ratio of superordinate to subordinate class power, the more autonomous the state from the capitalist class. Nora Hamilton (1981) has thus shown for the Latin American countries that, everything else being equal, state autonomy increases as dominant classes become more divided. Similarly, as a considerable body of research emanating mainly from Sweden has established (e.g., Korpi 1983; Korpi and Shalev 1980; cf. Rueschemeyer and Evans 1985), states tend to become more autonomous of the capitalist class as subordinate classes increase their capacity to use the state for their own ends.

This association is clearly evident if one examines variations in the degree to which advanced capitalist states undertake interventionist and redistributive policies that benefit subordinate classes. One recent study of seventeen advanced capitalist countries (O'Connor and Brym 1988) demonstrates that the more highly organized working classes are in trade unions, the greater the degree to which (a) left parties gain long-term cabinet participation, and (b) 'corporatist' structures are created for societal-level tripartite bargaining among unions, capitalist umbrella organizations, and the state. In turn, the establishment of mechanisms for societal-level bargaining is associated with increased state intervention as reflected in more non-military public expenditure. In other words, taking most of the advanced capitalist countries into account, it appears that the more powerful working classes are relative to capitalist classes, the greater is their capacity to cause the state to undertake redistributive initiatives. This capacity is, however, significantly mediated by the structure of state institutions.

The Canadian case illustrates the point well. In 1980 Canada ranked twelfth among seventeen OECD countries in level of welfare spending. This low rank may be attributed to three sets of factors. First, the Canadian capitalist class is relatively powerful: by international standards the economy is highly oligopolized, and corporate interlocking among top capitalists is relatively dense (Clement 1975; Ornstein 1989). Second, the Canadian working class is comparatively weak: its level of unionization places it at the low end among OECD countries, and no left party has ever been represented in a Canadian federal cabinet. Third, tripartite societal-level bargaining is minimal in Canada: the country's relatively weak working class and its decentralized

federal structure have inhibited unitary state action. For these reasons the Canadian state is less autonomous of the capitalist class and less interventionist and redistributive than most states in Western Europe (Banting 1987; Brym 1986b; Cameron 1986; O'Connor and Brym 1988; Panitch 1986).

Of course, power relations between superordinate and subordinate classes in Canada have fluctuated over time. In concluding, I will illustrate this point by outlining how increasing working class power between 1945 and 1981, and subsequent capitalist-class reaction to working-class gains, have influenced Canadian state policy.

The augmentation of working-class power between the end of the Second World War and the 1981-82 recession derived from the increasing prosperity, unionization, and militancy of the nonagricultural labour force. This was an era of unprecedented economic expansion. As Canada-US trade and investment grew, Canadians prospered from their close relationship with the world's wealthiest, hegemonic power. During this period the proportion of unionized workers in the nonagricultural paid labour force doubled, reaching 40 per cent in 1983. Strikes became an increasingly popular means by which workers expressed discontent—to the point where in the 1970s Canada lost more time because of strikes per 1,000 workers than any other country in the world. Increased radicalism was also reflected in the so-called 'breakaway' movement. Before 1977 over half of Canada's trade unionists were small minorities in international unions with large US memberships. Conditioned by American electoral and other circumstances, these unions were largely opposed to the idea that workers should support an independent labour party. In the 1970s, however, Canadian unionists became increasingly dissatisfied with the internationals for failing to support them in key labour disputes and collecting more in union dues than they reinvested in Canadian organizational and educational work. As a result many Canadians broke ties with the internationals and formed their own national unions. These nationals were more supportive of the NDP than the internationals had been, and they have apparently succeeded in gradually mobilizing a larger proportion of the trade-union vote for the NDP (Laxer 1976).

Propitious fiscal conditions, combined with mounting pressure from below, encouraged the expansion of health and education services, unemployment insurance and regional development programs, and so forth. In the 1970s state autonomy and intervention in the economy reached a stage where the Liberal government of Pierre Trudeau began adopting policies aimed at increasing Canadian economic independence. The Foreign Investment Review Act set up mechanisms to screen and inhibit takeovers of Canadian companies by foreign multinationals. The National Energy Program greatly increased Canadian ownership in the important oil and gas industry. And an expanded economic role was sought for Crown corporations.

Not surprisingly, the most powerful Canadian capitalists were increasingly troubled by these developments. In order to help to reduce the growing autonomy of the state they formed the Business Council on National Issues in 1976 (Langille 1987). Composed of the chief executive officers of the 150 leading multinational corporations operating in Canada, the BCNI has lobbied diligently and effectively for less government intervention in the economy, a smaller welfare state, free trade with the US, and wage restraint.

Heightened international competition in an era of global industrial restructuring rendered BCNI demands more urgent and compelling, and the 1984 election of a Conservative government under Brian Mulroney facilitated the implementation of the BCNI program. Since 1984 some Crown corporations have been privatized. The Foreign Investment Review Act and the National Energy Program have been scrapped. A government assault on the right of public-sector workers to strike began as early as 1982 (Panitch and Swartz 1985). But the most momentous development of the decade was the signing of a free-trade agreement with the US in January 1988.

Fully 30 per cent of Canada's GNP derives from international trade, and 80 per cent of the country's international trade is with the US. In the mid-1980s, however, this trade was threatened by US protectionism. Faced with an overvalued dollar, a growing trade deficit, and the prospect of increasing unemployment, the US administration restricted imports of Canadian steel, pork, beef, fish, potatoes, and softwood lumber. The senior executives of companies that rely on access to US markets—the largest companies in Canada—felt that mounting American economic nationalism could eventually ruin their businesses. As a result, they became the foremost proponents of free trade (Johnston 1985).

It seems likely that if the 1988 free-trade agreement is fully implemented it will help Canadian industry to become more efficient and competitive. For Canadian workers, on the other hand, increased competition could very well involve wage concessions and the erosion of welfare-state programs. After all, under free trade unionized Canadian workers would have to compete against non-unionized workers in the American Sunbelt (who earn less than half the Canadian wage) and in the Maquioladora free-trade zone of northern Mexico (who earn one-twentieth the Canadian wage).[9] In that sort of competitive environment Canadian workers could hardly be expected to maintain the living standards they achieved in the 1970s.

Recent public-opinion polls reflect widespread concern over these developments. The free-trade issue has become the top public problem worrying Canadians, and while three-quarters of the population thought free trade was a good step for Canada in 1985, fewer than half thought so just before the November 1988 election. Although opposition to free trade was insufficient to unseat the ruling Conservatives, most commentators agree that the free-trade controversy led to more politicized class conflict than Canada has ever seen, and modest gains for the NDP. In the 1960s and 1970s it was often said that Canada was a bastion of regional, non-class politics. Whatever validity this claim may have had, it hardly serves as an accurate interpretation of current events. Politicized class conflict is playing an increasingly prominent role in Canadian public life, and, in the light of the foregoing analysis, one may reasonably expect the distribution of class power to help in shaping the outcome of that conflict.

# 4

# Social Stratification:
# Class and Ethnic Dimensions

SOCIAL MOBILITY

John Porter's *The Vertical Mosaic* (1965) has been called 'the most important book in Canadian sociology' (Forcese 1980 [1978]: 43). If intellectual significance can be gauged by the extent to which a work sets the terms of a debate—by the degree to which it is paradigmatic—then the designation seems entirely appropriate.

As was the case for all the founding fathers of English Canadian sociology, Porter's perceptions of Canada were shaped by his apparent respect for American society. 'The liberal ideology of the United States . . . leavened his own work. . . . He implicitly or explicitly contrasted Canadian society and its flaws to the American' (Forcese 1981: 653). Thus the major theme of Porter's *magnum opus* is that Canada is a relatively inegalitarian society compared to the US. He held that there is less net upward mobility in Canada than in the US because educational opportunities are less widespread in Canada. (Net upward mobility refers to the amount of movement up the socio-economic hierarchy minus the movement down for a specific time period.) The mechanism ensuring this state of affairs is supposedly the Canadian government's traditional policy of encouraging the immigration of highly educated people from abroad rather than expanding the educational system. Presumably, this policy is an outcome of Canadians' value-orientations (cf. Naegele 1964 [1961]; Lipset 1963). 'Judging from its educational system,' wrote Porter (1965: 53-4), 'Canada has not been a mobility oriented society. Collective goals do not seem to have been defined, however vaguely, in terms of increasing opportunities through free universal education' (cf. Porter 1979: 89-101). Moreover, Porter maintained that there is a strong and persistent relationship between socio-economic location and ethnic origin in the country. For example, he showed that Canadians of English and Scottish origin occupied a disproportionately large number of élite positions. This relationship, he believed, explained the relative cohesion of Canadian ethnic groups, the comparative obduracy of ethnic identities and interactions in the country. He therefore regarded government policies aimed at preserving and enhancing ethnic culture as policies that simultaneously preserve and enhance ethnic inequality.

In this chapter I will first assess, in the light of Porter's own and subsequent research, the view that the rate of net upward mobility in Canada is comparatively low. I will then examine the evidence for the contention that Canada is a 'vertical mosaic', a society characterized by an enduring system of ethnic stratification that reinforces ethnic group cohesion. Finally, I will discuss the relationship between ethnic group cohesion and mobility in light of accumulated evidence on the subject.

## Mass mobility

Porter asserted that Canada's rate of net upward mobility was below that of the US and the industrially advanced countries of Western Europe. This assertion was made without the benefit of a Canadian national mobility study, the first such survey having been conducted only in the 1970s (Boyd *et al.* 1985). Instead, Porter based his contention on data concerning educational opportunity and élite recruitment; some of the élite data will be examined below. For the moment, let us consider the significance of Porter's observation that a disproportionately large number of well-to-do families had children attending college in 1956 (Porter 1965: 184, 186). As Harvey Rich (1976: 16) has shown, this is really a quite unremarkable fact. American data from the early 1960s reveal roughly the same distribution of university students by family income. About half the university students in both countries came from families in the top income quartile. Furthermore, if one examines the percentage of university students whose fathers were in manual occupations in Canada (1956) and major European countries (circa 1960) one discovers that Canada led the pack: 26 per cent of Canada's university students were from the manual working class, compared with 5 per cent of West Germany's, 8 per cent of France's, 14 per cent of Sweden's, and 25 per cent of Great Britain's. Porter's view that the

Canadian rate of net upward mobility is unusually low could be sustained only by his failing to report such comparative figures.

Nor do any of the subsequent studies of intergenerational occupational mobility in Canada support Porter's contention. Carl Cuneo and James Curtis (1974) studied the status achievement of about 500 males between the ages of 25 and 34 in Toronto and Montreal. Their aim was to replicate the standard American mobility model developed by Peter Blau and Otis Dudley Duncan (1967). When Cuneo and Curtis compared correlations of various measures of fathers' and sons' status for anglophone and francophone Canadians with identical measures for a similar group from the Blau and Duncan sample, the result was eighteen Canadian/American comparisons, only four of which indicated a statistically significant cross-national difference—three for the francophone group and one for the anglophone group. They concluded that, on the whole, inherited or 'ascriptive' factors were no more important in Canada than in the US in determining status. Anton Turrittin's (1974) study of 763 Ontario male eligible voters prompts a similar conclusion. Only one of the six comparative tests between his own and the Blau and Duncan data showed a statistically significant cross-national difference. Analyzing a national sample of 793 males, Peter Pineo (1976) found that only two of his six comparative tests revealed statistically significant cross-national differences. John Goyder and James Curtis (1979) conducted a four-generation mobility study on a national sample of 1,143 males. They discovered no difference in net upward mobility between Canada and other industrialized countries, including the US, and submitted that 'the impermanence of family status over adjacent generations does suggest [that Canada is] an achievement society rather than an ascriptive one' (Goyder and Curtis 1979: 229). In like manner, Michael Ornstein (1981: 209) concluded his study of some 2,200 Ontario men with the observation that

> comparisons of our measures of the extent of intergenerational
> occupational mobility with the corresponding values observed in
> other advanced capitalist nations demonstrate that . . . Ontario
> [where over 35 per cent of Canada's population lived in 1981] is
> not particularly unique. If anything, higher-than-average rates of
> mobility are observed. The suppositions of Porter, Clement, and

others as to the lack of mobility in Canadian society have no basis in any of the empirical research conducted to date.

Hugh McRoberts and Kevin Selbee (1981) analyzed subsamples from both the Blau and Duncan dataset and the largest national mobility study conducted in Canada to date. Canadian native-born males (n = 8,950) and US non-black males were compared. McRoberts and Selbee (1981: 417) concluded:

> The literature comparing Canada and the United States led us to expect that some differences would exist. Our findings concerning the nature of circulation mobility in the two countries speak directly to . . . functionalist discussions of values and value orientations. Taking as given a value difference between Canada and the United States, our analysis suggests two possibilities: first, value differences were in the past and are today not of sufficient magnitude to affect mobility; or, second, value differences (and hence values themselves) are spurious with respect to mobility—i.e., value differences, even if they can be shown to exist, have no effect on circulation mobility.

Finally, a team of American and Israeli researchers (Tyree, Semyonov, and Hodge 1979) constructed an index of social mobility from studies conducted in 24 countries including Canada and the US. They found that Canada had the second highest rate of net upward mobility; the US ranked fourth.

Porter's portrayal of mass mobility in Canada is clearly not borne out by available evidence. It is simply not the case that Canada is a '"low mobility" society . . . with few avenues through which the lower class can rise' (Clement 1977a: 293). Indeed, it is a tribute to Porter that when it became apparent in the early to mid-1970s that research was disproving some of the key theses of *The Vertical Mosaic*, he informed one of his chief collaborators that 'he would have written those parts of *The Vertical Mosaic* differently had [the new research] been available to him at the time' (Pineo 1981: 623).

## Elite mobility

As a means of substantiating his argument, Porter also analyzed patterns of *élite* recruitment. Is his viewpoint sustained by careful scrutiny of his own data and by subsequent research on the subject? For two reasons the answer must be no. First, patterns of recruitment to élite positions tell us nothing in and of themselves about mass vertical mobility and the relative rigidity of the entire class structure. Canada, after all, has only a couple of thousand élite positions but, as of 1988, over 25 million inhabitants. Thus, in principle, it may even transpire that élites become *more* of an upper-class preserve while net upward mobility *increases* for the mass of the population. As John Myles and Aage Sørensen (1975: 78-9) have demonstrated, increasing upper-class representation in élite positions *may* be caused by increasing rigidity of the entire class structure. But growing upper-class predominance in élite positions may also result from an increase in the number of élite offspring or from a decrease in the number of élite positions. Therefore it is conceptually inappropriate to draw conclusions about rates of movement through the whole class structure from élite-recruitment data.

Second, even if we ignore this conceptual problem, it turns out that patterns of élite recruitment are more egalitarian than Porter and some of his students made them out to be. There is even some evidence that recruitment to at least one Canadian élite is more egalitarian than recruitment to comparable élites in other countries, including the US.

Porter held that an unusually high percentage of people comprising the economic, political, bureaucratic, and ideological élites of Canada came from upper- and upper-middle-class backgrounds.[1] A serious problem, however, derived from the fact that Porter used published biographical information as his main source of data on élite social characteristics: the published sources sometimes lacked information on the occupation of an élite member's father. Porter decided to classify such élite members as people recruited from the upper or upper middle classes if they had a university education. Yet Porter's own data (Porter 1965: 186) showed that a majority of Canadian university students came from lower-middle-class, manual-working-class, and farm families in the mid-1950s. Hence educational attainment was in fact a very poor predictor of class origin; by using it Porter greatly overestimated the class exclusivity of Canadian élites (Rich 1976: 19 ff.).

Rich (1976) illustrated this point by comparing the results of his own study of higher civil servants in Ontario with Porter's data on the federal bureaucratic élite. Porter found that nearly 87 per cent of the federal bureaucratic élite came from upper- and upper-middle-class families. Using educational attainment to infer class origin, Rich found that a nearly identical proportion of higher civil servants in his sample came from these classes. But when he used his interview data to classify his respondents by father's occupation rather than educational attainment, he discovered that only 36 per cent of élite members were recruited from the upper and upper middle classes. Studies of higher civil servants in other major industrialized countries published between 1950 and 1971 showed that this was a relatively *low* proportion: in Great Britain, France, and Germany, between 62 per cent and 73 per cent of higher civil servants came from the upper and upper middle classes, while in the United States the figure was 45 per cent (Rich 1976: 20).

Subsequent research confirms that using educational attainment as a measure of class origin leads to a considerable over-statement of the restricted character of élite recruitment in Canada. On the other hand, when data on father's occupation are used, Canadian élites appear more open. Thus Robert Presthus and William Monopoli (1977), using father's occupation as their class indicator, found that 40 per cent of their sample of senior Ottawa bureaucrats came from upper- and upper-middle-class backgrounds. This figure is less than half that of Porter's and very close to Rich's. Colin Campbell and George Szablowski (1979) also used father's occupation as their class indicator in their study of Ottawa 'superbureaucrats'. Like Rich, they found that their respondents' 'socio-economic back-grounds resemble those of the country's general populace much more closely than do the backgrounds of bureaucratic élites in other advanced liberal democracies for which we have comparable data' (Campbell and Szablowski 1979: 105). This tendency was the reverse of an earlier one, reported by Presthus and Monopoli (1977), for the US bureacratic élite to be more open to middle- and lower-class recruitment than the Canadian bureaucratic élite.

The picture concerning the economic élite is less straightfor-ward. Clement (1975: 190) originally followed Porter's lead in using educational attainment as a class measure of last resort. This method allowed him to conclude that the Canadian economic élite was not only highly class-restrictive when Porter did his study (82 per cent coming from upper- and upper-middle-class origins), but that it became even more restrictive by the early 1970s (over 94 per cent from upper- and upper-middle-class origins). Moreover, Clement (1975: 204) found that the proportion of people from upper- and upper-middle-class origins was nearly the same in the 'comprador' and 'indigenous' segments of the economic élite. This result contrasts with Craig McKie's (1977) study of top executives of Ontario manufacturing companies with 100 or more employees. Using father's occupation as his class indicator, he found that 44 per cent of his sample came from upper- and upper-middle-class origins. He also discovered that US-born executives working in US branch plants in Canada were *more* likely to come from upper- and upper-middle-class origins than were Canadian-born executives. However, the population on which McKie based his research is not strictly comparable to the population studied by Clement (senior executives and board members of dominant corporations). To complicate matters further, in a subsequent study of American and Canadian economic élites Clement (1977: 208-9) dropped the higher-education measure of class origin, although he continued to use attendance at a private school as a class indicator. He found that 61 per cent of senior executives and board members of dominant Canadian corporations, including people working for US-controlled branch plants in Canada, came from upper-class origins alone. The comparable figure in the United States was 36 per cent. Figures on upper-middle-class origin were not reported in the later study. One is thus left with the impression that the indigenous Canadian economic élite is more class restrictive than both the American economic élite and other Canadian élites, but perhaps less class restrictive than the comprador segment of the economic élite in Canada. It also seems that using educational criteria for determining class origin exaggerates the proportion of upper- and upper-middle-class people in the economic élite.

Finally, let us consider the two major studies of the Canadian political élite—Porter's own, and that of his student Dennis Olsen (1980). Porter (1965: 394) reported that, if one uses educational attainment as a measure of class origin, some 86 per cent of the political élite in 1960 appeared to have been recruited from the upper or upper middle classes. Olsen, however, reanalyzed Porter's data. He did not employ university education as an indicator of upper- or upper-middle-class origin (Olsen 1980: 129), and he discovered that in 1960, 39 per cent of the political élite came from the upper and upper middle classes; in 1973 the figure was about 43 per cent. As for the other élites, so for the political élite: using educational attainment as an indicator of class origin increases the apparent proportion of upper- and upper-middle-class people in élite positions.

I conclude that at both the mass and élite levels, the Canadian class system is more open than Porter maintained—although, of course, élite members, and especially those in the economic élite, are still disproportionately recruited from the upper middle and upper classes, as they are elsewhere.

## Theoretical issues

Although Porter originally set the terms of the Canadian debate on social stratification, it is now widely recognized, in the light of the findings just discussed, that his perspective is seriously deficient. But its shortcomings are not just empirical. Theoretically questionable assumptions have also been found in *The Vertical Mosaic* and some of the research it generated. As a result a shift away from these assumptions has taken place in the 1980s. Specifically, Porter's work greatly invigorated the study of how individuals attain status and income levels, and how they are recruited to élite positions. These research areas have become quite sophisticated in Canada. Some Canadian students of social stratification, however, are now beginning to recognize that Porter's tradition of research may have been prompting researchers to ask insufficiently sophisticated questions.

As elsewhere, researchers in Canada have come up against some important limitations of traditional mobility models. Typically, these models measure the independent and joint effects of individual-level attributes—years of formal education, years of job experience, father's occupation, IQ, personal aspirations, parental expectations, etc.—on attained status or income. But this approach implies certain problematic theoretical assumptions (Breton 1979; Horan 1978). In particular, it takes for granted the existence of a free market guaranteeing that individual placement in the occupational structure is a reflection only of individual-level characteristics. At the same time, it ignores how the characteristics of the labour market itself—which is frequently very far from free—determine individual placement in the occupational hierarchy. The *structure* of market relations has consequently attracted the attention of Canadian sociologists over the past few years. Even more important (in terms of predictive power), Canadian students of social stratification are beginning to recognize that the structure of gender and class relations constrains and shapes status- and income-attainment processes. This observation dovetails with developments in the area of élite research, where attention is shifting from the individual characteristics of élite incumbents to the structure of relations (particularly class relations) among the incumbents.

The study of structural effects on status attainment and job income have led to the following conclusions. (1) 'Human-capital' factors, such as years of education and years of experience, and other socio-economic background factors, such as father's occupation and father's education, do not account for most of the explained variation in income and status attainment. (2) Labour-market factors sometimes perform marginally better, sometimes not. These factors include the unemployment rate at the time a person enters the job market and the industrial segment in which a person works (e.g., highly capitalized, high-wage, unionized establishments where male workers predominate versus less capitalized, low-wage, non-unionized establishments where female workers predominate). (3) Gender and class (the latter as defined by neo-Marxists such as Wright [1979]) account for more of the explained variation than do human-capital factors. (The influence of ethnic and racial factors on status attainment is discussed in the next section of this chapter.)

The results of several studies may be cited in order to illustrate these points. In research on 7,350 students who graduated from Ontario universities from 1960 to 1976, Edward Harvey and Richard Kalwa (1983: 447) found that the unemployment rate at the time of graduation had a larger independent effect on status attainment for women than did six socio-economic background factors combined, and that all seven variables explained only 14 per cent of the variation. For men, the effect of the unemployment rate was slightly less than the six socio-economic background factors combined, and all seven variables explained only 18 per cent of the variation. Richard Apostle, Donald Clairmont, and Lars Osberg (1985: 44, 47) studied wage attainment in 1,063 economic establishments in the Maritime provinces in 1979. They found that education and work experience accounted for only 17 per cent of the variation in wages (12 per cent for men alone), while structural factors related to labour-market segmentation, marital status, and occupational status (the latter interpreted as an index of class) accounted for another 31 per cent of the variation (15 per cent for men only). Michael Ornstein (1983a: 55-7, 60-1, 64-5) studied wage attainment in a national sample of 1,400 men and women. He found that only 20 per cent of the variation in job income could be explained by eight human-capital and socio-economic-background factors. But when gender was added to his regression equation he discovered that it had a stronger independent effect than any other variable and was nearly as powerful as all the other variables combined; explained variance increased to over 33 per cent. The inclusion of class and labour-market variables increased the explained variance to 48 per cent; and the addition of interaction effects brought the explained variance to 55 per cent. In the full regression model three different groups of variables had roughly equal independent effects on income: the human-capital and status-attainment variables; gender and its interactions; and social class (measured in neo-Marxist terms). Labour-market factors had only about a third as much impact as any of these three groups of variables.

In the light of these findings, the problems with traditional, mainstream stratification research may be summarized as follows. The older status- and income-attainment models explain a relatively small portion of the variation in their dependent variables chiefly because they regard stratification systems as sets of independent elements (individuals) whose attributes (education, experience, etc.) earn them money and status through the workings of a free market for labour. In contrast, higher levels of explained variation can be achieved only by drawing attention to broader structural issues, to patterns of interdependence among elements in stratification systems, to the manner in which opportunities to earn money and achieve status are constrained by the distribution of power among classes, between sexes, etc. Match a group of Canadian men and a group of Canadian women in terms of education, occupation, amount of time worked each year, and years of job experience, and one discovers that the women earn only 63 per cent of what the men earn (Goyder 1981: 328). It is difficult to understand how this fact might be explained without taking structured gender inequalities into account (see Chapter 5 for an extended discussion of this point). Similarly, structural boundaries shape mobility patterns. For example, it seems that more mobility takes place within classes than between them.

A precisely analogous argument may be made about older Canadian élite studies, such as those conducted by Porter (1965) and Clement (1975). Most of the data that were systematically collected and analyzed in these works concern the individual characteristics of élite members. For the most part only impressionistic evidence was used to support assertions about the relationship between élite attributes and broader class and socio-economic structures; the properties of these structures *per se* were not systematically analyzed. Clement, for example, used data on the attributes of individuals (which corporate boards of directors men sat on) to make claims about the clustering, centrality, and power of certain groups of enterprises in the Canadian economy. That is, individuals were considered to be nodes in a social network; corporations were considered to be the ties that bind the individuals together; and it was incorrectly assumed that the most densely connected individuals are the most powerful members of the élite and that they bind together central, and therefore powerful, corporations. From a structural viewpoint, however, the firms, not the men, are the nodes in the network; the men connect the firms; and the simple density of ties among men tells us little about the economic power of the firms that they connect or, indeed, about other important aspects of the socio-economic structure. Similarly, this general failure to examine structural properties in their own right allowed both Porter and Clement to reach opposite conclusions regarding the heights of the Canadian stratification system. On the basis of impressionistic evidence Porter claimed that Canadian élites do not form a ruling class, while Clement claimed that they do. What neither researcher fully appreciated is that, in order to offer more than impressions regarding these and other important issues of a related nature, one requires (a) techniques for measuring structural properties directly, and (b) testable hypotheses about how patterns of relations among élite members, and among the institutions they control, ought to look if one theory or another is valid.

Marxist theory and network-analytic techniques offer the most promising starts in this direction (for example, Berkowitz 1980; Carroll 1982; 1984; 1986; Carroll, Ornstein, and Fox 1977; Fox and Ornstein 1984; Ornstein 1976; 1984; and Wellman and

Berkowitz 1988 for general background). These approaches have prompted and facilitated examination of the network of relations among firms considered as a whole. Several important parameters of the economic élite system have been mapped out by researchers operating in this tradition—notably the overall level of network integration, the economic power of banks versus industrials and of foreign- versus indigenously-controlled enterprises, the clustering of enterprises into cliques, and the organizational versus class motives for forming interlocking directorates. The substantive and theoretical conclusions reached about the economic élite and its relation to the larger class structure are often radically different from, and always more sophisticated than, those arrived at by the preceding generation of élite researchers. (Many of these conclusions are reviewed in the discussion of élites and economic development in Chapter 2 and so need not be repeated here.) The extension of this approach to other élites is likely to improve further our understanding of the upper reaches of the Canadian class structure.

ETHNIC STRATIFICATION

## Canada/US comparisons

An important variation on the main theme of *The Vertical Mosaic* is that the Canadian stratification system is structured along ethnic lines. It seemed to Porter that ethnic inequalities and ethnic-group solidarity in post-Second World War Canada were persisting and, in some cases, even strengthening. In his opinion this tendency represented a step backwards from the meritocratic liberal ideal, supposedly embodied in American practice, which he valued highly. Porter felt that the retention of ethnic identity hampers upward mobility, creating what sociologists now call an 'ethnic mobility trap' (Wiley 1967). Hence, in his view, attempts by government and private bodies to encourage ethnic group cohesion have the effect of entrenching socio-economic inequalities.

In the mid-1960s Porter was inclined to contrast this situation with that in the United States. He held that

> [t]he retention of strong European ethnic affiliations is deeply imbedded in the Canadian value system. This strong emphasis

on ethnic pluralism . . . seems to have increased during the
twentieth century . . . as various groups were encouraged to
retain their European identities within a Canadian 'mosaic'. . . .
[T]here never has been in Canada, as in the United States, a
strong commitment to the creation of a new nation, a new ethnicity. . . . (Porter 1979: 91).

[I]t might be said that the idea of an ethnic mosaic, as opposed to
the idea of the melting pot, impedes the processes of social
mobility. This difference in ideas is one of the principal dis-
tinguishing features of United States and Canadian society at the
level of social psychology as well as that of social structure (Porter 1965: 70).

Similar statements may be found in the writings of other sociologists in the 1960s (see McKenna [1969] for the relevant observations of Clark, Lipset, Naegele, Porter, and Wrong).

It follows from this characterization that there might well be
dissimilarity between Canada and the United States in levels of
prejudice and discrimination against ethnic minorities; in immigration policies; in levels of ethnic stratification; and in ethnic-
group mobility. But despite the frequent invocation of the vertical-mosaic versus melting-pot theme in the 1960s and the first
half of the 1970s, no studies have been conducted that measure
Canadian/American differences, if any, in 'particularism/
universalism' (see Table 1.2). I have, however, come across two
explicit Canadian/American comparisons of the impact of
ethnicity on mobility and stratification, and a few socio-
historical articles that explicitly compare Canadian and
American immigration policies and the extent and depth of
ethnic prejudice and discrimination in the two countries.

One of these articles was actually written by Porter, who by
the late 1970s had done an about-face on the ethnic question
(Porter 1979: 139-62). He came around to the view that neither
the characterization of the US as a melting pot, nor that of
Canada as a cultural mosaic, was accurate; he now emphasized
the *similarities* of ethnic-group experience in the two countries.

The conclusions that Porter drew from his socio-historical
research in the late 1970s have been confirmed and elaborated
by others. It is now fairly widely accepted that assimiliationist
models of ethnic-group integration predominated in the US *and*
in Canada until the Second World War. Following the war the

idea of 'cultural pluralism' became popular on *both* sides of the 49th parallel (Palmer 1976).

The history of immigration policies is also similar in Canada and the US (Hawkins 1972; Richmond 1967; 1976). In both countries the annual rate of immigration has been closely attuned to labour-market demand and the selection of immigrants has been based on clearly ordered preferences: northern and western Europeans first, central, eastern, and southern Europeans second, non-Europeans last. In the 1960s Canadian immigration law was liberalized so as to eliminate the most discriminatory features of selection policy. Several attitudinal surveys conducted over the past decade nonetheless demonstrate that the old selection policy is still reflected in the distribution of mass prejudice in Canada (Berry, Kalin, and Taylor 1977; Dasko 1988; Goldstein 1978; Harpur 1982; Pineo 1977). According to one survey, in the early 1980s nearly 60 per cent of Canadians were prepared to limit the rights of non-white immigrants and a full 31 per cent of Canadians supported the idea of an all-white Canada; the proportion of Canadians wanting less immigration fluctuated in the 60 to 70 per cent range between 1977 and 1987.[2] By allowing for fine ethnic and racial gradations and regional and other comparisons, some of these surveys permit quite precise observations about the distribution of mass prejudice in Canada. For example, in Canada as a whole people of Pakistani and East Indian origin are negatively evaluated more frequently than members of any other minority group, while in western Canada alone prejudice against native Indians is most widespread.

As far as the actual treatment of minority groups is concerned, neither country has been a paragon of tolerance, and it is debatable whether Canada is the more magnanimous society. There is of course nothing in Canada to compare with the American history of institutionalized racism against Blacks. The treatment of native peoples has also been less brutal in Canada than in the US—but largely, it seems, for the pragmatic reason that natives were more useful to white settlers in exploiting the difficult Canadian frontier. On the other hand, the US was more lenient than Canada in its treatment of its Japanese citizens during the Second World War; one student of this subject failed to find 'the more humanistic, tolerant, less violent Canadian scenario some purport to discern. There was no indication that [in the] Canadian . . . mosaic respect for cultural diversity, etc., aided the Japanese minority' (O'Neil 1981). Similarly, Canada had a worse record than the US—in fact, the worst record of any Allied country—for admitting European Jews between 1939 and 1945 because of anti-Semitism among some high-ranking Liberals, who were then in power, and the readiness of that party's leaders to bow to pressure from Catholic Quebec (Abella and Troper 1979).

It must also be noted that the mean degree of occupational dissimilarity among ethnic groups is moderate in both the US and Canada, indicating that the degree of ethnic stratification is comparable in the two countries (Darroch 1980: 211). Moreover, the magnitude of the influence of ethnicity on mobility is similarly low in the US and Canada. National mobility studies conducted in both countries around 1970 show that ethnic differences in occupational status are largely attributable to differences in educational achievements, social origins, and background characteristics; very little of the variation in the occupational status of ethnic groups derives from ethnicity *per se* (Boyd, Featherman, and Matras 1981; Richmond and Zubrzycki 1981).

None of this evidence supports the view that Canadian and American orientations to ethnicity differ fundamentally, much less that such dissimilarities as do exist result from profound value differences. Canada and the US do, of course, exhibit some striking variations in ethnic composition. In 1981, for example, 12 per cent of the US population was Black and under 3 per cent of French origin, compared with 27 per cent of French origin and perhaps 1.5 per cent Black in Canada. Moreover, a considerably larger proportion of Canada's population consists of immigrants than is the case in the US because in the post-Second World War period Canada, with only a tenth of the US population, accepted about half as many immigrants as the US. These factors seem to account in large part for the different flavour and greater intensity of ethnic expression in Canada (Palmer 1976: 513, 524-5).

## The Canadian case

Canadian sociologists have done far more research on ethnic stratification and rates of ethnic mobility within Canada itself than on the question of cross-national differences. A review of this research prompts the following conclusions. Contrary to the view of Porter and other sociologists who wrote in the 1960s, (a) ethnicity is not a good predictor of socio-economic status or mobility in Canada when other causes are held constant; (b) ethnic inequality is decreasing over time; (c) the members of most ethnic groups experience considerable net upward mobility; (d) the effect of ethnicity on status attainment weakens as immigrants become more acculturated; (e) these generalizations do not hold as strongly for members of some groups—especially some racial minorities—as they do overall.

Consider, for example, Canada's two largest ethnic groups. Table 4.1 sets out some of the most frequently cited indicators of inequality between Canadians of British origin (45 per cent of the population in 1971, 40 per cent in 1981) and those of French origin (29 per cent of the population in 1971, 27 per cent in 1981) (*1981 Census* . . . 1984: Table 1, 1; Kalbach and McVey 1979 [1971]: 195). All indicators show that the degree of inequality between the two groups is pronounced. For example, in 1961 the mean income of British-origin males was 25 per cent greater than the mean income of French-origin males in the country as a whole (indicator a). In that same year inequality was greater inside Quebec than outside that province; the British-origin/ French-origin difference in earning power reached 49 per cent in Montreal (indicator b). Also in 1961 the degree of inequality was reduced when controls were introduced for education and occupation, but inequality increased with occupational/ educational level (indicators h through j; cf. Beattie and Spencer 1971; 1975).[3] Throughout the post-Second World War period inequality has been much greater at the élite level than at the mass level (compare indicators a through k with indicators l through p). At both levels and in all locations, however, Canadians of French origin are catching up to Canadians of English origin. Thus by 1971 the British-origin/French-origin income advantage for males in Montreal fell to 30 per cent from 49 per cent a decade earlier (indicators a and c; cf. Lanphier and Morris 1974; 1975; Raynauld, Marion, and Béland 1975). Similarly, in the national economic élite in 1951 the British-origin/French-origin ratio was nearly nine times higher than one could expect on the basis of the representation of these groups in the population; that figure fell to about six and a half times higher by 1972 (indicators m and

TABLE 4.1

SELECTED INDICATORS OF INEQUALITY BETWEEN
CANADIANS OF BRITISH AND FRENCH ORIGIN

| indicator | population or sample | British-origin as % French-origin |
|---|---|---|
| a.  mean income, males, 1961 | national | 125 |
| b.  mean income, males, 1961 | Montreal | 149 |
| c.  mean income, males, 1971 | Montreal | 130 |
| d.  % of lab. force in managerial/ professional occupations, 1970 | Quebec | 157 |
| e.  % of lab. force in blue-collar occupations, 1970 | Quebec | 45 |
| f.  probability of responding successfully to managerial/ professional job opportunity, 1951 | national | 175 |
| g.  probability of responding successfully to managerial/ professional job opportunity, 1961 | national | 162 |
| h.  mean income, unskilled workers with primary education, 1961 | national | 105 |
| i.  mean income, clerical and skilled workers with secondary education, 1961 | national | 111 |
| j.  mean income, managerial/ professional and sales workers with post-secondary education, 1961 | national | 116 |
| k.  rate of return for university education controlling for occupation, 1961 | national | 133 |
| l.  value-added, English- & French-origin owned manufacturing estabs., 1961 | Quebec | 2,074 (278) |
| m.  number in economic élite, 1951 | national | 882 (1,378) |
| n.  number in economic élite, 1972 | national | 657 (1,026) |
| o.  number in political élite, 1953 | national | 413 ( 646) |
| p.  number in political élite, 1973 | national | 173 ( 271) |

Note: Indicators l, m, n, o and p are weighted to take account of the ratio of French-origin to British-origin people in the census years 1951, 1961, and 1971. For example, indicator m is the ratio of British-origin to French-origin people in the economic élite in 1951 times the ratio of French-origin to British-origin people in the population in that year, expressed as a percentage. Unweighted figures are given in brackets.

SOURCES: Breton and Stasiulis 1980; Clement 1975; Kalbach and McVey 1971; 1979 [1971]; Morris and Lanphier 1977; Olsen 1980; Raynauld, Marion and Béland 1975; Reitz 1981; Royal Commission . . . , 1969.

n). The same holds for rates of net upward mobility (not shown in the table): the British-origin advantage over those of French origin has declined in the post-Second World War period (Boyd *et al.* 1981; Boyd *et al.* 1985; Dofny and Garon-Audy 1969; de Jocas and Rocher 1968 [1961]; McRoberts *et al.* 1976).

Although other ethnic groups (27 per cent of the Canadian population in 1971, 33 per cent in 1981) complicate this changing pattern of inequality, they do not alter it beyond recognition (*1981 Census . . .* 1984: Table 1, 1; Kalbach and McVey 1979 [1971]: 195). With some important exceptions, non-British, non-French minorities are becoming normally distributed throughout the stratification hierarchy. Moreover, they are doing so at a quicker pace than the French Canadians.

The evidence that Porter and his followers (especially Blishen 1970) used to arrive at the opposite conclusion consists of census cross-tabulations that show how the male labour force is distributed among broad occupational categories by major ethnic group. Porter measured group inequality by subtracting the proportion of each ethnic group's members in high-status (professional/financial) occupations from the proportion of the entire labour force in such occupations. If, for a given ethnic group, the difference in proportions increased over time, Porter inferred that inequality between that group and the rest of the labour force had also increased; and conversely, if the difference in proportions decreased he inferred that inequality had decreased. This led him to conclude that in the intercensal period 1951-61 inequalities between the French, Italian, Eskimo, and Indian ethnic groups, on the one hand, and all other ethnic groups, including the British, on the other, had increased.

As Jeffrey Reitz (1981) and others have shown, however, this index of group inequality has an undesirable property. It assumes that new high-status jobs will be distributed equally among individuals regardless of their group affiliation—that, in other words, the share of new high-status jobs allocated to each group will depend only on each group's size. Clearly, this is an untenable assumption if there is some group inequality.

Other measures, such as the index of dissimilarity and the index of net difference, do not make this assumption. Gordon Darroch (1980) has demonstrated that when census cross-tabulations are used to calculate these indices for Canadian ethnic groups, inequalities appear to be much more attenuated than in Porter's analysis. They also seem to be weakening over time. For example, the mean index of occupational dissimilarity for Canadian ethnic groups decreased from about 27 in 1931 to about 19 in 1951 to about 14 in 1961. This means that in 1961 an average of 14 per cent of the members of each ethnic group would have had to change their occupations in order to make each group's occupational distribution identical with the overall distribution of occupations. The degree of dissimilarity between the occupational distribution of most ethnic groups and the occupational distribution of the entire population was thus quite moderate even 25 years ago. Darroch also showed that the mean index of dissimilarity had fallen further by 1971, even though the larger number of occupational categories into which the 1971 data were divided inflated the value of the index.

Admittedly, the rank ordering of ethnic groups changed little from 1931 to 1971. Moreover, Jews and Asians had moderately high dissimilarity scores (23 for Jews and 21 for Asians in 1961), indicating their unusually high mean occupational status. At the other extreme, native Canadians had a very high index of occupational dissimilarity (43 in 1961), which reflected their miserable socio-economic conditions. Many of Canada's native people were displaced from traditional lands and forced onto reserves, where they have been kept in a state of impoverishment and administrative dependency and have found it difficult to be integrated in the national economy. Those who never had reserve status or who leave the reserves face tremendous handicaps: rampant alcoholism, very low educational levels, extremely high levels of discrimination, and so forth (Valentine 1980). The fact remains, however, that these are exceptions to the general rule. Jews, Asians, and native peoples (including status and non-status Indians, Métis and Inuit) amount to only about 7.5 per cent of the Canadian population. Recent research suggests that non-Caribbean Blacks born in Canada should be added to the list of groups with persistent and unusually low mean occupational status (Henry and Ginzberg 1988; Winn 1988). But the *overall* trend is for group occupational distributions to approach population values. Apparently, ethnicity influences occupational status significantly only in the case of a few, mainly racial, groups (cf. Kalbach 1970; Pineo 1976;

Richmond and Kalbach 1980.) And even in these cases the effect of ethnicity on occupational attainment seems to be non-linear. *Moderate* levels of discrimination may increase the resolve of minority-group members and facilitate *high* occupational attainment, as in the case of the Japanese. On the other hand, high levels of discrimination may frustrate the resolve of minority-group members and encourage *low* occupational attainment, as in the case of the Métis.

Studies of individual mobility allow direct measurement of the effect of ethnicity on income and status attainment, and they add considerable weight to the above interpretation. In 1961 Anthony Richmond (1964) studied social mobility in a small (n = 478) representative national sample of post-Second World War immigrants. He showed that immigrants from the UK began their occupational careers in Canada with strong advantages over other immigrants: the former had fewer language problems and their educational qualifications were more widely accepted by employers. These advantages diminished over time, however, as immigrants from other countries became acculturated, and as a result non-UK immigrants achieved more upward mobility in Canada than did UK immigrants. In a subsequent analysis of a much larger representative sample of Toronto households in 1969-70 (n = 11,652), Richmond and Goldlust (1974) discovered no association between ethnicity and income when the combined effects of father's occupation, education, present occupation, age, and length of residence in the country were taken into account. Similarly, only 1 per cent of the variance in mobility was explained by ethnicity when appropriate controls were introduced. Using data collected in 1971, Michael Ornstein (1981) analyzed mobility among more than 3,000 Ontario men. Controlling for education, occupation, and other variables, ethnicity explained only 5.2 per cent of the variance in the respondents' occupation and only 3.5 per cent of the variance in income. When additional controls were introduced for place of birth, mother tongue, and place of schooling, the effect of ethnicity on respondent's occupation and income was entirely indirect and fell still further. This finding supports the view that the effect of ethnicity on status attainment and income weakens as immigrants acculturate. Finally, Monica Boyd and others (1981; 1985) analyzed the effect of ethnicity on male status attainment in the 1973 National Mobility Study (n = about 44,000). They reported that ethnic stratification became less marked in Canada over time, as evidenced by the fact that the relationship between ethnicity and occupational status was weaker for sons than for fathers. Moreover, the effect of ethnicity on son's occupation was very weak in absolute terms; and ethnicity influenced son's occupation almost entirely indirectly, through father's occupation. Thus, holding constant father's occupational status, the partial correlation between ethnicity and son's occupational status was a negligible .01. They concluded:

> The non-French, non-English groups have markedly gained on the two charter groups [English and French] in terms of intergenerational changes in occupational status. The difference between the means for fathers and sons for Poles, for example, is 12.7 Blishen [SES] points, for Ukrainians 14.8. The difference for the English was 8.0 and the French 8.3. All the non-charter groups listed [Norwegian, Polish, German, Dutch, Ukrainian, and 'others'] gained dramatically . . . relative to the English, and they overtook the French (Boyd et al. 1981: 667).

At the level of élites, too, members of 'other' ethnic groups have registered gains since the Second World War (see Table 4.2). In the economic élite, Jews (who make up about 1.3 per cent of the population) quintupled their representation between c. 1951 and c. 1972. Similarly impressive gains have been registered by French-origin and other ethnic groups in the federal bureaucratic élite—the former doubling their representation and the latter quadrupling theirs in the time period considered. Much more modest gains have been registered by French-origin and other ethnic groups in the political élite. All these gains have been made at the expense of Canadians of British origin. On the whole, however, ethnic inequalities at the élite level appear to be considerably greater than at the mass level.

In sum, a number of key arguments in *The Vertical Mosaic* relating to ethnicity must be called into question on the basis of all—or nearly all[4]—the available evidence. Clearly, in his early work Porter exaggerated the contrast between Canadian and American attitudes towards, and treatment of, ethnic groups. Furthermore, neither he nor anybody else substantiated the claim that variations in values account for such differences as do exist between the two countries. The importance that Porter attached to ethnicity as a factor in the structuration of the

Canadian stratification system has also been disputed. A substantial body of research demonstrates that, with important exceptions—consisting mainly of racial minorities—ethnicity does not strongly influence status or income attainment. Nor is ethnic stratification in Canada becoming more deeply entrenched over time.[5]

TABLE 4.2
ETHNIC REPRESENTATION IN CANADIAN ÉLITES,
C. 1951 AND C. 1972

|  | British 1951 | British 1972 | French 1951 | French 1972 | Jewish 1951 | Jewish 1972 | Other 1951 | Other 1972 |
|---|---|---|---|---|---|---|---|---|
| economic | 1.9 | 1.9 | 0.2 | 0.3 | 0.6 | 3.0 | 0.1 | 0.2 |
| political | 1.6 | 1.5 | 0.7 | 0.9 | — | — | 0.2 | 0.3 |
| bureaucratic | 1.8 | 1.5 | 0.4 | 0.8 | — | — | 0.1 | 0.4 |

Note: 'Other' includes Jews. A value of 1.0 indicates that the proportion of a particular ethnic group's members in an élite is equal to the proportion of that ethnic group's members in the population. Values greater than 1.0 indicate ethnic group over-representation in an élite and values less than 1.0 indicate under-representation.

SOURCES: Clement 1975: 231, 234, 237; Kalbach and McVey 1979 [1971]: 195, 198; Olsen 1980: 22, 78.

ETHNIC-GROUP COHESION

The final theme of *The Vertical Mosaic* that I want to discuss concerns the relationship between ethnic-group cohesion, on the one hand, and upward mobility and high social status, on the other. Porter argued that there is an inverse relationship between the two sets of phenomena.[6] In his view, immigrants, many of whom have a low 'entrance status' when they arrive in Canada, can move up the social hierarchy only if they abandon their old culture and blend into the mainstream of Canadian life. Hence his disapproval of the federal government's 'multiculturalism' program instituted in 1971: Porter felt that by encouraging the persistence of ethnic particularism the government was in effect slowing down the immigrant's economic progress.

Many research findings appear to substantiate the argument

that there is an inverse relationship between ethnic-group cohesion and high mobility and status. For example, Tomoko
Makabe (1978) conducted in-depth interviews of 100 second-
generation Japanese in Toronto. Fifty-two of her respondents
were highly upwardly mobile and they all identified themselves
as 'Japanese Canadians'. Of the remaining, less upwardly mobile respondents, 43 identified themselves simply as 'Japanese',
thus reflecting a lower degree of identification with Canadian
society and a higher degree of identification with their ethnic
group than was the case for the highly upwardly mobile. On a
much larger scale, Reitz (1980) conducted a representative
sample survey of ethnic groups in Canada's major cities in the
mid-1970s (n = about 2,500). He found that measures of ethnic-
group interaction and ethnic-group identification varied mod-
estly, but significantly and inversely, with job status and income
(Reitz 1980: 186).

Consider also the phenomenon of ethnic residential segregation, which is frequently regarded as an independent source of
ethnic-group cohesion. Analyses of census and survey data
show that areas of high socio-economic status in Canadian cities
are less ethnically segregated than low SES areas. It has also been
demonstrated that, within ethnic groups, people with low SES
are more ethnically segregated than people with high SES (e.g.,
Balakrishnan 1976; 1982; Darroch and Marston 1971; Marston
1969). Again, this supports the view that ethnic-group cohesion
and high status vary inversely.

Finally, data on ethnic marriage patterns also show that high
SES usually results in low ethnic-group cohesion. Endogamy (in-
marriage) is an important basis of ethnic-group cohesion in
Canada, albeit to varying degrees for different groups (Driedger
1975). Significantly, there is a negative association between
propensity to marry within the group and the net difference in
occupational status between groups.[7] This association is strong
and in the direction predicted by Porter. For over 90 per cent of
Canadians, in-marrying is associated with low occupational
status and out-marrying with high occupational status. This,
too, is indicative of the larger fact that, everything else being
equal, disadvantaged ethnic groups are more cohesive than
advantaged ethnic groups. The disadvantaged frequently think
of their limited life chances as consequences of their ethnicity:
collective rather than individual attributes loom large because

individual mobility is by definition difficult to achieve for the disadvantaged (Breton 1978; 1979; Reitz 1980; cf. Hechter 1978).

There are, however, some exceptions to this overall pattern —exceptions that point to some important shortcomings in Porter's reasoning. For instance, Jews and Asians (mainly Chinese and Japanese) exhibit high mean occupational status and *high* rates of in-marriage (Brym, Gillespie and Gillis 1985). Jews and Asians are in fact such extreme exceptions that if they were included in the above calculations the correlations between in-marriage and occupational status for all ten ethnic groups would be strongly *positive*.[8] Reason to question the universal applicability of Porter's assertion that upward mobility leads to lower ethnic-group cohesion may also be found in the results of a large sample survey conducted in Toronto in 1969-70 by Richmond (1974: 192-6). Richmond found that for some types of mobility in some groups there was an association in the predict-ed direction. Intragenerational upward mobility among the foreign-born, for example, was associated with a decline in ethnic group identification. But the latter was also associated with intergenerational *downward* mobility among those born in Canada whose mother tongue was English. The result of these and other contradictory trends was to produce 'no significant overall association between social mobility and [patterns of ethnic] identification'. Similarly problematic for Porter's hypothesis is Reitz's (1980: 186) survey finding from the mid-1970s that some urban Canadians in all ethnic groups did not abandon their ethnic ties when they were upwardly mobile into the middle class. The maintenance of strong ethnic ties in the middle class was about a third as frequent as it was in the work-ing class. The fact that a considerable number of urban middle-class people in all ethnic groups tended to interact and identify with other members of their ethnic groups is not easily explic-able in Porter's terms.

Reitz singled out two main reasons why middle-class people may retain strong ethnic ties. First, members of an ethnic group may be employed in work settings where other members of their ethnic group predominate (cf. Hechter 1978). The degree to which this is the case indicates the group's concentration in particular *horizontal* economic locations (as opposed to their ver-tical economic location as measured by, say, mean SES). Consi-der the example of Italian-Canadian occupational segregation in the construction industry. Not just construction workers, but also owners, lawyers, accountants, and other professionals of Italian origin are employed in this industry. The professionals may achieve upward mobility without having to leave their ethnic group and without having to give up their ethnic identity. Indeed, ethnic-group affiliations may promote their upward mobility and they may therefore develop a vested interest in the preservation of the ethnic group. About a quarter of the middle-class people in Reitz's sample who maintained strong ethnic ties worked in such settings. In Toronto the ethnic groups that were especially highly segregated in high-status jobs included Jews, Chinese, people of British origin, and people whose families had resided in Canada for three or more generations (the great majority of the latter are also of British origin; see Reitz, Calzavara, and Dasko 1981: 55). It is particularly within these ethnic groups that, for reasons of economic interest, one would expect to find relatively high levels of middle-class ethnicity.[9]

Second, Reitz argued that middle-class ethnicity is associated not so much with present as with past discrimination, group conflict, and job segregation.[10] Jews, Japanese, and Chinese have such histories in common. High levels of discrimination against members of these groups in the past caused them to perform menial tasks in 'split labour markets' and/or to become 'middleman minorities' (Li 1979; Makabe 1981; cf. Bonacich 1972; 1973). As a result members of these groups have tended to develop relatively extensive and powerful ethnic institutions, as well as symbols and social-psychological mechanisms, to protect and advance their collective interests. These have helped to prolong group cohesion beyond the point that can be predicted just from knowledge of the current economic position of these groups. For example, ethnic institutions—newspapers, central political bodies, cultural organizations, and so forth—take on lives of their own after they are established, since their staffs develop vested interests in institutional continuity. Ethnic groups characterized by histories that generate institutional and other mechanisms of this sort *and* by current high-status job segregation may be expected to experience the highest incidences of middle-class ethnicity—an expectation that is given some support by Reitz's study and the data supplied above on ethnic outmarriage.

This argument suggests that Porter's conception of ethnicity is deficient. Recall that for Porter ethnicity is a residue of past culture that is dysfunctional in modern society. Ethnicity may therefore be expected to dissipate as society modernizes; or to retain some vigour if modernization lags, as is allegedly the case in Canada. But in the view of Reitz, Raymond Breton, and other contemporary students of ethnicity in Canada (Breton 1978; 1979; Breton and Breton 1980; Breton and Stasiulis 1980; Darroch 1981; Darroch and Ornstein 1980), there is no one-to-one correspondence between modernization and ethnic-group cohesion. In their view ethnicity is a contingent basis for identification and action, an achieved, not an inherited, status (cf. Yancey, Ericksen, and Juliani 1976).[a] Ethnic identification and group affiliation may have utilitarian value even in the most modern society and within any class. This is most clearly evident among lower-class people, who tend to seek collective solutions to mobility problems since by definition they find it difficult to achieve individual mobility. But ethnicity may also help some middle-class people to advance or protect their interests. And ethnic contacts and identities are likely to be strengthened in the middle class if for historical reasons a firm institutional, social-psychological, and symbolic superstructure cements the ethnic community.

The foregoing implies that a wide variety of ethnic phenomena are better understood if the individual is not assumed to be the only relevant unit of analysis; consideration of the class and organizational bases of ethnicity significantly enhances sociological analysis. Breton has demonstrated this point convincingly in his examination of how the degree of 'institutional completeness' of ethnic communities affects ethno-linguistic stratification and conflict (Breton 1964; 1978; 1979; Breton and Breton 1980; Breton and Stasiulis 1980). 'Institutional completeness' refers to the number and type of formal organizations in an ethnic community that service ethnic-group members: schools, churches, sports clubs, mutual-aid societies, credit unions, employment agencies, and so forth. According to Breton, if there is a low degree of institutional completeness within the ethnic groups of a society, the SES of an individual will depend chiefly on his or her occupation, level of education, and so forth. If, on the other hand, a broad range of parallel institutions service different ethnic groups, an individual's SES will also depend heavily on the position of the institutions to which he or she belongs *vis-à-vis* other institutions. In the latter case an individual is likely to attempt improving his or her position not just by trying to find a better job, but also by trying to improve the relative status of institutions to which he or she belongs; the question of organizational control may become more important for the disadvantaged than the conditions of individual mobility as such.

The problem of ethnic conflict is illuminated by Breton's organizational perspective. For example, even casual observation suggests that the level of institutional completeness is higher in Canada than in the US—partly because nothing in the American experience parallels the history of Canada's francophones. The French were at one time politically and numerically dominant in the area that became Canada; they have been concentrated overwhelmingly in Quebec; and, proportionately, francophones are more than twice as numerous as the largest minority group in the United States. A very complex and highly articulated system of formal organizations has consequently been developed to serve the large francophone community, with its strong sense of historical continuity and difference. In addition, a considerably larger proportion of Canada's population consists of immigrants and first-generation North Americans than is the case in the US. Ethnic organizations are more useful to less acculturated citizens, and therefore are more widespread in Canada.

Because of the comparatively high level of institutional completeness in Canadian ethnic communities, the conflict generated by inequality is elevated to the organizational level almost as a matter of course; inequality is often debated in terms of organizational control and jurisdiction, since individual status is so dependent on organizational status. The nature of the constitution, the distribution of powers between provincial and federal governments, the ethnic composition of the federal bureaucracy, the government-sanctioned use of French and English in schools, businesses, courts, and governments, the selection of party leaders, the status of Quebec in (or outside) Confederation—these are the issues that animate ethnic politics in Canada. In Breton's words, 'the structure of the state apparatus tends to be a regular object of conflict between ethnic communities' (Breton 1978: 155). In the US, by contrast, the structure of the state apparatus is less a subject of ethnic and racial controversy. Ethnic and racial conflict over the distribution of rewards in society tends to focus on such matters as the prevention of discrimination, the size of the welfare budget and, lately, the need for reverse discrimination. This is what one would expect in a society where a lower level of institutional completeness leads to a more individualistic interpretation of the sources of inequality.

The reorientation in thinking about ethnicity that has occurred since the mid-1970s follows a by-now-familiar pattern: as in other fields, a better appreciation of the social-structural roots of ethnicity is apparent in recent work. This change entails a shift away from the assumption, commonly held in the 1960s, that the individual is the unit of analysis in sociological research. Researchers now generally recognize that many ethnic phenomena can be better understood if they are viewed from class and organizational perspectives as well. Sociologists less commonly regard people's beliefs, symbols, and values as important independent causal agents. They less commonly make functionalist assumptions about the connection between modernization and ethnicity. And although they have underscored the importance of race as a cause of inequality, they have by and large been convinced that ethnicity in general structures the Canadian stratification system in a much less dramatic way than was formerly believed.

# 5

# The Feminist Challenge: A Reconsideration of Social Inequality and Economic Development

## BONNIE J. FOX

THE DEVELOPMENT OF FEMINIST THEORY

In the 1960s the large numbers of middle-class Canadian women leaving university faced an adulthood that was not substantially different from the one their mothers were living. These women were caught in a contradiction: despite their strong educational credentials and related aspirations, they encountered a labour market that offered few careers for educated women, and a community that offered neither child-care supports to dual-career couples nor role models of adult women successfully living lives that were not centred on domesticity. Many of them had been politicized by involvement in anti-poverty and native-rights struggles, participation in the Student Union for Peace Action (SUPA), or work in the NDP; their American counterparts were similarly politicized by involvement in the civil-rights movement and mobilization against the Vietnam War. For these women, Canadian and American, the need to choose between family and career seemed unfair; for many the reality of gender[1] inequality was intolerable. They were the people behind the most recent resurgence of the 'women's liberation movement'— a movement that poses a fundamental challenge to the social order and to sociology, which both studies and often supports that social order.

By the mid-1970s American and Canadian feminist sociologists were documenting gender inequality (see Huber 1973; Stephenson 1977 [1973]; Henry 1975). Primarily concerned with unequal opportunity, this work was permeated with the liberal assumptions characteristic of American sociology. As a result social structure was treated as given; what was under examination were the processes of recruitment of individuals into positions in the social hierarchy (as is typical of 'social stratification' research generally). Nevertheless, this investigation of gender inequality raised questions about some basic elements of social structure—such as the gendered division of labour. In turn, there emerged a sense of the profound sexism of sociology—a discipline that had been virtually silent on fundamental matters of gender inequality.

Especially important feminist criticisms of sociology were developed in Millman and Kanter's (1975) edited volume. The chief criticism was that sociology did not recognize that women and men inhabit different social worlds. Written by men, sociology involved the study of men and not humankind, much less women: sociology examined only half of social reality. Clearly, the first task of feminist sociology was to add the missing half. That task would transcend disciplinary boundaries.

These early-1970s arguments by feminist sociologists transcended the criticism that sociology was incomplete without a consideration of women and their typical experiences, however: more important, feminists declared sociology's understanding of society to be systematically distorted because it was informed by men's experiences alone. Dorothy Smith (1974) argued that sociological methods, concepts, and analyses were products of the 'male social universe'—what Mary O'Brien (1981) would later label 'male-stream thought'—and suffered accordingly. Because men were less involved than women in the daily negotiations necessary to meet family members' physical and emotional needs, their experience was less rooted in the immediacies of daily living. Consequently their sociology was needlessly abstract and often hopelessly uninformed by people's direct experiences. In a special issue of the *Canadian Review of Sociology and Anthropology* devoted to women's issues, Smith (1975: 367) called for 'a major critique of the existing disciplines and theoretical frames . . . subjecting it [knowledge] to exacting scrutiny and criticism from the position of woman as subject (or knower)'.

Thus the challenging second task of feminist social science was (and is) to rewrite sociology, incorporating the full significance of gender at the levels of social structure and interpersonal relations—the latter because one of the potentially most important insights of feminist theory comes from the various (and yet to be fully understood) implications of the fact that individuals have gender identities. That men as well as women act from a psychological and material condition rooted in gender socialization and gender relations is often overlooked by sociologists concerned with individual behaviour. Also problematic, however, is the analysis of sociologists so sensitive to social structure and the social forces acting over and against the individual that they ignore the power of human agency. A feminist sociology would retain the powerful idea of social structure, but simultaneously insist upon recognizing human agency, especially as it is influenced by gender ideology.

Meanwhile, Marxist, radical, and socialist feminists were developing the theory necessary to accomplish goals as ambitious as rewriting sociology.[2] Canadians have contributed disproportionately to such theory. There has been continual interchange and debate in Canada—more so than in the US—between political activists and academics. As a result academics have found meaningless abstraction hard to sustain in light of scrutiny of their writings by their activist sisters. As well, in contrast to the American scene, neither liberal feminism nor radical feminism has achieved hegemony in Canada. Here, no doubt as a consequence of the CCF/NDP legacy, Marxist and socialist feminists have provided vibrant political tendencies and fruitful theoretical currents. Additionally, and again in contrast to the case in other countries, Marxist feminists and radical feminists in Canada have engaged in debate with each other (Hamilton and Barrett 1986). Perhaps that is why the synthesis known as socialist feminism is so vital in Canada. These factors, coupled with the close attention Canadian feminists have paid to British theoretical debates, which tend to be more sophisticated than their American counterparts, have resulted in important theoretical contributions by Canadian feminists.

The 'domestic-labour debate' among Marxist feminists, for example, and the critical response to it, produced theoretical advances beyond the nineteenth-century roots of both Marxist feminism and radical feminism. While the debate was motivated by the desire to respond to 'wages for housework' arguments, and more generally to theorize women's work, a concern about the nature of the relationship of household production to capitalist commodity production quickly assumed prominence (Benston 1969; Morton 1971; Seccombe 1974; 1975; Fox 1980a). And while that preoccupation proved to be only indirectly useful to feminist concerns (Hamilton 1981; Miles 1983), it produced an understanding of the centrality of women's domestic labour to capitalist production. It became clear, as a consequence, that ignoring gender relations in general, and household labour in particular, produces distorted analyses of 'the economy'.

Wally Seccombe (1975) developed the argument that household work is central to capitalist commodity production. The persistence of capitalism requires the transformation of consumer commodities into 'use values' (e.g., meals, clean clothing), and the production and reproduction of 'labour power' (i.e., raising the next generation and maintaining people's capacity to work). Recognizing the fact that capital needs women's production of life and the means of life raises the possibility that capital somehow appropriates labour from the housewife.[3] Perhaps one legacy of this debate, then, was the introduction of the more general question of the role of women's unpaid family labour in capitalist development (a point I take up below).[4]

Critics of the domestic-labour debate had a telling condemnation: it overlooked *relations* between women and men, which are at the heart of the problem of gender inequality (Hamilton 1981; Miles 1983). Furthermore, the economistic focus of the debate ignored issues of sexuality, gender socialization, and gender ideology, which clearly are central to gender relations. More recent feminist work in Canada, as elsewhere, has turned to these matters (O'Brien 1981; Valverde 1985; Hamilton and Barrett 1986; Maroney and Luxton 1987).

Although they have reached a level of sophistication comparable to that of most other theoretical traditions in sociology, feminist theories have been recognized only superficially by most subfields of the discipline. Considerations of gender and women's experience are now standard in many areas of sociology; what this means, however, is that sociology has incorporated women by adding them onto otherwise unrevised models of individual behaviour and social process. Only sociology of the family has been fundamentally transformed by an understanding of the significance of gender. In contrast, the sociology of inequality (or 'social stratification') has applied its unamended concepts (e.g., socio-economic status [SES], class) to women, and inserted women into its unrevised models (e.g., of status attainment), with results that are less than illuminating. Indeed, these results should have raised questions about the concepts and models themselves. Unfortunately, fundamental questions and criticisms have not emerged. In the next section I shall review these attempts to incorporate women into sociological analyses of inequality, criticize sociology's concepts and models in the light of the results of these attempts, and argue that true incorporation of gender must involve a complete *recasting* of analyses of social organization.

The challenge of feminist theory to sociology is obvious in the case of social inequality. Much less apparent is its significance for an issue such as Canadian economic development as it is discussed by political economists. Like feminism, recent Canadian political economy springs from the politicization of the 1960s (in its nationalist current), and grounds itself in Marxist theory (though often that of the Canadian Marxists Macpherson, Pentland, and Ryerson rather than of Marx himself) as well as Innis's work. Yet the concerns of Canadian 'dependency theorists' and feminist theorists are different indeed. Nevertheless, much of the feminist critique of sociology applies to the 'Canadian political economy tradition'—at least to the proponents reviewed above—and is now being articulated (Armstrong and Armstrong 1983b; Cohen 1985; Maroney and Luxton 1987; Porter 1987).[5] Expanding on that critique below, I shall show that recognizing women's contributions adds to our understanding of Canadian economic development. More generally, I shall argue that feminist concerns entail a focus on social relations and social process that is superior to the usual focus of political economists attempting to explain development in Canada, and that a feminist analysis of development can reorient the discussion in a fruitful way.

SOCIAL STRATIFICATION AND CLASS DIVISION

Social inequality is understood by Marxists in terms of a distinct structure in which class divisions based on ownership or non-ownership of the means of production are fundamental. According to this perspective, social inequalities other than those of class assume particular forms because of the organization of production, which ultimately determines social organization. In contrast, non-Marxist sociologists usually assume that society is stratified along a number of different lines—that there are a number of sources of inequality, without clear relationships to each other. While the latter perspective is conducive to simply adding gender inequality to the list of social inequities, many feminists argue that understanding the effects of gender should produce a fresh analysis of social inequality in general.

Rather than attempt such an analysis, this section will examine some of the problems with the concepts and models used to study inequality that become evident when women are considered. In the course of reviewing research in the quantitative stratification tradition of 'status attainment', I first indicate problems with the application of its unrevised status-attainment models to women. Then I review derivative research focussed on women's position in the labour market, and draw out the implications of findings in this area for the analysis of social inequality. As well, I look at some of the important work on social class. While the older work on class suffers from the omission of women, the newer work acquires other problems when models developed by men to study men are simply applied to women. With respect to both research traditions—those of status attainment and Marxist theories of class—the attempt to introduce gender to 'sex-blind' models not only reveals distortions in those models but also suggests more satisfactory approaches to the study of inequality. After sketching some of these lessons, I conclude the section by reflecting on recent debates among Canadian feminists about the relationship of gender to social class, and thus to social inequality in general.

### Socio-economic status and its attainment

Developed by American sociologists (especially Blau and Duncan 1967) and reflecting key ideological preoccupations of American sociology, status-attainment research focusses on the relative effects of the ascribed and achieved characteristics of individuals on the prestige of their occupations. The prestige of individuals' work is held to summarize their life circumstances and social position. In turn, it is *personal characteristics*, rather than social structure, that determine people's allocation to particular statuses (Boyd *et al.* 1985: 2). Indeed, this research tradition is decidedly anti-structural—a stance assumed by its American pioneers, Blau and Duncan (1967), and common to mainstream sociology (a point elaborated below; see also Fox 1988b).

While status-attainment research focusses on the individual, it nevertheless makes certain assumptions about social structure. As in economists' human-capital models, an open, competitive market-place is assumed to evaluate and differentially reward the traits that individuals embody; the rewards vary according to the importance of these traits to society. This functionalist perspective on society reduces social structure to a hierarchy of jobs of varying social value (Horan 1978). Just as it ignores social-structural constraints, status attainment also takes occupation to be the most important foundation of stratification (Blau and Duncan 1967; Goyder 1981), and one that is unrelated to other sources of inequality (Breton 1973). Nevertheless, what is assumed in status-attainment models does undergo empirical test whenever such models are used. As we shall see, the findings from research in the status-attainment tradition are ultimately informative about social structure.

### Women and 'status attainment'

The concept of SES and the status-attainment models related to it were developed to study men. The exclusive study of men followed from the assumptions that the family is the basic unit of stratification, and that its status is established by the occupation of the male household head (Acker 1973). On the basis of Parsonian theory, it was assumed that 'the woman's fundamental status is that of her husband's wife, the mother of his children' (Parsons quoted in Sampson and Rossi 1975: 201). In short, women were viewed as having no status aside from that derived from their husbands—a judgement rendering invisible all women unattached to men.

A desire to avoid these sexist assumptions has led a number of researchers to study women; but to do so they have used the unrevised concepts and models designed to study men (Cuneo and Curtis 1975; Boyd *et al.* 1981; Boyd 1985; Goyder 1985). Monica Boyd's work is typical. Using data from the 1973 Canadian Mobility Study, she compared the process of status attainment for women and men, including as (ascribed) family-background characteristics father's and mother's education, father's occupational status, and mother's labour-force particip-ion. Respondent's education, first-job status, and current occupational status were examined as achieved characteristics. Boyd (1985) found that women's occupational status is less influenced by family background than men's, and that for women the effect of family background is largely mediated by education and the status of the first job—even more so than for men. Additionally, she found that women typically begin their careers in jobs of higher status than men, although they experience less career mobility thereafter. This curious finding is in line with several studies that have shown the female labour force to have an average SES that is equal to or higher than that of the male labour force (Boyd and McRoberts 1982; Boyd 1986).

The 'finding' of women's higher occupational status indicates the lack of relevance of status-attainment models (especially the concept of SES) for women. For example, this odd result must be reconciled with the huge body of research documenting women's disadvantaged position in the labour market (see below). In response to this literature, Boyd (1985: 269) argued that the higher-status social origins and greater educational attainment of women than men in the paid labour force 'compensates' for their lower earnings in determining their SES.

The equality of men's and women's SES cannot be so easily dismissed, however, since it suggests that SES is insensitive to gender. It is significant that the direct prestige ratings on which these researchers base their index (i.e., Pineo and Porter 1967) were made without any reference to the gender of the workers in the rated occupations (Fox and Suschnigg 1988: 7). Statistical analysis of these prestige scores by Fox and Suschnigg (1988) shows that the gender composition of the occupations had no effect on their status rating independent of differences among occupations with respect to levels of education and earnings. Even the marginal relationship between status and the gender composition of occupations was very small.

Measuring the prestige of housework also produces odd, but informative, results. Margrit Eichler (1976) included housework in a list of 'occupations' rated for prestige in the usual manner, and found it to have relatively high status: housework ranked above average—equivalent to, or higher than, occupations common to women in the paid labour force. In other words, the most fundamental division in the occupational structure—between privatized, unpaid work and socialized, paid work—and the one most related to gender, is not reflected in prestige.

In their concern that SES scales should register gender differences, researchers have ignored the fundamental question of the sensitivity of prestige to gender, and have focussed instead on the construction of alternative scales. Thus Blishen and Carroll (1978) and Boyd (1986) have proposed different revisions of the SES index. While the different indices generate very similar results, the efforts of these researchers to assess their revised scales are revealing: the scales were judged according to their ability to produce results similar to those generated in research using more directly interpretable measures, such as income. In adopting this criterion, these researchers implicitly acknowledged the social centrality of *material conditions* in shaping peoples' lives.

The assumption that the prestige of a person's work is a good indicator of the nature and quality of that individual's life is problematic (Coser 1975). While the social significance of occupation is unquestionable, the 'socioeconomic "goodness" or desirability' (Boyd and McRoberts 1982: 131) of jobs, or the 'intersubjective assessment of the honour due to specific forms of work' (Blishen et al. 1987: 466)—which SES purports to represent—is of doubtful importance. Certainly, variations among individuals with respect to the material conditions shaping their lives are not captured by a measure of the prestige of their work. Focussing on the prestige of paid occupations is fanciful, if not scandalous, for a society in which such fundamental matters as life chances, material standard of living, opportunities for self-fulfilment, and degree of personal autonomy are *significantly* different for different groups of people.

Considered carefully, 'occupational status' seems particularly inappropriate when used to encapsulate women's lives. This is so partly because paid jobs do not mean the same thing for women as they do for men: for instance, a relationship to a man can be more critical than the work a woman does (although the two often go hand in hand) in determining her living standard.[6]

In fact, assuming that women's life course is parallel to men's is generally problematic. First, women's lives resist—more than men's—reduction to a single dimension of goodness. Even

women's 'status' derives from several sources, involving at least
family relations and work. Specifically, women have not oriented their lives primarily to market-place achievement. Not only
does the notion of a career (in the usual sense) not fit most
women's lives, but the ranking of different outcomes makes no
sense because many of women's 'accomplishments' occur
outside the market-place. Second, the constraints of social structure loom especially large in women's lives: the notion that
achieved traits determine an individual's future is even more
questionable for women than it is for men. As Smith (1987: 64-5)
has argued, while some men can assume the ability to act upon
the world in a planned, rational, and effective manner, most
women view their life histories as 'not so much a career as a
series of contingencies, of accidents'.

Third, as long as social arrangements dictate gender inequality in the labour market, modelling the economic outcome
in women's lives will require some indication of their relationship to men. While it is sexist simply to consider the household
as embodied in its male head, it is also of doubtful value to study
the individual without due consideration both of his or her gender and of the household as the typical unit of income sharing
and daily maintenance. Thus the laudable attempt to rid sociological models of sexist assumptions by treating women as individuals entails some problems, because many women are not
economically autonomous. In other words, neither assumption
—that the family is the appropriate economic unit of analysis, or
the alternative notion that the individual is the appropriate
one—is wholly satisfactory. Reality demands a more complex
approach. Overall, then, one can only conclude that 'status
attainment' is a very poor model of women's lives.

### Women's position in the labour market

The concern in status-attainment research with the relative effects of ascribed and achieved characteristics is indirectly a concern with social organization—whether current levels of intergenerational mobility indicate individual allocation through
open competition or through simple inheritance. Significantly,
the blindness that has allowed researchers to restrict themselves
to the study of white men (e.g., Blau and Duncan 1967) precluded a sound answer to this question. In representing ascription

narrowly, by indices of the SES of family background, and omitting consideration of sex and race—the two most significant ascribed characteristics—status-attainment researchers grossly underestimated the importance of ascription (Burawoy 1977). In the end, it is precisely the research that examines male-female (and racial) differences in the labour market that has been most revealing about social structure.

Quantitative research on women's position in the labour market has been primarily concerned with the gap between men's and women's earnings, and with the factors that are assumed to cause the gap. Most Canadian studies employ status-attainment (or human-capital) models of labour-market processes. Thus they typically assume that personal characteristics allocate individuals to positions in the labour market: the chief independent variables in these studies are human-capital factors like education and labour-force experience. In turn, intergroup differences for which these factors cannot account are taken to constitute 'discrimination'.

The presumption—implicit among most status-attainment researchers—is that social inequalities that follow from factors supposedly in people's control, such as educational attainment, are somehow 'fair', while those due to other factors are discriminatory or unjust. On the contrary, some researchers have pointed out that while the unaccounted-for differences in income may indicate the extent of direct pay discrimination, most of the variables being considered also represent differential treatment of women (Ornstein 1983a; Fox and Fox 1987: 375). For example, 'human-capital' differences between men and women reflect different socialization experiences as well as differences in opportunity. Hence when researchers assess the significance of different factors they are identifying the locus and nature of discrimination against women, not determining 'how much' discrimination there is—as is usually argued.[7]

Perhaps the best measure of gender discrimination, then, is the size of the earnings gap: women's average earned income is between 50 per cent and 60 per cent of men's (Boyd and Humphreys 1979; Goyder 1981; Denton and Hunter 1982; Ornstein 1983a). Goyder's (1981) analysis of 1973 Canadian Mobility Study data—which involved a statistical adjustment for education, occupational status, career continuity, and hours worked—showed that only the number of hours worked annually and career continuity significantly affected the discrepancy between men's and women's earnings. The obvious implication of this finding is that women's typical pattern of marrying and assuming domestic responsibilities is a chief cause of their disadvantaged position in the labour market. Nevertheless, the adjustment for these variables still left Goyder with the major part of the earnings gap unexplained: women's earnings were raised to only 67 per cent of men's.

Goyder (1981) and others (Boyd and Humphreys 1979; Denton and Hunter 1982) have also found gender differences in dollar returns to personal (i.e., human-capital) characteristics (cf. Ornstein 1983a). The conclusion researchers have drawn is that the earnings gap is due not to gender differences in relevant personal characteristics (not all of which are in men's favour) but to the differences women and men experience in the *process* of finding a job and earning an income (Denton and Hunter 1982). In other words, the labour market operates differently for women and men, which suggests the importance of barriers to women's success in the labour market.

The only Canadian researcher to undertake a systematic examination of the causes of the gender gap in earnings from a perspective critical of 'status attainment' is Michael Ornstein (1983a). Ornstein assessed the relative importance of human-capital factors, occupational structure, part-time work, and characteristics of the employer. Like many American studies (reviewed in Fox and Fox 1986), Ornstein's analysis showed human-capital factors to have relatively little causal significance to the earnings gap. While women's part-time work appeared to have a sizeable effect on the gap, occupational structure (i.e., average wage levels and the gender composition of occupations) had the greatest impact.

Ornstein's findings highlight a problem with studies done from the 'status-attainment' perspective: in omitting structural indicators, especially variables such as occupation (which is replaced by 'occupational status'), these studies attribute differential returns to personal traits that are probably largely matters of differential occupational placement (e.g., different returns to education are mostly the result of obtaining different jobs). Like the US studies (Fox and Fox 1986), Ornstein's work suggests that the gender segregation of the labour market is the main proximate 'cause' of the wage gap in Canada. It is lamentable, and no doubt the 'fault' of the near-hegemony of the status-attainment perspective, that researchers have barely begun to examine the structure of the labour market. Nevertheless, what status attainment hid, the recent concern over gender inequality puts into focus.

One systematic assessment of the gender segregation of the Canadian labour force between 1931 and 1981 (based on detailed census occupations matched between adjacent censuses) showed the persistence of the pattern of men's and women's employment in different occupations (Fox and Fox 1987). As of 1981, over 60 per cent of the male or female labour force would have had to change occupations to equalize the male and female job distributions. This high level of segregation existed even after two decades (the 1960s and 1970s) of slightly declining segregation, as some women entered jobs preponderantly held by men in earlier years. Moreover, as Armstrong and Armstrong's (1983a) in-depth interviews indicate, census data underestimate the actual degree of separation of men and women in paid work.

Structural features of the labour market less obvious than its gender segregation have also been discussed by sociologists. In the US most of the concern with structure has centred on theories of labour-market segmentation developed by radical and Marxist economists. Even the most sophisticated of these segmentation theories is more descriptive than analytical, however, so quantitative researchers have not always found them useful (Ornstein 1983a). Nevertheless, statistical analyses in Canada by Boyd and Humphreys (1979) and Apostle, Clairmont, and Osberg (1985) successfully specified different segments of the economy and then found different income returns to personal characteristics by sector. This research indicates not only that women receive different returns to human-capital characteristics than men, but also that the difference varies by sector.

Until recently the classical Marxist concept of a 'reserve army of labour' has received more attention than segmentation theory among Canadian scholars concerned with labour-market structure and process. Connelly (1978) developed the argument that housewives constitute an institutionalized latent reserve of labour: they are not only increasingly available for wage work but are also cheap and competitive within the range of jobs open to them. While limited in its explanatory power, the concept of a reserve labour pool was useful when applied to women because it made clear another way in which housewives are important to the labour market, and raised the issue of low-paid labour that increases competition in the labour market. Addressing this question of competition, Fox and Fox's (1986) statistical analysis of census occupations (matched across censuses) indicated that women's wages exert competitive pressure on men's earnings (noticeable ten years later), in occupations where both the proportion of women and the wage gap are large. While the finding is important for confirming male trade-unionists' historic fears about the competitive threat that women's low wages represent, it is more broadly important in suggesting that gender inequality is a matter of general consequence in the labour market: the gender division is a structural feature of the labour market that affects men as well as women.

The ultimate source of the difference between women's and men's earnings is the gender division of society. While contemporary quantitative research supports this conclusion, such research unfortunately draws attention away from the historical process that created women's unequal position in society in general, and in the labour market in particular. To capture that process fully, an explanation must take into account the sexual division of labour characteristic of European society before the development of capitalism and the industrial reorganization of production. Some writers have argued that it is then important to consider capitalism's erosion of the household as a unit of production, and the eventual individualization of people as sellers of labour power (Fox and Fox 1986). In that context, for a variety of reasons (especially women's family responsibilities), women's bargaining power in the labour market has been extremely poor, and their wages relatively very low—factors that have enforced a dependence on marriage. Other writers have argued that women's low wages are due to the continued existence of the family as the unit of maintenance in advanced capitalist societies, with men's wages partly covering the costs of women's daily maintenance (Connelly 1978). While the 'family wage' (paid to men) has never been a reality for many families, both men's and women's wages assume family membership; these facts explain why women's earnings are both necessary and low (Connelly 1978). In both explanations, women's domestic responsibilities and their location in the family are seen as the basis of their position in the labour market.

While the gendered division of labour is the basic cause of women's poor labour-market position, the actions of skilled male workers responding to the threat of women's low wages compounded the impact of this structural factor: the gender-segregated occupational structure was in part actively created. Gaskell (1983) has described how organized male workers responded to the threat posed by the capitalist reorganization of work by fighting for the labelling of certain jobs as 'skilled' and by demanding control over entry into these jobs.[8] Apparently, men's reaction to the erosion of craft work through the industrial division of labour involved a feeling of threat to masculinity as well as to the status of craftsman. Valverde (1988) and others have shown that gender ideology strongly influenced this reaction. Consequently, women workers were not only unorganized, and thus unable to undertake similar defensive or offensive action, but they were also often defined as the enemy in struggles of labour against capital (see Taylor 1983 for a more nuanced account). Of course, capital also had a hand in promoting gender divisions, by using women not only as cheap labour but also as strikebreakers.

What is important here about this historical gender conflict is that it provides another indication of the centrality of gender to labour-market processes. Gender is both a key structural feature of the labour market and an ideological force shaping the human actor, whether that actor is the collective labourer or management.

The quantitative research on gender differences in the labour market is informative not only about gender inequality but also about the nature of social inequality in general in advanced capitalist society. Perhaps most important, this research highlights the significance of social structure relative to individual status characteristics in allocating individuals to work and related material and social rewards. Considering women's occupational accomplishments alone, sex itself is more important than the variables included in status-attainment models (i.e., superiority/inferiority of family background and number of years of schooling). That is, 'ascription' is more important than 'achievement'.

Let us reconsider the process of 'attainment' of an occupation with respect to women's typical life experience. Even today, the capacity and propensity to bear children shape all women's lives, because social organization is only slowly changing from an equation of womanhood with motherhood and domesticity. Not only does the gender difference correspond to the most significant division of work—that between unpaid, privatized and paid, socialized work—but also women's position in the labour market reflects practices and laws equating womanhood with domesticity (e.g., protective legislation), and past conflict between labour and management shaped by gender ideology (as I argued above). As well, the lives of individual women are always distinguished from men's by the necessity to weigh responsibilities for children against all else—in the decision whether to have children, or the daily demands of caring for them. Indeed, given that parents continue to bear the responsibility of caring for young children, the presence of children is likely to entail for women a commitment that assumes precedence over everything else.

Aside from sex, gender socialization bears great significance in women's lives. One among many implications of gender is that it appears to inscribe a power dimension in personality. The acquisition of masculine identity has been argued to involve a repression of the passive aspects of character, and the development of a psychic predisposition for interpersonal dominance, while feminine identity encourages empathy and interpersonal sensitivity (Chodorow 1978; Kaufman 1987; Hamilton 1987). As well as directly affecting labour-market success, these personality differences have far-reaching implications in intimate relations (Rubin 1983).

Beyond the gender dimension of personality, social structure is gender-divided. While women in Canada no longer receive fewer years of schooling than men, gender segregation still characterizes the educational system. Gaskell (1982) has shown that secondary schooling segregates especially those teenagers not in the university stream. Community colleges, which are assuming some of the job-training functions traditionally served by the workplace, are also characterized by very marked gender segregation. In universities as well, women and men tend to study different subjects (Fox 1986a). And beyond this obvious division by gender, Russell (1987) has identified the variety of ways in which teachers and guidance counsellors in secondary schools undervalue female students, encourage them to make traditional 'choices' about their future, and thus reinforce gender differences.

The occupational gender segregation and the male-female earnings gap characterizing the labour market are well documented. Less discussed is the evidence that gender is as important a determinant of employment earnings as any other variable—even when only those women who are working for wages are considered. Ornstein (1983b: 58) examined human-capital and status-attainment variables (i.e., education, experience, and occupation), gender, class, and employer characteristics (i.e., size of firm, sector, and unionization), and concluded that 'gender has a stronger effect than any other variable. It is nearly as powerful as all the other variables combined' in explaining employment earnings for people working 20 or more hours per week.

In sum, the social significance of sex challenges the assumption, typical in the status-attainment literature, that achieved traits shape peoples' lives more profoundly than ascribed traits. Moreover, the focus on individual characteristics in status-attainment research must be criticized in the light of research showing that the basic sources of gender inequality are structural. In turn, another premise of the status-attainment tradition (Fox 1988b), that occupation is the basis of social inequality, cannot be sustained when account is taken of gender. Occupational structure itself is significantly affected by gender. The gender division constitutes a basic structural feature of the occupational structure. Ornstein's (1983b) and Fox and Fox's (1986) research only begins to uncover the significance of gender to earnings in the labour market.

## Men and women in the ruling class

Canadian research on social mobility suffers from its grounding in the status-attainment tradition; that the classic Canadian studies of the capitalist class have their roots in élite theory is similarly problematic. At the minimum, like status attainment, this theoretical tradition places emphasis on the individual rather than on social structure. Thus power was conceptualized by John Porter (1965: 201) in terms of the personnel in positions allowing effective decision-making, and by Wallace Clement

(1975: 23) as a property of individuals who can mobilize resources or make decisions of consequence.

Élite theory must be criticized for its omission of larger social forces, such as market forces, and the power of social structure in general and the mode of production in particular. Yet there is some promise in the social-psychological approach common in studies of élites. In shifting the concern from economic processes and structures to individuals and relationships, élite studies have the potential to reveal the processes by which the 'ruling class' sustains and reproduces itself, including the creation and maintenance of élite solidarity.

Both Porter and Clement were concerned with the generational reproduction of élites and the establishment and maintenance of a 'confraternity of power' (or élite solidarity) in each generation (Porter 1965: 522). Porter argued that kinship is important to both processes, and Clement held that the social dimension of class—family and other personal relations, along with ideology — is critical to the existence of the élite. Nevertheless, instead of analyzing—or even describing—the creation, maintenance, and dynamics of the personal relationships that sustain the élite, both Porter and Clement concentrated on personal status characteristics. For both sociologists, kinship primarily signified class origins, or the characteristics ascribed by virtue of family of origin that equip individuals either well or poorly for material success (Clement 1975: 206). Had these studies focussed instead on the processes of generational and daily reproduction of élites, a consideration of women, social relations, and even gender ideology would have been imperative. Since both men's arguments called for exactly such an analysis, its absence is direct testimony to the sexist bias in their work. More important, its omission renders these analyses lifeless, because they pay insufficient attention to the informal organization of social and economic power.

To the extent that Porter and Clement did show some concern with the social bases of power, both followed the tradition of élite studies in assuming that the social similarity of members of the élite was central to their ongoing power. Similarity was seen to comprise values and attitudes (i.e., a world view), as well as ways of living; this idealist emphasis was especially strong in Porter's work. Both he and Clement, however, ignored three fundamental ingredients of élite homogeneity: first, masculinity, or gender ideology; second, the socialization for which women are responsible; and third, the social relations that create and express élite solidarity.

The 'confraternity of power' is, as the term implies, a brotherhood. Masculinity not only provides men with a basic sense of identity; it also bestows on them an elusive sense of membership in a superior caste. Moreover, because masculinity is so fragile—a social construction rather than a biological 'given'—men seem to need continual assurance about their gender identity (Kaufman 1987: 13), which in turn generates activities that confirm male identity and solidarity (e.g., men's recreational and sports activities, men's clubs). Thus masculine identity represents a powerful basis of commonality and even bonding —not just because it defines men as superior, but also because it seems to require and generate activities that promote male bonding.[9]

Socialization in general is largely responsible for élite attitudes and values, although class interests, as they become apparent in adult positions, are arguably as important. Indeed, the separation of socialization practices from class interests is itself questionable. Porter's and Clement's treatments of élite practices implied that élite schools play a larger role than parents in socializing children. The importance of the mother, then, in preparing her children to assume their adult roles, was overlooked despite Porter's finding that a higher percentage of élite men had mothers with élite origins than had élite fathers. Maxwell and Maxwell's (1971) studies of élite girls' schools have made clear the high degree of social control these schools exercise over their students, and the obvious goal of producing a uniform and strong class identity among their students. Such practices would make little sense were the girls not future agents of social control, as reproducers of the next generation and important public representatives of their class.

In addition to gender ideology and women's role in socialization, Porter and Clement overlooked the social relations necessary to class solidarity. When analysis shifts from wealthy men's similar values to the relationships among them that produce and express that commonality, women's role is obvious. Indeed, weighing the importance of social relations, Ann Duffy (1986) has argued that women create and sustain the foundations of upper-class existence. She contends that maintaining power requires that money be transformed into 'social capital'—the kin and friendship networks, and the social events and institutions that maintain such relationships—and that the people largely responsible for this 'social capital' are women.

Porter recognized the centrality of marriage and argued that kinship is the most important relationship connecting élite members. Nevertheless, while he recognized how crucial alliances among families are to the ongoing existence of a ruling class, the impression his work conveys is one of women as passive bearers of future generations and links between families, rather than as active socializers (involved in ideological reproduction) and as the main creators of the ties that daily reproduce an ideological hegemony and bind men together in a community capable of 'ruling'.

Despite their virtual silence on women's role in creating and sustaining critical relations, both Porter (1965) and Clement (1977a: 234) acknowledged that women 'reproduce' the ruling class socially through their involvement in community affairs. Their failure to describe this process, however, implicitly understated its significance. Upper-class women's involvement in service organizations, philanthropic groups, social and educational reform bodies, and other community organizations typically protects class interests. Wayne Roberts (1979) has argued that the social-reform activities of upper-class women in the late nineteenth and early twentieth centuries were especially important in legitimating upper-class power, since Canada had no entrenched class system based on inherited wealth and ruling-class men were absorbed in building their businesses. The reforms these women initiated under the guise of protecting 'the family' served to deflate the radical potential of the newly formed working class, according to Roberts.

Social historians have provided a variety of examples that support Roberts' argument. Noble (1979), for example, maintained that wealthy women's charity work in the mid-nineteenth century served both to construct the boundaries that defined social classes and to deal with poverty without attacking its sources. Similarly, Barbara Roberts (1979) showed that upper-class women's involvement in the immigration of young British women—ostensibly charity work—directly served class interests. Recognizing that the Victorian family was the cornerstone of imperial England, agencies run by upper-class women recruited girls who were suited to be 'good' wives and mothers in the long run, and domestics in wealthy homes in the short.

In sum, then, Porter's and Clement's examinations of the 'ruling class' initially ignored women because they failed to give adequate consideration to the informal activities through which class power is reproduced and maintained. That is, they failed to examine processes critical to ruling-class existence in addition to its control of capital.

## Men and women in the working class

In contrast to élite theory, the Marxist theory of social class connects the position and power of individuals to structural sources of power and inequality. The emergence in recent decades of work grounded in a Marxist conceptualization of class is therefore a welcome development. Research by Michael Ornstein (1983c) on the historical emergence of a Canadian class structure, for example, provides a promising alternative to the tradition represented by Porter and Clement. Nevertheless, given the origins of Marxist quantitative research on social class, it is disconcerting that researchers in this emerging tradition accommodate the issue of gender simply by slotting women into categories constructed without any consideration of the gender division of labour and non-wage work. As with status-attainment studies, the results of such a treatment of gender suggest inadequacies in the original conceptualization of class, even with respect to men.

Building on the work of the American sociologist Eric Olin Wright (1979), Carl Cuneo (1985) used census data (1931 to 1981) and Labour Force Survey data (1946 to 1984) to determine which sex has become more 'proletarianized' in Canada in recent decades. Cuneo defined two basic modes of production—capitalism and 'independent commodity production'—and two classes within each—the bourgeoisie and working class in the former, the petty bourgeoisie and unpaid family labour in the latter. In justifying his unconventional designation of unpaid family labourers (other than housewives) as a class, Cuneo invoked the 'Marxist definitional requirement' that a mode of production have two classes. Not settling for a definitional solution, however, he also developed the argument that these workers provide labour in return for subsistence (room and board), and in turn reduce business costs and thus contribute to profits.

Cuneo found that women were under-represented—and increasingly so—in the property-owning classes (i.e., the bourgeoisie and petty bourgeoisie) and over-represented among both wage workers and unpaid family workers. While women's over-representation had lessened among wage workers, they were increasingly under-represented among those employees who were managers, supervisors, and in similar positions of power. Meanwhile, unpaid family workers were increasingly female.

While these findings are informative, Cuneo—oddly—interpreted them to show women as experiencing 'proletarianization' when they moved from full-time housework to work outside the home. Yet dependence on wage labour—the essence of the proletarian condition—surely does not begin for a woman living with a man when she begins working outside the home. Most full-time housewives depend on wages for their personal survival, as well as for the performance of their domestic labour. Their relation to wage earnings is indirect, but no less critical than men's. The full-time housewife is, in effect, doubly dependent: directly on her husband and indirectly on his wages.

In almost every detail, the argument that Cuneo made for unpaid family labour applies to housework: it is unpaid labour exchanged for the spouse's support, which makes possible a higher standard of living than his wage could otherwise purchase (Fox 1980b). Housework differs from the unpaid family labour involved in a small business only in that it does not contribute directly to profits. Arguments have been made (e.g., Fox 1980b), however, that domestic labour does contribute indirectly to profits (by lowering the value of the labour socially necessary for the reproduction of labour power, and thus lowering capital's wage bill). Particulars of the analysis of domestic labour and its relation to capital aside, the failure of Marxist theory to give full-time housewives a class position confirms women's invisibility; in other words, it confirms superficial appearances, which Cuneo partly penetrated with his classification of 'unpaid family labour'. More important, Cuneo based his analysis on Marxist definitions that were unexamined in the light of feminist critiques, and he thus failed to address adequately the demanding question of changes in women's material position.

William Carroll (1987) has carried out an interesting elaboration of Cuneo's research. Adding occupation to the analysis, he found that the chief reason women are more 'proletarianized' than men is their occupational segregation: women are more likely than men to be in occupations with relatively high proportions of employees. For Carroll as for Cuneo, however, housewives have no class position.

As Cuneo pointed out, it is essential to analyze the relationship between gender and social class. In fact, that task necessarily precedes assessment of the relative degrees of proletarianization of women and men. Conceptualizing the intersection of gender and class requires analysis, in class-theoretic terms, of the material position of the housewife, who is involved in a production process and arguably carries out work essential to capitalist commodity production (Seccombe 1975; Fox 1980a). But more than an analysis of domestic labour is required. To meet seriously the challenge of a conceptualization of gender and class probably requires a reconceptualization of social class itself.

Just as writers in the status-attainment tradition have assumed that a woman shares her spouse's status, class analysts have assumed that the prototypical proletarian condition is that of the family (or, rather, household), and that economically the housewife is totally dependent on her wage-earning spouse. Indeed, it is the household that undergoes proletarianization (in the classic case, with the loss of farm land). Yet the proletarian condition of dependence on wages actually unfolds differently for women than for men.

Changes in women's relation to capital first of all must be recognized as occurring within the context of women's dependence on marriage for access to the means of production—both in economic modes, such as family farming, that predated industrial capitalism, and in capitalist economies with their characteristic gender gap in earnings. Among peasants or family farmers, marriage has typically been essential for women to acquire access to the means of production (Hedley 1981; Bennett 1987; Ghorayshi 1988); in industrial capitalist societies it is still largely through men that women have access to wage earnings sufficient for a decent standard of living, especially when children are involved (Fox 1980b; 1986a).

Once a woman is married, however, dependence on a spouse's earnings is not the sole determinant of her material position. Until the end of the nineteenth century even women living in towns and cities (e.g., in Montreal) had access to the means of much of their domestic production. Working-class women typically raised animals such as chickens, pigs, and cows, and cultivated vegetable gardens, thus producing the bulk of the family's foodstuffs (Bradbury 1979; 1984a; 1984b; Hollingsworth and Tyyska 1988). Dispossession from the means of household production—and thus a proletarianization particular to women—came only gradually, with changes in urban space, and more abruptly with city ordinances outlawing the keeping of barnyard animals in cities (Bradbury 1984a).

Consequently, while the proletarianization of households produced men's immediate dependence on wage work, women's full dependence on wages came only after a gradual loss of the means of domestic production. During the period of housewives' possession of the means of household production and the partial conversion into commodities of subsistence goods, women contributed substantially to household subsistence: men and women were thus mutually dependent economically, as they had been for centuries. In turn, as women lost those means of production their economic dependence on their husbands increased, especially since the availability of wage work for married women was limited. Simultaneously, subsistence goods were increasingly available only as commodities and the household became mechanized, which meant that women's domestic labour was progressively commodity-dependent and thus subject to market influences. In other words, the process of women's proletarianization antedated their entry into the labour market, the point at which Cuneo's and Carroll's analyses begin.

The availability of jobs for married women, and their mass influx into the labour market in recent decades, involve a more direct relationship of housewives to capital, but no greater dependence on wages. Moreover, women's wage work entails a *lessening* of women's economic dependence on their spouses. At the minimum, therefore, an examination of women's class position, such as that attempted by Cuneo and Carroll, requires a more considered conceptualization of social class for women. The details of proletarianization and working-class status are different for women and men.

Furthermore, an understanding of the relationship of gender and social class may require some reconceptualization of class, or at least a different interpretation of the concept. In the attempt to adapt class analysis to the exigencies of survey research, there has been a tendency to interpret social class as a (material) position in the social structure that individuals *occupy* rather than as a position that *enters and shapes the social relations* involved in particular activities. Yet if 'class' is a facet of certain social relations—specifically, relations of production—class analysis should result from the study of work processes and not simply from the categorization of individuals. Moreover, if production is seen as occurring in the household as well as under the aegis of capital (as feminists insist), then it is essential to recognize in an examination of social class that a single in-dividual may maintain different sets of production relations.

It is therefore problematic to think of certain individuals as occupying a single, uncomplicated class position. For example, a man whose labour is exploited by capital through wage work may exploit a woman's labour at home. That is, there are aspects of class division in some male-female relations—specifically those involving work. Men often appropriate the unpaid labour of their wives in family businesses, and arguably also in house-holds where women do the housework (Burstyn 1985).

In sum, a more fruitful way of approaching class analysis is to examine specific social *relations* in the process of their creation and daily unfolding rather than purporting to capture the es-sence of social class by classifying *individuals*. A focus on both class structure and relations will not only generate a recognition that men and women in the same household may not be in the same class position, but in the process will also produce more informative social research.

### Gender and social inequality

It is clear that analyses of social inequality suffer when they fail to consider gender. Less obvious is how the issue of gender should be accommodated in treatments of social inequality. A basic amendment would be to consider women's experience of the social world in addition to men's. As my review of the power-élite literature showed, this added concern about women's lives turns attention towards the dynamics and social relations of daily living, especially with respect to raising children and creating and maintaining both family life and kin and friendship networks.

My critique of recent research on class indicated, however, that a more profound change is required. Social structure, social forces, and social relations that typically are not considered to involve gender actually do involve it. As a result, the feminist revision of sociology must consist of more than simply 'adding on' women. New conceptualization is called for. Fortunately, some recent debates in feminist theory indicate how that reconceptualization might proceed.

The debate about 'patriarchy', or male dominance, addresses the issue of the relationship between class inequality (and the organization of production), on the one hand, and gender inequality on the other. The point of contention has been whether gender is an aspect of class and 'patriarchy' a characteristic of capitalism, or, alternatively, whether patriarchy should be seen as a system in itself, with gender relations considered comparable to but different from class relations. Proponents of the latter notion (often referred to as 'dual-systems theorists' [Fox 1988a]), argue that while class relations are rooted in production or economic activities, gender relations are rooted in 'reproduction' or family activities. The implication here is that gender is one of many sources of inequality (though perhaps the most basic one).

While the dual-systems view of patriarchy and capitalism is typically American (and radical-feminist), a few Canadian theorists have made such arguments. Varda Burstyn (1985), for example, has maintained that gender relations resemble class relations in that men appropriate women's domestic labour, which provides for much of men's daily maintenance and affords them leisure time that they otherwise would not have. Thus while economic-class exploitation occurs in the production of commodities, 'sex-class' exploitation arises out of the organization of sexuality (i.e., heterosexuality and monogamous marriage), child care, and housework (i.e., the privatized family household).

Mary O'Brien (1981) too has argued that gender relations are autonomous. She has proposed an elaborate theory that assumes that 'the *biological* process of reproduction' (O'Brien 1981: 185, my emphasis) produces patriarchy. According to O'Brien, men are alienated in the process of biological reproduction because they are separated from their 'seed' during sexual intercourse. To achieve some sense of continuity, they develop an appropriative stance *vis-à-vis* women and the world in general: they create institutions such as marriage that control and subordinate women. For both Burstyn and O'Brien, then, male dominance is distinct from other types of social inequality. With its own dynamics and sets of social relations, patriarchy is a distinct dimension of social inequality or stratification.

Critics of dual-systems theory argue that capitalism is patriarchal, and that because 'sex differences pervade every aspect of human activity' (Armstrong and Armstrong 1983b: 7), gender inequality cannot be seen as separate from class inequality and other social inequalities. Pat Armstrong and Hugh Armstrong (1983b) have suggested that notions of class as 'sexless' are distorted because the sexual division of labour is inherent in capitalism. According to the Armstrongs (1983b: 9),

> free labour, which is essential to the very definition of capitalism, entails the reproduction of labour power primarily at another location [other than the workplace]. This separation under capitalism between commodity production and human reproduction . . . in turn implies a particular division of labour between the sexes.

Furthermore, the Armstrongs maintained, women are assigned to the household because they bear children. Women's subordination follows from the domination of commodity production over other forms of production (e.g., household production) in capitalist societies.

The Armstrongs have been criticized for a biological reductionism that too simplistically assigns social consequences to women's reproductive capacity (Connelly 1983; see also Fox 1986b for a discussion of a similar British debate). As well, following British theorist Michele Barrett (1980), Patricia Connelly (1983) contended that the division of labour between men and women is not necessary to the capitalist mode of production, but rather is a historical product of a gender ideology (antedating capitalism) that informed the collective struggles out of which capitalism (as a social formation) arose. Connelly emphasized that the origins of capitalist patriarchy must be distinguished from its current form. She agreed with the Armstrongs that gender inequality is integral to advanced capitalist society; she disagreed that such a situation is necessary.

Many, perhaps most, socialist feminists would now hold that capitalism and patriarchy cannot be considered as separate systems (see Fox 1988a for a critique of dual-systems theory). Indeed, appreciation of the pervasive character of gender differences in this society grows daily among feminists. Yet there is neither consensus about the full meaning of 'patriarchy' nor a clear sense of how to incorporate gender in social analysis.

Elsewhere, in attempting to define patriarchy, I have argued that the term refers to the 'system of practices, arrangements and social relations that ensure biological reproduction, child rearing and the reproduction of gendered subjectivity', as well as gender ideology, or the sense of gender identity, itself (Fox 1988a: 175). While the social relations organizing 'reproduction' are distinct from other relations, once it is recognized that men and women differ in their personal identities, it is no longer possible to separate gender from other aspects of social organization. Hence including gender in social analysis means two things. First, any political-economic analysis must include production that occurs via gender relations and primarily through women's work—the production of children and more broadly all productive activities that occur in the household. Moreover, just as household production is the other half of total social production (Engels 1972), so too what goes on in so-called 'personal life' is often a central component of the more 'public' activities that sociologists usually write about. As I argued above in reviewing élite studies, the informal social relationships that women are largely responsible for are at the heart of matters apparently outside the sphere of family life. Second, because gender identity is a basic component of all human subjectivities, all analyses of social relations—even those outside family and personal life—must consider gender ideology, and recognize that gender is always salient to men as well as to women.

CANADIAN DEPENDENT DEVELOPMENT: DEPENDENT ON WOMEN

Women's invisibility in élite studies was coupled with an under-emphasis on the processes and social relations that provide for the existence and daily maintenance of the élite. Likewise, in failing to examine women's situation seriously, studies of the working class have overlooked women's domestic production (which sustained early proletarian families). Similar problems, involving omission of productive processes, plague the treatment of Canada's economic development by the political economists reviewed in Chapter 2. Feminist theory, then, may offer a more general critique of the arguments of the political economists than those developed elsewhere (McNally 1981; Panitch 1981; Schmidt 1981; Carroll 1985). Rather than addressing directly the issue of distorted economic development, the following feminist critique questions whether the Canadian political economists reviewed above provide an adequate understanding of the development process—a prerequisite for assessing issues of dependency and distorted development.

As is true of sociology in general, the political economists' view of development has abstracted too much from what is basic in shaping the Canadian economy, Canadian society, and therefore the daily lives and experiences of Canadians. Just as Innis derived the major contours of social organization from the character of staples, Canadian political economists have tended to emphasize single factors, such as the nationality of capital, in order to derive from them the nature of Canadian economy and society. Generally, discussions of Canada's development have been concerned with the nature and structure of the capitalist class rather than the economy itself.[10] Related to this pattern is the tendency in discussions of development to omit consideration of the requisites and the process of development itself. More precisely, the production, stressed by Marx, of the surplus necessary for development—i.e., 'primitive accumulation' (1967 [1887])—has not been examined, and the social relations of production—e.g., the relations between labour and capital [Panitch 1981]—have been neglected as well. Adequate treatment of the basis for Canada's development requires discussion of the fur trade, the fisheries, and especially agriculture—as well as industrialization. In turn, discussion of these types of production necessarily highlights women's central role in Canadian economic development. I shall first demonstrate this centrality by examining women's work in fur, fish, and agricultural production, and in early industrialization. Second, to correct the distortion due to gender-blind analysis, I shall present some elements of a different analysis of development, including a modest reassessment of the nature of 'development' itself.

## Women's role in development

While the fur trade is usually portrayed as a man's world, it is clear that native women were central to it. Sylvia Van Kirk (1980) and Jennifer Brown (1980) have shown that although the European traders relied largely on native men for trapping, they depended on native women for cementing ties with the trappers, keeping them alive in the bush, and providing the emotional connection that made their isolated lives endurable.

Because women occupied a powerful position in native culture (Leacock 1981; Anderson 1985; 1987), 'in order to secure good trade relations it was necessary to cultivate the women' (Van Kirk 1980: 71). Marriage to native women was, then, an effective way for Europeans to establish liaison with the natives—and such 'country marriages' were common (Van Kirk 1980). In turn, the inland journeys required by the fur trade depended on women to make and 'man' the canoes, and to act as guides and translators. In the words of a Chipewyan guide in 1772, 'there is no such thing as traveling any considerable distance, for any length of time, in this country, without their [women's] assistance' (quoted in Van Kirk 1980: 63). Finally, their 'tender ties' with native wives kept the Europeans alive not only emotionally but also literally: the women provided food (pemmican) and clothing (moccasins, snowshoes), and taught the men the skills necessary for living in the bush, about which the Hudson Bay Company initially knew little.

Just as gender relations were at the heart of the fur trade, the partnership of a man and a woman—simultaneously the union of ownership and labour—has constituted the primary relationship governing the inshore fishery in Newfoundland and the Maritimes, and family farming across the continent: in both types of production the family has been the principal unit of production.

Recently, feminist researchers in the Atlantic region have been developing a political economy of the fishing industry that shows the importance of gender relations and the family household. As Marilyn Porter (1983; 1985a; 1987) has shown, from the late eighteenth century to the 1950s, the husband/wife partnership constituted the team that carried out the two tasks that were necessary to the family fishery in Newfoundland and the Maritimes and are still present in some rural areas of Atlantic Canada: men fished and women processed the catch. Processing (skilled work that was apparently more time-consuming and complex than fishing, and was essential for sale of the catch) was carried out partly by the women themselves and partly by hired labour that they supervised (Porter 1985a). As well, women in fishing communities typically did work that ensured family subsistence (e.g., caring for animals and gardens, producing dairy products and household linen) and that brought cash into the household. As a result women in the inshore fishery not only produced enough basic subsistence goods to reduce significantly the pressure on men for family support, but also provided both cash and major labour inputs that were appropriated by their husbands to sustain their businesses.

Since the 1950s processing and the women who perform it have moved into factories, though women's factory work varies with changes in the economy (Connelly and MacDonald 1983). The cash that women earn not only raises the standard of living of their families, but also is necessary to the permanently cash-starved businesses of the fishermen. Ironically, as Patricia Connelly and Martha MacDonald (1983) have argued, women's contributions—whether in the form of home production or of wage earnings—sustain an economic mode in which the 'semi-independent' fisherman[11] can persist in business while receiving a price for his fish that is below the cost of production (a point I shall take up later).

Like the inshore fishery, Canadian agriculture has featured the family as the primary unit of production. Agribusiness notwithstanding, in 1981 'capitalized family farming'[12] represented 99.3 per cent of Canadian farms and 90.4 per cent of farm sales (Ghorayshi 1988: 4). Furthermore, 'for most farms, the wife's contribution is indispensable for the survival of the family enterprise' (Ghorayshi 1988: 7). Women have been essential both because of the varied types of labour they perform and because of their pivotal role in securing the labour of others.

In frontier conditions women worked in the fields (Johnson 1973; Fairbanks and Sundberg 1983; Silverman 1984). Indeed, when the farmer was forced to work off the farm for wages, his wife was left to run the farm, often doing all the work (Hedley 1981). More important, with respect to the processing and production of food, women's labour provided a pattern of self-sufficiency that was the norm on family farms—a norm that lasted until recently in many places (Hedley 1979; Fink 1987). In the pioneer conditions that existed in the west even in this century,

> where one had to cope with virgin land, fickle weather and exploitative grain handling agencies, . . . people were chronically short of cash with which to buy manufactured goods. As a result, they had to keep their purchases to a minimum by producing everything they could at home, whether it was a pound of lard or a cake of soap (Rasmussen 1976: 42).

It should also be recognized that frontier farming involved 'unrequiting toil' (Johnson 1973: 52), which married men apparently found more bearable than single men (Rasmussen 1976; Light and Prentice 1980; Sundberg 1986). Most obviously, women's daily presence reduced loneliness; but it also ameliorated the conditions of the struggle to survive. Homemade curtains and rugs, which 'civilized' the crudest of wilderness homes, were among the more common products of feminine sensibilities (Gorham 1976). Moreover, whether as wives and mothers or as members of religious orders, women provided the social services essential to pioneer life, especially health care (Rasmussen 1976; Noel 1985). And it was usually women who created the organizations and institutions at the heart of community: libraries, churches, schools (Kohl 1976; Luxton 1980).

Once in possession of the standard range of household equipment, farm women typically raised chickens and hogs; milked the cows and manufactured butter and cheese; planted and harvested large vegetable and fruit gardens and processed the produce; sheared the sheep and (partly) processed the wool; and helped with the field work when there were labour shortages—in addition to raising children and keeping house (Fairbanks and Sundberg 1983; Cohen 1985). Farm wives generally took the surplus products of their labour to market, including textile goods in the early nineteenth century, dairy products until the twentieth, and eggs until after the Second World War (Jensen 1980; 1986; Cohen 1985). Furthermore, while the literature has emphasized the complementary nature of farm wives' work, recent research by Ghorayshi (1988) indicates that these women do significant amounts of field work (now made easier by mechanization and necessitated by male farmers' wage work off the farm). Estimates of the field work done by farm wives range from 17 to 40 hours per week (Ghorayshi 1988: 11), apparently varying substantially by type of farm. Perhaps this is not a new pattern.

The 'reproductive' work done by farm wives is as important as their subsistence work. Because family farms traditionally have recruited their main labour force from their own ranks, a basic requisite is the continual reproduction of the family.[13] Thus 'children are the best stock a farmer can possess' (an informant quoted in Guillet 1963: 172), which explains in part the high birth rates that characterized the early years of Canadian settlement (Cohen 1985).

Yet far more is involved than women's bearing and rearing of children. Because the family is the production unit and source of labour, kin relations govern the production process (Ghorayshi 1988). Moreover, co-ordination of the activities of the family and the enterprise is a basic ingredient in economic success (Kohl 1976; Bennett 1982). Usually the farm wife is in this pivotal co-ordinating position, since women generally are responsible for the creation and maintenance of harmonious family relations. There are many ways in which farm success depends on family members' subordination of personal desires to the needs of the enterprise. And it is typically the wife and mother who procures the next generation's 'consent' both to work and to sacrifice for the sake of the farm. In general, the degree to which the wife and mother is supportive of the male farmer's authority and his expectations of the children matters greatly in shaping the next generation's orientation to farming and to the family farm (Kohl 1976; Bennett 1982).

Women are also pivotal in securing labour from the larger kin network and the community. The responsiveness of these people depends on the man's reputation as a farmer—a public image that his wife helps to produce—and on the nature of the relations that the woman has cultivated (Kohl 1976). For example, a woman's relations with her daughter have economic import: the daughter's in-laws are frequently key sources of assistance (Jensen 1986). Even the reputation of a woman's cooking can be a factor in procuring and keeping hired help at harvest (Silverman 1984). Generally, the complementarity of the household and the farm enterprise means that some of women's domestic labour contributes directly to the running of the farm (Ghorayshi 1988: 11).

The unity of family and enterprise is the chief factor constituting the family farm's strength and ensuring its survival. Because production relations are family relations, difficult times can be survived by intensified self-exploitation of family labour and by underconsumption. As Harriet Friedmann (1978) has pointed out, family farms can persist in years of zero or even negative surplus production more easily than capitalist enterprises with their paid workers. In other words, by consistently subordinating their own and the household's consumption needs and desires to those of the enterprise, family members contribute substantially to the enterprise and indeed may be the key to its survival. And it is women who motivate and orchestrate this dedication.

The literature on family farms has emphasized the complementarity of men's and women's work. The argument has been made that farm men and women typically have invested their surpluses differently: his in the farm enterprise and hers in the family (Kohl 1976; Sachs 1983; Cohen 1985). While men have concentrated on expanding their capital, women have focussed on ensuring subsistence, devoting any surplus product to household consumption or to personal relationships (Fink 1987). While this emphasis on the complementarity of men's and women's farm work may exaggerate the differences in the work they do, it highlights an important pattern: when farmers have shifted to market production, the drain on the net surplus product due to subsistence needs has been minimal because of women's subsistence production.

Women's market profits have at times also supported necessary cash expenditures for the farm (e.g., for machinery). Historically, women's contributions have been so important that their erosion has seriously undermined the survival of family farms. For example, when New England mills destroyed the market for homemade textiles in the nineteenth century, the loss of women's earnings from this production apparently forced many farm families to abandon their land (Jensen 1980).

Overall, the fur trade, the inshore fisheries, and family farming have depended on women's work not only to ensure subsistence but also, as I shall argue below, to make possible the surplus production that formed the basis of economic development. In discussing self-propelled economic development, political economists have appropriately given much attention to industrial production. What they have been silent about is the centrality of women's low-paid labour to industrial development. Nevertheless, there is evidence that in Canada, as in England, women's labour subsidized the industrial revolution.

The factors that made women a cheap labour pool in England —their domestic responsibilities, coupled with differential treatment by employers and active exclusion by trade unionists— were present in Canada as well. What was different here were the implications of women's dependence on marriage (and men's wages). During industrialization in England, stable marriage was unlikely for working-class women, given the patterns of behaviour that the proletarian condition prompted in men— including avoidance of marriage, temporary separation, and permanent abandonment of women and children (Pinchbeck 1930).

The Canadian situation was better for women. Because of the continued availability of land in Canada, the degree of proletarianization was less extensive than in England. Because of a perpetual shortage of women, the 'marriage market' here was good for them. And since married women typically did not work outside the home, Canada did not have the kind of female labour pool that England had.

Nevertheless, women's economic role during Canada's industrial development was structurally similar to that in England. In nineteenth-century Montreal (which was surrounded by an agricultural region that was stagnant and thus proletarianizing), women aged 15 to 29 vastly outnumbered men (Cross 1977). As in England, industrialization in Montreal featured 'heavy reliance on child and female labour' (Bradbury 1979). According to Suzanne Cross (1977: 84), the 'existence of a pool of cheap female labour encouraged the growth of the garment, boot and shoe, textile and tobacco trades'. Women and children composed over 80 per cent of the labour force in Montreal's clothing industries, over 40 per cent of workers in the leather, boot, and shoe industries, and 60 per cent of the labour force in tobacco-processing and cigar-making—respectively, Montreal's first, second, and fourth largest industries—between 1861 and 1881 (Bradbury 1984b: 117).

As elsewhere, 'outwork'[14] was an important component of Canadian industrialization (Steedman 1986). Outworkers, who were overwhelmingly female, not only accepted wages far below factory levels, but also bore capital costs (e.g., by paying rent on their machinery) and absorbed much of the instability caused by market-place fluctuations in demand. The vast majority of work in Montreal's garment industry was done as outwork by women, often assisted by their daughters, in small sweatshops or at home (Cross 1977; Lavigne and Stoddart 1977; Bradbury 1979).

Mercedes Steedman (1986) has argued that the use of female outworkers in Canada's garment trade enabled its industrialization, not only because of the attendant low wage bill, but also because of the division of labour and erosion of skilled work that outwork allowed. Management initially destroyed tailors' jurisdiction over skilled labour by giving out simple garments to women sewing on machines outside the factories (Cohen 1985; Steedman 1986). That practice paved the way for the twentieth-century use of less skilled labour in factories (Steedman 1986: 155). In this century women in the needle trades have done the work that is labelled 'unskilled' and paid little (Gannage 1985). It is interesting that the failure of trade unions to organize, include, and support women workers undermined unions' attempts to curb homework and contracting-out, mechanization, and factory piecework, which eroded workers' control over the labour process (Steedman 1986).

Aside from research on the garment industry, evidence of women's role in Canadian industrialization is hard to find. The size of the gender gap in wages, the degree of gender segregation, the degree to which women's participation in waged work represented competitive pressure on men's jobs and wages, are questions about the nineteenth century that have yet to be fully explored.

Instead, Canadian researchers have focussed on the subsidization of industrial capitalism that women have provided by their housework, both stretching and supplementing men's wages. Industrialization was predicated on women's domestic labour: women compensated for men's low wages either by producing at home what would otherwise have had to be purchased or, in the absence of the means of home production, by somehow wresting a minimal subsistence from an inadequate wage (Fox 1980b). Bettina Bradbury's (1984b: 124) research shows that in the early years of industrial development '[w]omen's work in the home could and often did make the difference between adequate survival and hunger and discomfort'.

In Montreal, until the 1870s, working-class housewives regularly kept animals (e.g., pigs, cows, poultry), cultivated gardens, and sold eggs, butter, cheese, and vegetables for extra cash (Bradbury 1984a). When such activities became more difficult, housewives used the home itself to squeeze out extra cash, by sharing residential space with other families or by taking in boarders (Medjuck 1979; Bradbury 1984a). Given their greater resources, middle-class women were able to contribute more in these ways than working-class women (Fox 1980b; Bradbury 1984a; Darroch and Ornstein 1983). Working-class housewives' loss of these means of domestic production pushed them into outwork, into unskilled domestic drudgery for cash (e.g., 'charring' or housecleaning), and even into prostitution (Hollingsworth and Tyyska 1988) to accomplish the same ends.

## A different view of Canada's development

Recognition of women's central role in the productive activities characteristic of Canada's past raises the question of whether this understanding changes our approach to the issue of economic development and alters our understanding of the country's economy. Adding women to economic history does not answer the questions typically posed by political economists (for example, whether and in what way Canada's economy is distorted). It does, however, underscore the importance of matters often forgotten, and raises questions and issues of a different sort. In general, examining women's role in the development process entails a focus on the *internal* factors important to the development of what is now Canada—and thus promises to counter the emphasis of both Canadian 'dependency theorists' and 'internationalists' on external forces.

The discussion in the preceding section indicated, first, how the family is important in economic development. Second, it turned attention to production, and especially to the surplus production that is at the heart of development. Third, it indicated how non-capitalist economic arrangements (e.g., family farms) survive, and consequently turned the usual concern with development—which is predicated on the demise of such arrangements—on its head. And in the end it has recast the issue entirely, to question the social significance of economic development itself.

Understanding that families are essential to economic development does not require sophisticated theory. Moreover, the insight is not a novel one. Colonial governments and single-company towns in the British North American colonies recognized how important families were, not only to produce the next generation, but also to build the institutions that create community and to embody the responsibilities and loyalties that bind men to their jobs.

A seventeenth-century Newfoundlander noted that 'for the permanent growth of a colonial population every single man who is sent out in excess of the number of single women is absolutely useless' (quoted in Porter 1985a: 109). In New France the family was clearly recognized as the foundation of colonial development, and women therefore were deemed essential, especially as reproducers and mothers (Foulche-Delbosc 1977). There, because the state 'treated the family as a matter of vital public concern' (Noel 1985: 24-25), it used financial incentives to encourage high birth rates and imposed financial penalties on bachelors (Noel 1985). Similarly, in company towns management sought workers who were married and had families (Luxton 1980: 27). The vigorous recruitment of women to the pioneer west was no doubt prompted by an understanding of how essential family was to development.

There is, however, a more specific way in which families are critical to economic development. The 'primitive accumulation' of the surplus on which economic development is built involves either the importation of capital from outside the country or the internal production of a surplus product, or a combination of the two. Canadian political economists imply that capital importation was the basis of economic development. Such a foundation is problematic: it is when the surplus is locally produced that the conditions contributing to sustained and self-propelled development are present. But perhaps industrialization in nineteenth-century Canada was supported by local surplus accumulation as well as the importation of foreign capital. If so, family farming was probably the source of that surplus production.

Gordon Laxer (1985a) has argued that the late-industrializing countries that overcame domestic shortages of capital and generated strong manufacturing sectors were those with strong agrarian sectors. Indeed, it is generally the case that industrial development follows prosperous agriculture (Brenner 1977). That is, farming and the surplus it produces seem to be the primary propellants of industrial capitalism. First, local farms represent the home market essential for industrial production, buying consumer goods and farm machinery. Second, the net surplus farm product feeds urban populations and industrial work forces: the more productive the agricultural sector is, the lower capital's wage bill needs to be. Finally, the agricultural population represents a reserve labour pool, available for and periodically in need of wage work. While Vernon Fowke (1957) and Clare Pentland (1981 [1960]) recognized the importance of agriculture to development, the scant attention paid it by recent political economists discussing Canada's 'distorted development' is both interesting and telling.

Not only agriculture in itself but family farms in particular are important to self-propelled development. The union of a man and a woman in possession of their land constitutes a very effective production unit: as I argued above, the gender division of labour with the wife producing much of what is required for subsistence makes it possible for the man to concentrate on the production of a surplus product for the market. Arguably, this surplus is the source of the 'primitive accumulation' on which development is predicated—assuming that the state and industrial capital (e.g., farm-implements companies, CN, CPR) appropriate much of the surplus.

Nevertheless, arguing that economic development is predicated on family farming is speculative. Less speculative is the more modest claim that the family as a combined unit of production and consumption is especially durable. When kin relations govern production and consumption, and the two are combined in the same unit, the potential for self-exploitation and under-consumption for the sake of the farm enterprise makes for a very durable production unit. Harriet Friedmann (1978) has argued that because family farms recruit the bulk of their labour force internally, the household is the unit best able to establish and reproduce itself as a 'form of production'. In turn, according to Friedmann (1978), the family farm is well suited to surplus production: because production relations are kin relations, the consumption needs of the labour force can be directly subordinated to the needs of production (as we saw above).

It is important here to note that such surplus production involves the farmer/owner's appropriation of his wife's surplus labour: while the man's is invested in the farm enterprise, the woman's surplus farm labour is invested in her children, whose labour he employs. Her surplus labour is thus indirectly expropriated by the farmer. As well, in doing much of the work that ensures subsistence—from basic production to processing and preparation—women have systematically minimized the costs of the man's and the children's subsistence (e.g., the need to purchase food), and thus subsidized development of the farm, allowing more for reinvestment. To argue, then, that the expropriation of women's unpaid labour is at the heart of self-propelled economic development is not unreasonable.

If the argument about the importance of family farming is correct, it is significant that the Hudson Bay Company forbade the entry of European women to the new world after 1684 and prohibited even retired employees with native wives from establishing settlements independent of trading posts—only eventually meeting their desire to remain in the new world by establishing the Red River settlement (Brown 1980). In short, in Hudson Bay country the fur trade inhibited precisely what was necessary for self-propelling economic development. Compared with the colonies to the south, therefore, Canadian settlement had institutional as well as climatic and locational inhibitors.

Marjorie Cohen (1985) has developed a more specific argument about the centrality of the family farm, and thus of women's labour, to development. Examining the ability of the area that would become Ontario to develop economically, she argued that the key inhibitor of the development of an economy based on staples is the instability of the labour force. An economy so vulnerable to market fluctuations tends to lose its labour force—south of the border, in this case. To maintain a population available for industrial employment a subsistence base is necessary: free land for homesteading solved that problem. On the other hand, industrial development is predicated on a landless, proletarianized population. These contradictory requirements posed a major problem in Canadian economic history, a problem obscured by Canadian political economists' focus on trade and the structure of capital. Cohen asserted that responsibility for Ontario's industrial development ultimately rested on the development of agriculture, which ensured the population's subsistence and sustained a work force that periodically worked for wages (largely so as to purchase industrial products).

There are, then, reasons to believe that family farming was important to Canada's industrialization. Yet the viability of family farming, and the implications of that viability for simultaneously inhibiting the formation of an industrial proletariat and raising the price of wage labour, must not be minimized. The possibility, for most Canadians, of remaining involved in work such as family farming, and thus avoiding total dependence on wages, might be another reason—aside from small population and relatively late settlement—that in Canada industrialization was on a smaller scale and slower than in the US.

It may be significant as well that Canada did not have the kind of female labour pool apparently available in England and New England. As I argued above, a female proletariat provides a special subsidy to industrializing capital. While England was notorious in the nineteenth century for its surplus of single women, Canada had a shortage of women and hence made constant efforts to import them; there was a steady demand for wives for pioneer settlers throughout the 1800s. As well, the demand for domestic servants was high: because daughters' labour was in such high demand on family farms, young women were less likely to be sent into service in Canada than in England (Cohen 1985).

The necessity for women to work at home in family production units explains why the rates of female involvement in the labour force recorded by Canadian census-takers were lower than those in England and New England (Bradbury 1979; 1984b). This lower rate of women's involvement in industrial work is significant in itself, since it meant less female subsidy to Canadian industrialization; but it is also significant as an indicator of the degree of proletarian impoverishment of the population in general. The fact that proletarianization was lower in Canada because of a survival of 'independent commodity production' may be one reason why the Canadian labour force was relatively expensive (Panitch 1981) and industrialization more modest in Canada than in the US: land was still available here when Americans were being pushed off farms and into industrial work.

It is a short step from understanding women's importance in independent commodity production to focussing on the survival of this precapitalist mode of production—a survival that, given an aggressive capitalist world economy, cannot be taken for granted (Connelly and MacDonald 1983; Ghorayshi 1988; Porter 1987). In turn, explaining the persistence of economic activities that are less progressive technically than capitalism addresses the matter of Canada's uneven regional development, but does so by inverting the political economists' usual concern with the failure of certain regions to 'develop'.

In the case of the Maritimes and Newfoundland, fishermen have been able to resist complete proletarianization and maintain some of the elements of self-employment largely because of the major contribution to family subsistence made by their wives, who regularly adjust their work to ensure household survival (Connelly and MacDonald 1983). The processing that wives traditionally performed not only was a necessary complement to fishing, but also afforded the men some leverage in the market-place: the family's control over processing as well as catching fish apparently gave the men some choice about when to offer their product for sale (Antler 1977), although unequal exchange relations, then as now, undermined their position in the market-place. As well, then as now, housewives directly produced a variety of subsistence goods, with a minimal expenditure on equipment (Porter 1987). Many fishermen's wives now work in processing plants, earning wages that provide the bulk of household income. These earnings allow the fishermen to continue fishing while receiving prices for their catch that are below the costs of their subsistence (Porter 1987). In other words, in contributing significantly to family survival, women's work has a role in the economic subordination of Newfoundland and the Maritimes: it sustains the subordinated labour force (Porter 1987).

But there is another respect, too, in which consideration of gender is essential to understanding the history of the fishing industry and related development/underdevelopment. Paul Thompson's (1983) study of fishing communities in northern

England, Wales, and Scotland, exploring people's responses to their incorporation into a capitalist market-place in an area where the offshore fishery has died out and the inshore fishery revived, is important here. Thompson argued that the nature of gender relations, especially those between spouses, most crucially determines the collective response of a community to its situation. More precisely, the nature of gender relations indicates how forcefully people will fight the economic domination and destruction of a traditional economy. With evidence from several case studies, Thompson maintained that where gender relations are relatively egalitarian, men and women —together and singly—*fight* for autonomous survival, and also raise children who are likely to be independent, aggressive, even entrepreneurial, rather than pliant, conformist, and obedient. For these reasons, he argued, communities in which there is rough gender egalitarianism are likely to produce a vibrant family fishing industry—one that resists capitalization. In other words, Thompson suggested that the relationship between men and women is critical in determining the future because the nature of this relationship affects the kinds of adults who are produced, and thus (ultimately) the stance that a community will take to prevent domination.

Marilyn Porter (1985a) has argued that in Newfoundland fishing communities women's economic contribution brings them power in the household, which is the centre of the community. Probably as a consequence, women's public community involvement is greater than men's (Porter 1985b). And women's organizations, while seemingly concerned with community rather than 'political' affairs, have latent political power, according to Porter. Women's groups constitute strong grass-roots formations characterized by efficient internal organization; their impressive informal communications networks bridge local communities (unlike men's associations); and they remain uninvolved in the formal, powerless, and inappropriate political institutions that were imposed on these communities by outside forces (Porter 1985b).

Barbara Neis (1988) has described an instance where women's sense of responsibility for their families and community activated the power latent in their organizations and political culture. When the only major employer in the town of Burin, in outport Newfoundland, threatened to close in 1983, local women organized and staffed a 'protest line' that effectively shut down plant operations until the employer changed his mind. Lasting nearly six months, and 'manned' 24 hours a day, seven days a week, the protest line was no doubt responsible for the plant's remaining open in the town.

In summary, I have sketched here some of the elements of a view of economic development that focusses on the productive activities of which it consists. Starting from the Marxian idea that economic development occurs on the basis of surplus production, I have suggested that family farms are especially suited to the production of that surplus because they consist of the union of production and consumption, as well as that of a woman and a man. As important as economic development, however, is the matter of the struggle to maintain a way of life based on family ownership of the means of production. Women's efforts are central to both processes: that of producing the surplus that generates development, and that of resisting the development of industrial capitalism. This does not mean that an examination of women's activities and gender relations can indicate whether economic development will occur: the position a region holds in the capitalist world economy and that area's social and economic structure largely determine the likelihood and nature of development. The reason studying women and the relations in which they are involved is important is that it emphasizes the *work* that is at the heart of human existence—whether in the context of development or of underdevelopment.

## *A reconsideration of 'development'*

Nineteenth-century social anthropologists and social theorists (e.g., Maine, McLennan, Morgan, reviewed in Coward 1983; Luxton n.d.) assumed that examination of the family could reveal the nature of the wider social relations and the dynamics of social development in a society. The study of the family, gender relations, and women's position was therefore at the centre of the work of many of the nineteenth-century precursors of modern sociology and especially anthropology. In marked contrast, the study of gender relations is marginalized and self-contained today. While the main theme of this chapter is that marginalization of gender produces poor social theory, I propose in this final section that focussing on social relations in general, and gender relations in particular, brings a better understanding of social organization than does the approach of political economists interested solely in the issues of dependency and distortion in the Canadian economy.

Political economy purports to be an analysis of society in general (Maroney and Luxton 1987). Moreover, Canadian dependency theorists' concern about a distorted economy is, of course, ultimately a concern about the *material basis* of people's lives—whether economic expansion or stagnation, stability or instability, will occur, and thus whether high or low, steady or unsteady employment can be expected; whether Canadians can anticipate a high standard of living in the future; etc. Unfortunately, in their preoccupation with the ways in which the Canadian economic profile differs from that of the US (or any other country) and, especially, with the structure of the capitalist class rather than with the structure of the economy, they overlook the object of the exercise: understanding the organization of Canadian society. More recent work that emphasizes the capitalist character of the Canadian economy (Laxer 1985a; 1985b; Carroll 1986) is a major improvement over the early studies by the nationalists, in that the newer perspective has greater potential for defining the important forces that shape people's lives. Yet this work seldom draws out the implications for daily life of its typically abstract analyses.

Following the nineteenth-century social theorists cited above, I propose that a focus on gender relations in a society provides a perspective on its social organization that will be extremely revealing. Canada's native foraging societies may serve as an example. In at least some of these societies the constellation of factors that promoted egalitarian relations between women and men was so fundamental that an analysis that begins with gender should reveal the basic contours of their social organization. Specifically, the daily co-operation essential to survival in foraging societies was a feature of social structure that informed household and community organization as well as gender relations (Leacock 1981; Anderson 1985; 1987). The importance of community, and a sense of collective identity, precluded privatization of family households. As well, the necessity of every individual's contribution to community and family survival ensured that individuals had an autonomy rare in other societies (Leacock 1981).

Foraging societies are the simplest of human societies; moreover, gender and kin relations govern all activities in them. Thus a focus on gender relations in the attempt to understand these societies is obviously fruitful. For understanding Canada, the value of this approach may be less clear. But it is important to recognize that 'the economy' in advanced capitalist societies involves the privatized production that occurs in the household as well as the socialized production of commodities: the work of procuring subsistence is divided significantly by gender. More generally, social structure is divided by gender in a variety of fundamental ways. When this recognition is combined with some appreciation that gender is a primary component of individuals' subjectivity, it is hard to refute the argument that the study of societies as complex as our own will benefit from an approach that takes gender into account from the outset.

Furthermore, the gender egalitarianism at the heart of many of these early Canadian societies raises the issue of the social effects of 'development'. For Canadian history mirrors all of human history in featuring a general (though uneven) decline in women's economic position until recently.

In Canada the long process of development began with native societies in which women had no less autonomy or power than men. Leacock (1981) attributed this egalitarianism to the absence of class relations: because all individuals had access to the means of production, no individuals or groups had the structural means to impose their will on others. Anderson (1985; 1987) elaborated Leacock's analysis by contending that it was also crucial that kinship (and not class) organized access to the means of production and products of labour, establishing mutual rights and obligations among all kin. Women's strong position in these societies eroded when the means of production were no longer collectively controlled by kin groups (for instance, because the men became trappers working for the French [Leacock 1981]), or because whole camps moved into French settlements where Europeans gave the men control over the means of production and conditions of existence [Anderson 1985]).

European culture, transplanted to the new world, entailed male dominance. Nevertheless, in colonial New France, partly because the family was the important social, economic, and political unit, women's social position, though not their legal one, was nearly equal to men's (Foulche-Delbosc 1977; Noel 1985). Farming in pioneer conditions also warranted only minimal male dominance, at least on many farms (Sundberg 1986). In the case of fishing families Porter (1985a) has noted a rough egalitarianism in which the woman was 'skipper of the shore crew': women's contribution to the family business merited power in the household, which in fact was the centre of community life.    The transfer of processing to factories, and women's new position as wage labourers, may have eroded women's power in fishing communities. In agriculture, according to Cohen (1984; 1985), the industrialization of the dairy involved a kind of proletarianization of women, in that marriage no longer gave them access to the means of production. For reasons largely involving the gender division of responsibilities (e.g., women's time and monetary commitment to domestic responsibilities), when dairying—which was traditionally women's sphere—industrialized, men took over its operation.

In general, then, primarily because the long process of economic development has displaced the family as the unit of production, women's work has undergone varying degrees of marginalization. Especially with the destruction of communal foraging societies, women's economic position declined. Even though industrialization afforded single women individual earnings and thus some autonomy from patriarchal families, it led to the eventual marginalization of household work and women's incorporation into wage work only as cheap labour. At the same time, of course, the social, political, and even economic changes that attended economic development opened possibilities for improvements in women's social position (e.g., greater autonomy from family and kin relations).

Recognizing that women generally experienced a worsening economic position in the historical process of 'development' leads to several conclusions. First, certainly, any account of development must include this negative note. Second, Canadian political economists' preoccupation with Canada's failure to replicate some presumably normal pattern of development should be challenged, because it implies unquestioned positive assumptions about economic development itself. In short, upholding capitalist development as the standard for emulation is questionable. In its concern with Canadian capital and its behaviour, the internationalist critique of dependency theory is especially guilty of minimizing the unevenness in Canadian development and also the retrograde effects of development itself in the context of a capitalist world economy. For capitalist 'development' is based on the subordination of labour, in that it entails proletarianization; it also entails the particular marginalization of women's work.

More broadly, a definition of development on capital's terms acknowledges neither the social relations of production nor important related political, social, and ideological matters. As Fernandez Kelly (1981) has argued, 'development'—reasonably defined—should involve an increase in equitable access to the resources that make possible life with dignity, and greater participation in the decision-making processes that shape people's lives. If that is what we mean by 'development', we must conclude that Canada's development has been worse than dependent and distorted.

# 6

# Conclusion

In Chapter 1 I noted that European sociology owes its first debt to conservative thinkers. In the wake of the French Revolution, the conservatives opposed individual liberty and equality of opportunity; they sought to justify the maintenance of order by stressing the importance of hierarchy and authority in social life. For the conservatives, society was a real organic entity, not just an agglomeration of individuals, as the liberals thought. In the conservative view, society constrains human aspirations and actions, thereby preventing disorganization and anarchy. From this ideological animus derived the unique orientation of European sociology—the study of how external, coercive forces shape human will (Durkheim), of how people make history, but not just as they please (Marx).

As my reference to Marx indicates, this orientation was compatible not just with conservative, but also with socialist thought. However, it had little in common with—indeed, was utterly opposed to—the celebration of the free individual that characterized the work of Rousseau and other liberals. Hence the difficulty of sociology when transplanted to liberal North America in the late nineteenth century: context and pedigree fought against each other for the minds of North American sociologists (cf. Bramson 1961).

In the 1950s and the first half of the 1960s, context seemed wholly victorious. As Harrison White, Chair of the Department of Social Relations at Harvard University, said in a 1968 lecture:

> Most sociology and social science, especially in the US, takes the view [of] voluntaristic individualism: basic reality is in individuals' values and choices, social structure, being derived therefrom, being merely epiphenomenal. . . .
>
> The fruit of much sociological theory is this deception: social structure must be the sum of individual values so you can define it a priori out of your head. Or in recent versions, you can find it

by pooling responses of populations to questionnaires. . . . (quoted in Wellman 1983: 163-4).

In the United States there was a close affinity between liberal ideology in politics and voluntaristic individualism in sociology. For example, the principle of free choice was embodied in Parsons' 'action frame of reference'; his 'pattern-variables' expressed the notion of social structure as the aggregate of individual values.

Why did voluntaristic individualism become as influential in English-Canadian social thought in the 1950s and 1960s as it did in the US? Leaving aside the question of just how pervasive liberalism was in Canada versus the United States thirty years ago, there is no denying that it was the dominant ideology in both countries. Voluntaristic individualism thus fitted the ideological terrain in Canada about as well as it did south of the border. Moreover, the ease with which prominent sociologists could move between the two countries facilitated a high level of intellectual cross-pollination. Also influential—perhaps decisive —was the political and economic context. Canadian sociologists lived next door to the wealthiest and most powerful country in the world. The United States seemed to be the natural standard against which all things should be judged. It was certainly deemed to be worth emulating.

Since the 1960s a growing number of sociologists in English Canada have been moving away from the notion that social stucture is the sum of individual values and towards the view that social structure is an external and coercive force.[1] This shift has greatly advanced our understanding of the workings of Canadian society. It is now evident, however, that the rejection of liberal assumptions was initially accompanied by some oversimplifications about the nature of Canadian society. Here are some examples that recapitulate the main themes of the preceding chapters:

1. Circa 1965 it was widely believed that economic development results from the presence of such *internal* factors as abundant raw materials, proximity to markets, and especially entrepreneurial talent. It follows that differences in level of development between regions (e.g., Atlantic Canada and Ontario) and between countries (e.g., Canada and the US) are related to variations in the availability of these factors. Partly

because researchers failed to find the hypothesized internal differences between regions, an alternative interpretation emerged in the 1970s. An *external* force—*bilateral* power inequality between states or between regions within states—came to be viewed as the fundamental cause of development and underdevelopment. Today power inequalities are still widely regarded as the foundation of patterns of development and underdevelopment. But at the cutting edge of the discipline, the power inequalities typically studied are *multilateral* and both internal *and* external. That is, the focus of attention now rests squarely on relations between and within classes, between and within regions and states—and between and within the sexes. It is the feminists, of course, who have underscored this last point. By convincingly showing how economic life is crucially underpinned by household production, they have secured a place for gender on the list of social relations that must be examined in any full discussion of Canadian development and underdevelopment.

2. In the mid-1960s a 'bottom-up' view of politics was common. That is, a wide variety of political phenomena—electoral behaviour, party formation, social-movement etiology, state policy formulation—were seen to derive from the wishes and values of the electorate. True, Canadian and US political cultures supposedly differed in details. It was presumed that a blend of liberalism and toryism in Canada, and a pure liberal tradition in the US, accounted for some political differences between the two countries. But both countries were democracies, and in both the electorate was held to be sovereign.

A decade later the opposite view—a 'top-down' theory of politics—had gained considerably in popularity, in part because mass values turned out to be poor predictors of political behaviour. The Marxists of the mid-1970s did not deny that the electorate is legally sovereign. But they felt that this matters little in practical terms, since ownership of property, not citizenship, determines political influence: the capitalist class rules, and in the long run the citizenry as a whole has little say in political affairs.

The popularity of both these extremes has waned in the 1980s. Increasingly, sociologists appreciate the consequences of the fact that Canada is both a democracy *and* a capitalist system, that political phenomena therefore derive from the interaction of 'top-down' *and* 'bottom-up' processes. This view represents a considerable advance over earlier formulations, and it draws attention to the political outcomes not just of superordinate or subordinate class power, but of the shifting *balance* of power between superordinate and subordinate classes.

3. Finally, important changes have taken place in the way sociologists study inequality. Two decades ago the agenda of stratification research derived from a classic liberal assumption: in societies where there is true equality of opportunity, the individual's position in the socio-economic hierarchy is determined less by ascribed characteristics (notably gender, race, and ethnicity) than by his or her abilities and achievements. It follows that societies with presumably greater equality of opportunity (such as the US) are more egalitarian and exhibit greater net upward mobility than societies with presumably less equality of opportunity (such as Canada).

Empirical research soon demonstrated the implausibility of the US-Canada contrast. But for a time the view prevailed that Canada's stratification system, like that of the US, is based much more on achievement than ascription. The negligible effect of ethnicity on income and mobility helped to support that view. So did the substantively quite small effect of gender on mobility for men and women in the full-time paid labour force. But the largely achievement-based view of Canada's stratification system could be sustained only as long as mobility research was restricted to men and women in the full-time paid labour force, as long as class and occupational prestige were confused, and as long as *individual* characteristics were assumed to be the all-important determinants of one's place in the socio-economic hierarchy.[2] Once *structural* barriers to equality of opportunity were taken into account, a somewhat different picture began to emerge. Increasingly, sociologists began to appreciate how patriarchal forces prevent most women from entering the full-time paid labour force, and how class (in the neo-Marxist sense) places certain barriers on individual mobility and income. Feminists in particular have played a major role in drawing our attention to the structure of social inequality. They have accomplished this by showing how unpaid and under-recognized productive activities that occur in the family and personal life sustain the more public activities that constitute the subject matter of traditional sociology.

Each of these changes in sociological outlook may fairly be regarded as an advance. This is not, however, to suggest that all is rosy. As was briefly noted in Chapter 1, the recent development of sociology in English Canada has been sullied by both parochialism and subjectivism. In this book I have played down the degree to which some contemporary English-Canadian sociologists—including many Marxists and feminists—shun the rigorous theory-testing that serves as the best guard against subjectivism. Nor have I made much of the tendency among some scholars to think of Canadian society as a unique historical case. It nonetheless seems to me that there has been an overreaction in some circles to the valuable empirical and universalizing tendencies of American sociology. Now that English-Canadian macrosociologists have gained an appreciation of the European problematics of the discipline, one hopes that in coming decades more of its practitioners will appropriate the best elements from American sociology as well.

# Notes

## 1: The European and North American Backgrounds

1. Of course, capitalism developed quite differently, partly because capitalist states stepped in to limit the length of the working day and improve working conditions. As a result, employers began focussing their profit-maximizing strategies on increasing productivity through technological and other innovations.

2. Many modern sociologists, particularly in the US, have trivialized Weber and rendered him much more anti-Marxist than he in fact was by exaggerating the independence of the various bases of inequality, unnecessarily multiplying the number of bases, regarding inequality as a continuous ranking of statistical categories, and highlighting the subjective evaluation of prestige as the major basis of inequality (Parkin 1972 [1971]: 13-47).

3. In fact, as will be seen in Chapter 5, some researchers have argued not only that gender is an important determinant of inequality, but that gender inequality is inextricably linked to property relations.

4. These tendencies have been weaker in some periods than in others. For example, my characterization of American sociology does not hold for the first half of this century, when the Chicago school dominated the discipline in the US.

## 2: Economic Development and Underdevelopment

1. GNP and standard-of-living measures do not take into account such factors as safety from crime and accessibility of health-care facilities. I have little doubt that if a more general quality of life measure were employed, Canada would rank higher than the US. Significantly, however, a quality of life measure would imply a notion of development quite different from that assumed by GNP and standard-of-living measures.

2. The first correlation is -0.35 ($F = 1.41$). The second correlation is -0.37 ($F = 1.6$). These correlations were not significant at the .05 level.

3. Staples theory explains regional patterns of development and underdevelopment little better than the entrepreneurial thesis. See Brym (1986c) and Copithorne (1979).

4. Jorge Niosi (1978: 14-67; 1981 [1980]: 5-10; 1983: 135) argues that this last point cannot be taken to mean that the banks actually control industry. For the contrary view, see Carroll (1986).

## 3: Politics

[1] Horowitz's interest in tracing the tory (and therefore British) roots of Canadian democratic socialism led him to underestimate the disproportionately important role played by workers of French, Scandinavian, Jewish, Italian, and Ukrainian origin in the history of the Canadian left. See, for example, Avery (1979); Milner (1978); Zakuta (1964: 31).

[2] How drastically the political landscape has changed since the 1960s! Today, in both economic and social terms, the Social Credit government in British Columbia is undoubtedly the most right-wing government in the country.

[3] It does not necessarily follow that provincialism stifles class politics (Bell and Tepperman 1979; Stevenson 1982 [1978]). Indeed, a stronger appeal to autonomist sentiment on the part of the NDP in Quebec appears to have increased support for the party in that province since 1984.

[4] The distribution of power between employers and employees has also influenced short-term fluctuations in the level of strike activity since 1945. This is clearly evident in the close association between the phase of the business cycle and the level of strike activity. During boom periods, increased job opportunities, wage levels, strike funds and union membership have given workers a greater strike capability, while during troughs in the business cycle workers have experienced a decline in these determinants of power. See, for example, Hibbs (1976), Korpi and Shalev (1980), Smith (1981).

[5] But see Shalev (1978) for some important qualifications regarding the intervening role played by the institutional framework of industrial-relations systems.

[6] But see Lipset and Rokkan (1967), which is the closest Lipset has come to the orientation outlined here.

[7] The following discussion has profited from van den Berg and Smith (1980).

[8] The following discussion draws on Alford and Friedland (1985), Esping-Andersen, Friedland and Wright (1976), Evans, Rueschemeyer, and Skocpol (1985), and Skocpol (1980).

[9] Maquiladora industries represent the second largest and fastest growing economic sector in Mexico. The 1,200 US factories in the zone employ 300,000 mainly teenage workers at about 65 cents an hour. About 40 per cent of manufactured goods imported by the US now come from Mexico. As a Texas senator recently stated: 'The progress of the Maquiladora plants keeps the United States competitive with the Far East' (quoted in Saul 1987).

# 4: Social Stratification

1. As Rich (1976: 19) notes, Porter used 'middle class' to refer to occupations generally regarded as upper middle class. I adopt the latter usage here.

2. Interestingly, however, Canadians' attitudes towards immigrants already in the country are substantially more positive than their attitudes towards additional immigration (Dasko 1988).

3. The reduction of measured inequality through the introduction of these controls should not be interpreted as evidence of meritocracy, since educational and occupational distributions may themselves be explained in part as the outcome of historical discrimination.

4. See, however, Lautard (1983), Lautard and Loree (1984), and Li (1978), whose work I have criticized in Brym (1986a: 110-11).

5. Analyses of 1861 and 1871 census data cast doubt on the *historical* validity of the vertical-mosaic concept too. See Darroch and Ornstein (1980; 1985).

6. Actually, he referred to 'assimilation' rather than 'cohesion'. But because assimilation is such an imprecise and value-laden term, I will follow Reitz (1980) and use cohesion instead. Reitz defined ethnic-group cohesion as the frequency of a person's interaction with other members of his or her ethnic group, and the degree to which a person identifies with other members of his or her ethnic group.

7. For eight ethnic groups—British, French, German, Italian, Dutch, Scandinavian, Polish, and Ukrainian—amounting to 91 per cent of the Canadian population in 1961 and 1971, data are available on (a) the percentage of male family heads with wives of the same ethnic origin and (b) the net difference in average male occupational status between ethnic groups. For each ethnic group the value of (a) may be divided by the proportion of group members in the total population to yield (c) an index that expresses the propensity to in-marry over and above what one would expect on the basis of chance, given the relative size of the ethnic group. In 1961 the zero-order correlation between (c) and (b) was -.68; in 1971 the correlation was -.64 (calculated from data in Kalbach and McVey 1979 [1971]: 195, 198-9, 321; Lautard and Loree 1984: 340).

8. The correlations are .44 for 1961 and .63 for 1971.

9. As members of the dominant ethnic group, people of British origin may not *perceive* their expressions of middle-class ethnicity as such; they may define themselves as 'non-ethnic dispensers of a universalistic ideology' (Vallee 1981: 639), although the reality, in terms of in-group interaction, is very different.

10. Reitz (1980: 173-4) found little indication that present inequality of opportunity encourages middle-class ethnicity. Nor does his analysis

support the view that the revival of middle-class ethnicity is an expression of the search for community roots in a technological and
bureaucratic society (Isajiw 1978). He thus found that ethnic-group
cohesion declined steadily and markedly over time: fully 50 per cent
of the variance in ethnic-group cohesion was explained by length of
residence in Canada (cf. Richmond 1974; Goldlust and Richmond
1974). An additional 17 per cent of the variance was explained by the
independent effects of SES (which varied inversely with cohesion)
and job segregation (which varied proportionately).

## 5: The Feminist Challenge

1 As do many feminist scholars, I distinguish between 'sex', which
refers to biology, and 'gender', which refers to social constructions or
products.

2 I am making a fairly standard distinction among perspectives within
feminism today. 'Liberal feminism' refers to an approach to gender
equality predicated on the assumption of women's and men's equality, based on the rational nature they have in common. Because differential treatment is held to be responsible for perceived differences
between women and men, the primary aim of liberal feminism is
'equal opportunity'. 'Radical feminism' refers to fairly diverse
feminist approaches that have in common both the assumptions that
women and men have essentially different natures and that men
universally oppress women, and the aim of creating a positive
cultural assessment of feminine characteristics, if not a wholly
separate women's culture. 'Marxist feminists' assume that the
organization of production is the ultimate determinant of social
organization (so gender relations take different forms in different
economic orders), that class divisions are the chief exploitative
divisions in society, and that Marx's concepts and methods can be
used to analyze women's oppression. 'Socialist feminism' involves a
synthesis of radical and Marxist feminisms, which recognizes the
significance of class, but also confirms the need to understand gender relations in their own terms—and thus to examine sexuality and
subjectivity (or how we see ourselves) as well as work.

3 The issue on which the debate floundered—whether or not domestic
labour was 'productive' in the Marxist sense of producing surplus
value—was essentially about this matter.

4 Chris Middleton (1983) has argued brilliantly that women's labour of
various kinds was basic to the 'primitive accumulation' on which
capitalism in Britain was based—see below for a similar discussion of
Canadian development.

5 In addition to these direct critiques, a host of feminist researchers in the Maritimes and Newfoundland have been attempting for nearly a decade to provide a political-economic analysis of the fishing industry that incorporates women (Connelly and MacDonald 1983; Neis 1988; Porter 1983; 1985a; 1985b; 1987).

6 Stevens and Boyd (1980) attempted to address this issue by considering housework as an occupational outcome. Not surprisingly, they found that with this amendment of status- attainment models a woman's occupational attainment is fairly easily predicted from her mother's. There are problems, however, with this model of social mobility. First, as I have already argued, the relatively high prestige attached to housework hides the significant material liabilities inherent in this 'occupation' (e.g., the economic dependence it entails because it is unpaid). Housework-as-attained-status poorly represents women's situation. Second, Eichler (1976) has shown that full-time housewives' status varies with the prestige of the husband's occupational status. So women derive status not only from the work they do but also from their husbands'.

7 It should be noted that there is a methodological problem with all the studies of the labour market reviewed here. Because none involves causal modelling of the variables, none provides an accurate assessment of the effects of the variables: indirect effects are not taken into account. Thus the effect of education on income, for example, is underestimated because its indirect effect, through occupational status, is ignored.

8 Gannage's (1986) case study of a small garment factory provided evidence of recent actions by a male-dominated union to keep women out of skilled jobs, even if that required the immigration of male workers from Europe.

9 I thank Kathy Kopinak for this insight.

10 The major exception to this tendency in Canadian political economy is the body of work carried out on the fisheries in Newfoundland and the Maritimes, and on the general underdevelopment of the Atlantic region (e.g., Brym and Sacouman 1979).

11 'Semi-independence' indicates that fishermen own their boats and gear but are so vulnerable in the market-place that the prices they get for their fish are like low wages.

12 Ghorayshi defines these as farms with fewer than five person- years of hired labour.

13 Ghorayshi (1988: 4) reports that '[f]amily enterprises relying solely on family labour accounted for 63.8% of total farms'.

14 'Outwork' refers to work done for factory owners, but performed outside the factory—in homes or in the small shops of contractors (sometimes called 'sweatshops').

## 6: Conclusion

[1] My impression is that a proportionately smaller number of sociologists in the US have been affected by this trend.

[2] In the US, the persistence of the achievement-based view was also aided by the initial avoidance of racial comparisons.

# References

AJS   *American Journal of Sociology*
ASR   *American Sociological Review*
CHAHP   *Canadian Historical Association Historical Papers*
CJPS   *Canadian Journal of Political Science*
CJS   *Canadian Journal of Sociology*
CRSA   *Canadian Review of Sociology and Anthropology*
GM   *Globe and Mail*
SPE   *Studies in Political Economy*

Abella, Irving, and Harold Troper
   1979   '"The line must be drawn somewhere": Canada and Jewish refugees, 1933-9'. *Canadian Historical Review* (60) 178-209.

Abrams, Philip
   1968   *The Origins of British Sociology: 1834-1914*. Chicago: University of Chicago Press.

Acheson, T. W.
   1972   'The National Policy and the industrialization of the Maritimes, 1880-1910'. *Acadiensis* (1) 3-28.

Acheson, T. W.
   1977   'The Maritimes and "Empire Canada"'. Pp. 87-114 in Bercuson 1977.

Acker, Joan
   1973   'Women and social stratification: a case of intellectual sexism'. *AJS* (78) 936-45.

Alford, Robert
   1963   *Party and Society*. Chicago: Rand McNally.

Alford, Robert
   1967   'Class voting in the Anglo-American political systems'. Pp. 67-93 in Lipset and Rokkan 1967.

Alford, Robert R., and Roger Friedland
   1985   *Powers of Theory: Capitalism, the State, and Democracy.* Cambridge: Cambridge University Press.

Allen, Richard
   1973   *The Social Passion: Religion and Social Reform in Canada, 1914-28.* Toronto: University of Toronto Press.

Ames, Herbert Brown
   1972   *The City Below the Hill*. Toronto: University of Toronto Press.
   [1897]

Anderson, Karen
   1985   'Commodity exchange and subordination: Montagnais-

Naskapi and Huron Women'. *Signs* (11) 48-62.

Anderson, Karen
  1987   'A gendered world: women, men and the political economy of the seventeenth century Huron'. Pp. 121-39 in H. J. Maroney and M. Luxton, eds. *Feminism and Political Economy.* Toronto: Methuen.

Anderson, Perry
  1968   'Components of the national culture'. *New Left Review* (50) 3-57.

Antler, Ellen
  1977   'Women's work in Newfoundland fishing families'. *Atlantis* (2) 106-14.

Apostle, Richard, Donald Clairmont, and Lars Osberg
  1985   'Segmentation and wage determination'. *CRSA* (22) 30-56.

Archibald, W. Peter
  1978   *Social Psychology as Political Economy.* Toronto: McGraw-Hill Ryerson.

Armstrong, Pat, and Hugh Armstrong
  1983a   *A Working Majority: What Women Must Do For Pay.* Ottawa: Canadian Advisory Council on the Status of Women.

Armstrong, Pat, and Hugh Armstrong
  1983b   'Beyond sexless class and classless sex: towards feminist marxism'. *SPE* (10) 7-43.

Armstrong, Pat, and Roberta Hamilton, eds.
  1988   'Feminist Scholarship'. Special issue of the *CRSA* (25,2).

Arnold, Stephen J., and Douglas J. Tigert
  1974   'Canadians and Americans: a comparative analysis'. *International Journal of Comparative Sociology* (15) 68-83.

Avery, Donald
  1979   *'Dangerous Foreigners': European Workers and Labour Radicalism in Canada, 1896-1932.* Toronto: McClelland and Stewart.

Baer, Douglas E., and James E. Curtis
  1984   'French Canadian-English Canadian differences in values: national survey findings'. *CJS* (9) 405-27.

Balakrishnan, T. R.
  1976   'Ethnic residential segregation in the metropolitan areas of Canada'. *CJS* (1) 481-98.

Balakrishnan, T. R.
  1982   'Changing patterns in ethnic residential segregation in the metropolitan areas of Canada'. *CRSA* (19) 92-110.

Banfield, Edward C.
  1958   *The Moral Basis of a Backward Society.* New York: Collier-Macmillan.

Banting, Keith G.
   1987   'The welfare state and inequality in the 1980s', *CRSA* (24) 309-38.

Barrett, Michele
   1980   *Women's Oppression Today: Problems in Marxist Feminist Analysis*. London: Verso.

Beattie, Christopher
   1975   *Minority Men in a Majority Setting: Middle Level Francophones in the Canadian Public Service*. Toronto: McClelland and Stewart.

Beattie, Christopher, and Byron G. Spencer
   1971   'Career attainment in Canadian bureaucracies: unscrambling the effects of age, seniority, education, and ethnolinguistic factors on salary'. *AJS* (77) 472-90.

Bell, David, and Lorne Tepperman
   1979   *The Roots of Disunity: A Look at Canadian Political Culture*. Toronto: McClelland and Stewart.

Bennett, John
   1982   *Of Time and the Enterprise: North American Family Farm Management in a Context of Resource Marginality*. Minneapolis: University of Minnesota.

Bennett, Judith
   1987   *Women in the Medieval English Countryside*. New York: Oxford University Press.

Benston, Margaret
   1969   'The political economy of women's liberation'. *Monthly Review* (21) 13-27.

Bercuson, David Jay, ed.
   1977   *Canada and the Burden of Unity*. Toronto: Macmillan of Canada.

Berger, Carl
   1976   *The Writing of Canadian History: Aspects of English-Canadian Historical Writing: 1900 to 1970*. Toronto: Oxford University Press.

Berkowitz, S. D.
   1980   'Structural and non-structural models of elites: a critique'. *CJS* (5) 13-30.

Berkowitz, S. D., ed.
   1984   *Models and Myths in Canadian Sociology*. Toronto: Butterworths Canada.

Berry, John W., Rudolf Kalin, and Donald M. Taylor
   1977   *Multiculturalism and Ethnic Attitudes in Canada*. Ottawa: Minister of Supply and Services Canada.

Bierstedt, Robert
   1974   'An analysis of social power'. Pp. 220-41 in *Power and Progress: Essays on Sociological Theory*. New York: McGraw-Hill.

Black, Don, and John Myles
  1986    'Dependent industrialization and the Canadian class struc-
          ture: a comparative analysis'. *CRSA* (23) 157-81.
Blau, Peter, and Otis Dudley Duncan
  1967    *The American Occupational Structure*. New York: John Wiley.
Blishen, Bernard R.
  1970    'Social class and opportunity in Canada'. *CRSA* (7) 110-27.
Blishen, Bernard, and William Carroll
  1978    'Sex differences in a socioeconomic index for occupations in
          Canada'. *CRSA* (15) 352-71.
Blishen, Bernard, William Carroll, and Catherine Moore
  1987    'The 1981 socioeconomic index for occupations in Canada'.
          *CRSA* (24) 465-89.
Blishen, Bernard R., *et al.*, eds.
  1968    *Canadian Society: Sociological Perspectives*, 3rd edn. Toronto:
  [1961]  Macmillan of Canada.
Bonacich, Edna
  1972    'A theory of ethnic antagonism: the split labor market'. *ASR*
          (37) 547-59.
Bonacich, Edna
  1973    'A theory of middleman minorities'. *ASR* (38) 583-94.
'Border exchanges'
  1987    *GM* (21 March) D6.
Bottomore, T. B.
  1967    *Critics of Society: Radical Thought in North America*. London:
          George Allen & Unwin.
Bottomore, T. B.
  1975    *Sociology as Social Criticism*. London: George Allen & Unwin.
Boulet, Jac-André, and Calvin Veltman
  1981    'Socio-economic achievements of Montreal language groups
          in 1971'. *CRSA* (18) 239-48.
Boyd, Monica
  1985    'Educational and occupational attainment of native-born
          Canadian men and women'. Pp. 229-95 in Boyd *et al*. 1985.
Boyd, Monica
  1986    'Socioeconomic indices and sexual equality: a tale of scales'.
          *CRSA* (23) 457-80.
Boyd, Monica, David L. Featherman, and Judah Matras
  1980    'Status attainment of immigrant and immigrant origin catego-
          ries in the United States, Canada, and Israel'. *Comparative So-
          cial Research* (3) 199-228.
Boyd, Monica, *et al.*
  1981    'Status attainment in Canada: findings of the Canadian
          mobility study'. *CRSA* (18) 657-73.

Boyd, Monica, and Hugh McRoberts
    1982    'Women, men and socioeconomic indices: an assessment'.
            Pp. 129-59 in M. Powers, ed. *Measures of Socioeconomic Status:
            Current Issues*. Colorado: Westview Press.

Boyd, Monica, *et al.*
    1985    *Ascription and Achievement: Studies in Mobility and Status
            Attainment in Canada*. Ottawa: Carleton University Press.

Bradbury, Bettina
    1979    'The family economy and work in an industrializing city:
            Montreal in the 1870s'. *CHAHP, 1978* (Ottawa) 71-96.

Bradbury, Bettina
    1984a   'Pigs, cows and boarders: non-wage forms of survival among
            Montreal families, 1861-91'. *Labour/Le Travail* (14) 9-46.

Bradbury, Bettina
    1984b   'Women and wage labour in a period of transition: Montreal,
            1861-1881'. *Histoire Sociale/Social History* (17) 115-31.

Bramson, Leon
    1961    *The Political Context of Sociology*. Princeton: Princeton Univer-
            sity Press.

Brenner, Robert
    1977    'The origins of capitalist development: a critique of neo-
            Smithian Marxism'. *New Left Review* (104) 25-94.

Breton, Albert, and Raymond Breton
    1980    *Why Disunity? An Analysis of Linguistic and Regional Cleavages
            in Canada*. Montreal: Institute for Research on Public Policy.

Breton, Raymond
    1964    'Institutional completeness of ethnic communities and the
            personal relations of immigrants'. *AJS* (70) 193-205.

Breton, Raymond
    1972    *Social and Academic Factors in the Career Decisions of Canadian
            Youth*. Ottawa: Queen's Printer.

Breton, Raymond
    1978    'Stratification and conflict between ethnolinguistic communi-
            ties with different social structures'. *CRSA* (15) 148-57.

Breton, Raymond
    1979    'Ethnic stratification viewed from three theoretical perspec-
    [1973]  tives'. Pp. 270-94 in Curtis and Scott 1979 [1973].

Breton, Raymond
    1984    'The production and allocation of symbolic resources: an
            analysis of the linguistic and ethno-cultural fields in Canada'.
            *CRSA* (21) 123-44.

Breton, Raymond, Jeffrey G. Reitz, and Victor Valentine, eds.
    1980    *Cultural Boundaries and the Cohesion of Canada*. Montreal: In-
            stitute for Research on Public Policy.

Breton, Raymond, and Howard Roseborough
    1968    'Ethnic differences in status'. Pp. 683-701 in Blishen *et al.* 1968
    [1961]  (1961).

Breton, Raymond, and Daiva Stasiulis
    1980    'Linguistic boundaries and the cohesion of Canada'. Pp. 137-328 in Breton, Reitz, and Valentine 1980.

Britton, John N.H., and James M. Gilmour
    1978    *The Weakest Link: A Technological Perspective on Canadian Industrial Development.* Ottawa: Science Council of Canada.

Brown, Jennifer
    1980    *Strangers in Blood: Fur Trade Families in Indian Country.* Vancouver: University of British Columbia Press.

Brym, Robert J.
    1979    'Political conservatism in Atlantic Canada'. Pp. 59-70 in Brym and Sacouman 1979.

Brym, Robert J.
    1980    'Regional social structure and agrarian radicalism in Canada: Alberta, Saskatchewan and New Brunswick'. Pp. 344-53 in A. Himelfarb and C. Richardson, eds. *People, Power and Process: A Reader.* Toronto: McGraw-Hill Ryerson.

Brym, Robert J.
    1984    'Social movements and third parties'. Pp. 29-49 in Berkowitz 1984.

Brym, Robert J.
    1985a  'The Canadian capitalist class, 1965-1985'. Pp. 1-20 in Brym 1985b.

Brym, Robert J., ed.
    1985b  *The Structure of the Canadian Capitalist Class.* Toronto: Garamond Press.

Brym, Robert J.
    1986a  'Anglo-Canadian sociology', *Current Sociology* (34, 1) 1-152.

Brym, Robert J.
    1986b  'Incorporation versus power models of working class radicalism: with special reference to North America'. *CJS* (11) 227-51.

Brym, Robert J.
    1986c  'An introduction to the regional question in Canada'. Pp. 1-45 in Brym 1986d.

Brym, Robert J., ed.
    1986d  *Regionalism in Canada.* Toronto: Irwin.

Brym, Robert J.
    1988    'Foundations of sociological theory'. Pp. 4-12 in L. Tepperman and J. Curtis, eds. *Readings in Sociology: An Introduction.* Toronto: McGraw-Hill.

Brym, Robert J.
1989    'Canada'. Pp. 177-206 in T. Bottomore and R. Brym, eds. *The Capitalist Class: An International Study*. New York: New York University Press pp. 177-206.

Brym, Robert J., and Barbara Neis
1978    'Regional factors in the formation of the Fishermen's Protective Union of Newfoundland'. *CJS* (3) 391-407.

Brym, Robert J., and R. James Sacouman, eds.
1979    *Underdevelopment and Social Movements in Atlantic Canada*. Toronto: New Hogtown Press.

Brym, Robert J., Michael W. Gillespie, and A.R. Gillis
1985    'Anomie, opportunity and the density of ethnic ties: another view of Jewish outmarriage in Canada'. *CRSA* (22) 102-12.

Brym, Robert J., Michael W. Gillespie, and Rhonda L. Lenton
1989    'Class power, class mobilization, and class voting: the Canadian case'. *CJS* (14) 25-44.

Burawoy, Michael
1977    'Social structure, homogenization and the process of status attainment in the United States and Great Britain'. *AJS* (82) 1031-42.

Burstyn, Varda
1985    'Masculine dominance and the state'. Pp. 45-89 in Burstyn and Smith 1985.

Burstyn, Varda, and Dorothy Smith, eds.
1985    *Women, Class, Family and the State*. Toronto: Garamond.

Cairns, Alan C.
1968    'The electoral system and the party system in Canada, 1921-1965'. *CJPS* (1) 55-80.

Cairns, Alan C.
1977    'The government and societies of Canadian federalism'. *CJPS* (10) 695-709.

Cameron, D. R.
1986    'The growth of government spending: the Canadian experience in comparative perspective'. Pp. 21-51 in K. Banting, ed. *State and Society: Canada in Comparative Perspective*. Toronto: University of Toronto Press.

Campbell, Colin, and George J. Szablowski
1979    *The Superbureaucrats: Structure and Behavior in Central Agencies*. Toronto: Gage.

Campbell, Douglas F.
1983    *Beginnings: Essays on the History of Canadian Sociology*. Port Credit, Ont.: Scribblers' Press.

Carroll, William K.
1982    'The Canadian corporate elite: financiers or finance capitalists?' *SPE* (8) 89-114.

Carroll, William K.
  1984    'The individual, class, and corporate power in Canada'. *CJS*
          (9) 245-68.
Carroll, William K.
  1985    'Dependency, imperialism and the capitalist class in Canada'.
          Pp. 21-52 in Brym 1985b.
Carroll, William K.
  1986    *Corporate Power and Canadian Capitalism*. Vancouver: Univer-
          sity of British Columbia Press.
Carroll, William K.
  1987    'Which women are more proletarianized than men?' *CRSA*
          (24) 465-95.
Carroll, William K., John Fox, and Michael D. Ornstein
  1982    'The network of directorate interlocks among the largest
          Canadian firms'. *CRSA* (19) 44-69.
Chamard, John, Victor M. Catano, and Colin Howell
  1983    'Entrepreneurial motivation: some evidence to contradict
          McClelland'. *Journal of Small Business Canada* (1) 18-23.
Chodorow, Nancy
  1978    *The Reproduction of Mothering: Psychoanalysis and the Sociology of
          Gender*. Berkeley: University of California Press.
Clark, S.D.
  1942    *The Social Development of Canada: An Introductory Study with Se-
          lect Documents*. Toronto: University of Toronto Press.
Clark, S.D.
  1948    *Church and Sect in Canada*. Toronto: University of Toronto
          Press.
Clark, S.D.
  1963    'Group interests in Canadian politics'. Pp. 64-78 in J. Aitchi-
          son, ed. *The Political Process in Canada: Essays in Honour of R.
          MacGregor Dawson*. Toronto: University of Toronto Press,
          1963.
Clark, S.D.
  1968    *The Developing Canadian Community*, 2nd edn. Toronto:
  [1962]  University of Toronto Press.
Clark, S.D.
  1976    *Canadian Society in Historical Perspective*. Toronto: McGraw-
          Hill Ryerson.
Clark, S.D.
  1979    'The changing image of sociology in English-speaking
          Canada'. *CJS* (4) 393-403.
Clark, S.D.
  1980    'Development of the social sciences in Canada and the issue

of national autonomy', an inaugural address in the University of Edinburgh.

Clarke, Harold D., *et al.*
1980 *Political Choice in Canada*, abridged edn. Toronto: McGraw-Hill Ryerson.

Clement, Wallace
1975 *The Canadian Corporate Elite: An Analysis of Economic Power.* Toronto: McClelland and Stewart.

Clement, Wallace
1977a *Continental Corporate Power: Economic Linkages Between Canada and the United States.* Toronto: McClelland and Stewart.

Clement, Wallace
1977b 'The corporate elite, the capitalist class, and the Canadian state'. Pp. 225-48 in Panitch 1977b.

Clement, Wallace
1977c 'Macro-sociological approaches toward a Canadian sociology'. *Alternate Routes* (1, 1) 1-37.

Clow, Michael
1984 'Politics and uneven capitalist development: the Maritime challenge to the study of Canadian political economy'. *SPE* (14) 117-40.

Cohen, Marjorie
1984 'The decline of women in Canadian dairying'. Pp. 61-84 in Prentice and Trofimenkoff 1984.

Cohen, Marjorie
1985 *The Razor's Edge Invisible: Women, Markets and Economic Development, 1800-1911.* Unpublished Ph.D. thesis, York University.

Connelly, Patricia
1978 Last Hired, First Fired: Women and the Canadian Labour Force. Toronto: Women's Press.

Connelly, Patricia
1983 'On Marxism and feminism'. *SPE* (12) 153-63.

Connelly, Patricia, and Martha MacDonald
1983 'Women's work: domestic and wage labour in a Nova Scotia community'. *SPE* (10) 45-72.

Copithorne, Lawrence
1979 'Natural resources and regional disparities: a skeptical view'. *Canadian Public Policy* (5) 181-94.

Coser, Lewis
1975 'Two methods in search of a substance'. *ASR* (40) 691-700.

Coward, Rosalind
1983 *Patriarchal Precedents: Sexuality and Social Relations.* London: Routledge & Kegan Paul.

Craib, Prudence W.
1981 'Canadian-based research and development: why so little?'
Pp. 7-22 in K. Lundy and B. Warme, eds. *Work in the Canadian Context: Continuity Despite Change*. Toronto: Butterworths.

Crawford, Craig, and James Curtis
1979 'English Canadian-American differences in value orientations: survey comparisons bearing on Lipset's thesis'. *Studies in Comparative International Development* (14) 23-44.

Cross, D. Suzanne
1977 'The neglected majority:the changing role of women in 19th century Montreal'. Pp. 66-87 in Trofimenkoff and Prentice 1977.

Cuneo, Carl J.
1980 'State mediation of class contradictions in Canadian unemployment insurance, 1930-35'. *SPE* (3) 37-65.

Cuneo, Carl
1985 'Have women become more proletarianized than men?' *CRSA* (22) 465-95.

Cuneo, Carl J., and James E. Curtis
1974 'Quebec separatism: an analysis of determinants within social-class levels'. *CRSA* (11) 1-29.

Cuneo, Carl J., and James E. Curtis
1975 'Social ascription in the educational and occupational status attainment of urban Canadians'. *CRSA* (12) 6-24.

Curtis, James E., Desmond M. Connor, and John Harp
1970 'An emergent professional community: French and English sociologists in Canada'. *Social Science Information* (9) 113-36.

Curtis, James E., and Ronald D. Lambert
1980 'Culture and social organization'. Pp. 79-121 in R. Hagedorn, ed. *Sociology*. Toronto: Holt, Rinehart and Winston.

Curtis, James E., and William G. Scott, eds.
1973 *Social Stratification: Canada*. Scarborough, Ont: Prentice-Hall of Canada.

Curtis, James E., and William G. Scott, eds.
1979 *Social Stratification: Canada*, 2nd edn. Scarborough, Ont:
[1973] Prentice-Hall of Canada.

Curtis, James E., *et al.*, eds.
1988 *Social Inequality in Canada: Patterns, Problems, Policies*. Scarborough, Ont.: Prentice-Hall of Canada.

Darroch, A. Gordon
1980 'Another look at ethnicity, social stratification and social mobility in Canada'. Pp. 203-29 in J. Goldstein and R. Bienvenue *Ethnicity and Ethnic Relations in Canada: A Book of Readings*. Toronto: Butterworths.

Darroch, A. Gordon
  1981    'Urban ethnicity in Canada: personal assimilation and politi-
          cal communities'. *CRSA* (18) 93-100.
Darroch, A. Gordon, and Wilfred G. Marston
  1971    'The social class basis of ethnic residential segregation: the
          Canadian case'. *AJS* (77) 491-510.
Darroch, A. Gordon, and Michael D. Ornstein
  1980    'Ethnicity and occupational structure in Canada in 1871: the
          vertical mosaic in historical perspective'. *Canadian Historical
          Review* (61) 305-33.
Darroch, A. Gordon, and Michael D. Ornstein
  1983    'Family coresidence in Canada in 1871: family life cycles,
          occupations and networks of mutual aid'. *CHAHP, 1982*
          (Ottawa) 31-55.
Darroch, A. Gordon, and Michael D. Ornstein
  1985    'Ethnicity and class, transitions over a decade: Ontario, 1861-
          1871'. *CHAHP, 1984* (Ottawa).
Dasko, Donna
  1988    'Surveys show the other side of Canadians'. *GM* (23 Jan.) D2.
Dawson, C.A.
  1940    *Group Settlement: Ethnic Communities in Western Canada.*
          Toronto: Macmillan.
Dawson, C.A., and R.W. Murchie
  1934    *The Settlement of the Peace River Country: A Study of a Pioneer
          Area.* Toronto: Macmillan.
Dawson, C.A., and E. R. Younge
  1940    *Pioneering in the Prairie Provinces: The Social Side of the Set-
          tlement Process.* Toronto: Macmillan.
de Jocas, Yves, and Guy Rocher
  1968    'Inter-generation occupational mobility in the province of
  [1961]  Quebec'. Pp. 711-23 in Blishen *et al.* 1968 [1961].
Denton, Margaret, and Alfred Hunter
  1982    'Economic sectors and gender discrimination in Canada: a
          critique and test of Block and Walker . . . and some new evid-
          ence'. Ottawa: Women's Bureau, Labour Canada.
Dofny, Jacques, and Muriel Garon-Audy
  1969    'Mobilités professionelles au Québec'. *Sociologie et sociétés* (1)
          277-301.
Douglas, John D.
  1967    *The Social Meaning of Suicide.* Princeton: Princeton University
          Press.
Downey, Lawrence W.
  1968    'A Canadian image of education'. Pp. 213-14 in Blishen *et al.*
  [1961]  1968 [1961].

Drache, Daniel
  1976    'Rediscovering Canadian political economy'. *Journal of Canadian Studies* (11, 3) 3-18.
Driedger, Leo
  1975    'In search of cultural identity factors: a comparison of ethnic students'. *CRSA* (12) 150-62.
Driedger, Leo, ed.
  1978    *The Canadian Ethnic Mosaic: A Quest for Identity.* Toronto: McClelland and Stewart.
Duffy, Ann
  1986    'Reformulating power for women'. *CRSA* (23) 22-47.
Durkheim, Emile
  1966    *The Rules of the Sociological Method*, 8th edn., G. Catlin, ed., S.
  [1895]  Solovay and J. Mueller, trans. New York: Free Press.
Durkheim, Emile
  1951    *Suicide: A Study in Sociology,* G. Simpson, ed., J. Spaulding
  [1897]  and G. Simpson, trans. New York: Free Press.
Eichler, Margrit
  1976    'The prestige of the occupation housewife'. Pp. 151-76 in P. Marchak, ed. *The Working Sexes.* Vancouver: Institute of Industrial Relations.
Eichler, Margrit
  1985    'And the work never ends: feminist contributions'. *CRSA* (22) 619-44.
Engels, Frederick
  1972    *The Origin of the Family, Private Property and the State.* New
  [1942]  York: International Publishers.
Esping-Andersen, Gösta, Roger Friedland, and Erik Olin Wright
  1976    'Modes of class struggle and the capitalist state'. *Kapitalistate* (4-5) 186-220.
Evans, Peter B., Dietrich Rueschemeyer, and Theda Skocpol, eds.
  1985    *Bringing the State Back In.* Cambridge: Cambridge University Press.
Fairbanks, Carol, and Sara Sundberg
  1983    *Farm Women on the Prairie Frontier.* New Jersey: Scarecrow Press.
Felt, Lawrence
  1975    'Nationalism and the possibility of a relevant Anglo-Canadian sociology'. *CJS* (1) 377-85.
Fernandez Kelly, Maria Patricia
  1981    'Development and the sexual division of labor: an introduction'. *Signs* (7) 268-78.
Fink, Deborah
  1987    'Farming in open country, Iowa: women and the changing

farm economy'. Pp. 121-44 in M. Chibnik, ed. *Farm Work and Fieldwork*. Ithaca: Cornell University Press.

Forbes, E.R.
  1977  'Misguided symmetry: the destruction of regional transportation policy for the Maritimes'. Pp. 60-86 in Bercuson 1977.

Forbes, E.R.
  1979  *The Maritime Rights Movement, 1919-1927: A Study in Canadian Regionalism*. Montreal: McGill-Queen's University Press.

Forcese, Dennis
  1981  'The macro-sociology of John Porter'. *CRSA* (18) 651-6.

Forcese, Dennis, and Stephen Richer
  1975  'Social issues and sociology in Canada'. Pp. 449-66 in D. Forcese and S. Richer, eds. *Issues in Canadian Society: An Introduction to Sociology*. Scarborough, Ont: Prentice-Hall of Canada.

Foster, Cecil
  1985  'Buck in luck'. *GM* (12 Jan.) 1-2.

Foulche-Delbosc, Isabel
  1977  'Women of Three Rivers:1651-63'. Pp. 14-27 in Trofimenkoff and Prentice 1977.

Fowke, V.C.
  1973  *The National Policy and the Wheat Economy*. Toronto: University
  [1957]  of Toronto Press.

Fox, Bonnie, ed.
  1980a  *Hidden in the Household: Women's Domestic Labour Under Capitalism*. Toronto: Women's Press.

Fox, Bonnie
  1980b  'Women's double work day: twentieth-century changes in the reproduction of daily life'. Pp. 173-217 in Fox 1980a.

Fox, Bonnie
  1986a  'An examination of "the longest revolution": women's position in Canada, the 1960s to the 1980s'. Unpublished paper presented at the 'Trends in Social Inequality' Conference, University of Western Ontario.

Fox, Bonnie
  1986b  'Never done: the struggle to understand domestic labour and women's oppression'. Pp. 180-90 in Hamilton and Barrett 1986.

Fox, Bonnie
  1988a  'Conceptualizing "patriarchy"'. *CRSA* (25) 163-83.

Fox, Bonnie
  1988b  'Feminist considerations of recent work on status attainment and social class'. Working papers series, Sociology Department, University of Toronto.

Fox, Bonnie J., and John Fox
  1986  'Women in the labour market, 1931-81: exclusion and
        competition'. *CRSA* (23) 1-21.
Fox, Bonnie J., and John Fox
  1987  'Occupational gender segregation in the Canadian labour
        force, 1931-1981'. *CRSA* (24) 374-97.
Fox, John, and Carole Suschnigg
  1988  'Gender and the prestige of occupations'. Working paper, In-
        stitute for Social Research, York University.
Fox, John, and Michael Ornstein
  1986  'The Canadian state and corporate elites in the post-War
        period'. *CRSA* (23) 481-506.
Frank, André Gunder
  1969  Latin America: Underdevelopment or Revolution. New York:
        Monthly Review Press.
Friedmann, Harriet
  1978  'World market, state, and family farm: social bases of house-
        hold production in the era of wage labour'. *Comparative
        Studies in Society and History* (20) 545-86.
Friedmann, Harriet, and Jack Wayne
  1977  'Dependency theory: a critique'. *CJS* (2) 399-416.
Frost, James
  1982  'The "nationalization" of the Bank of Nova Scotia, 1880-1910.'
        *Acadiensis* (12) 3-38.
Gamarnikow, E., *et al.*, eds.
  1983  *The Public and the Private* (London: Heinemann).
Gannage, Charlene
  1986  *Double Day, Double Bind: Women Garment Workers.* Toronto:
        Women's Press.
Gaskell, Jane
  1982  'Education and job opportunities for women: patterns of en-
        rolment and economic returns'. In N. Hersom and D. Smith,
        eds. *Women and the Canadian Labour Force.* Ottawa: Social Sci-
        ence and Humanities Research Council of Canada.
Gaskell, Jane
  1983  'Conceptions of skill and the work of women: some historical
        and political issues'. *Atlantis* (8) 11-25.
George, Roy E.
  1970  *A Leader and a Laggard: Manufacturing Industry in Nova Scotia,
        Quebec, and Ontario.* Toronto: University of Toronto Press.
Gerth, H.H., and C. Wright Mills
  1946  'The man and his work'. Pp. 1-74 in *From Max Weber: Essays in
        Sociology,* H. Gerth and C. Mills, eds. and trans. New York:
        Oxford University Press.

Ghorayshi, Parvin
    1988    'Wives' work and the survival of the farm family enterprise'.
            Unpublished paper.
Goffman, Erving
    1959    *The Presentation of Self in Everyday Life*. Garden City, N.Y.:
            Anchor.
Goldlust, John, and Anthony H. Richmond
    1974    'A multivariate model of immigrant adaptation'. *International
            Migration Review* (8) 193-225.
Goldstein, Jay E.
    1978    'The prestige of Canadian ethnic groups: some new evid-
            ence'. *Canadian Ethnic Studies* (10, 1) 84-95.
Gonick, Cy
    1975    *Inflation or Depression: The Continuing Crisis of the Canadian
            Economy*. Toronto: James Lorimer.
Gorham, Deborah
    1976    'The Canadian suffragists'. Pp. 48-57 in G. Mathesan, ed.
            *Women in the Canadian Mosaic*. Toronto: Peter Martin.
Goyder, John C.
    1981    'Income differences between the sexes: findings from a na-
            tional Canadian survey'. *CRSA* (18) 321-42.
Goyder, John
    1985    'Occupational mobility among women'. Pp. 297-334 in Boyd
            *et al*. 1985.
Goyder, John C., and James E. Curtis
    1979    'Occupational mobility over four generations'. Pp. 221-33 in
    [1973]  Curtis and Scott 1979 [1973].
Goyder, John C., and Peter C. Pineo
    1979    'Social class self-identification'. Pp. 431-47 in Curtis and Scott
    [1973]  1979 [1973].
Grayson, J. Paul, and Dennis William Magill
    1981    'One step forward, two steps sideways: sociology and
            anthropology in Canada'. Paper presented at the annual
            meetings of the Canadian Sociology and Anthropology
            Association. Halifax, Nova Scotia.
Guillet, Edwin
    1963    *The Pioneer Family and Backwoodsman*. Toronto: Ontario Pub-
            lishing Co.
Guindon, Hubert
    1964    'Social unrest, social class and Quebec's bureaucratic revolu-
            tion'. *Queen's Quarterly* (71) 150-62.
Guinsburg, T.N., and G.L. Reuber, eds.
    1974    *Perspectives on the Social Sciences in Canada*. Toronto: University
            of Toronto Press.

Guppy, L. Neil
    1983    'Dissensus or consensus: a cross-national comparison of occupational prestige scales'. *CJS* (9) 69-83.

Hamilton, Nora
    1981    'State autonomy and dependent capitalism in Latin America'. *British Journal of Sociology* (32) 305-29.

Hamilton, Richard F., and Maurice Pinard
    1976    'The basis of Parti Québécois support in recent Quebec elections'. *CJPS* (9) 3-26.

Hamilton, Richard F., and James Wright
    1975    *New Directions in Political Sociology.* Indianapolis: Bobbs-Merrill.

Hamilton, Roberta
    1981    'Working at home'. *Atlantis* (7) 114-26.

Hamilton, Roberta
    1987    'Misogyny'. *SPE* (23) 123-41.

Hamilton, Roberta, and Michele Barrett
    1986    *The Politics of Diversity: Feminism, Marxism and Nationalism.* London: Verso.

Hartmann, Heidi I.
    1984    'The unhappy marriage of Marxism and feminism: towards a
    [1978]    more progressive union'. Pp. 172-89 in A. Jaggar and P. Rothenberg, eds. *Feminist Frameworks: Alternative Theoretical Accounts of the Relations between Women and Men*, 2nd edn. New York: McGraw-Hill.

Harvey, Edward B., and Richard Kalwa
    1983    'Occupational status attainments of university graduates: individual attributes and labour market effects compared'. *CRSA* (20) 435-53.

Hawkins, Freda
    1972    *Canada and Immigration: Public Policy and Public Concern.* Montreal: McGill-Queen's University Press.

Hechter, Michael
    1978    'Group formation and the cultural division of labor'. *AJS* (84) 293-318.

Hedley, Max
    1979    'Domestic commodity production'. Pp. 280-98 in D. Turner and G. Smith, eds. *Challenging Anthropology.* Toronto: McGraw-Hill Ryerson.

Hedley, Max
    1981    'Relations of production of the 'family farm': Canadian prairies'. *Journal of Peasant Studies* (9) 71-86.

Henry, Frances
    1975    Special issue of the *CRSA* (12, 4, part I).

Henry, Frances, and Effie Ginzberg
  1988   'Racial discrimination in employment'. Pp. 214-20 in J. Curtis
         *et al.* 1988.
Hibbs Jr., Douglas A.
  1976   'Industrial conflict in advanced industrial societies'. *American
         Political Science Review* (70) 1033-58.
Hibbs Jr., Douglas A.
  1978   'On the political economy of long-run trends in strike activi-
         ty'. *British Journal of Political Science* (8) 153-75.
Hiller, Harry H.
  1979a  'The Canadian sociology movement: analysis and assess-
         ment'. *CJS* (4) 125-150.
Hiller, Harry H.
  1979b  'Universality of science and the question of national sociolo-
         gies'. *American Sociologist* (14) 124-135.
Hiller, Harry H.
  1980   'Paradigmatic shifts, indigenization, and the development of
         sociology in Canada'. *Journal of the History of the Behavioral
         Sciences* (16) 263-74.
Hiller, Harry H.
  1982   *S.D. Clark and the Development of Canadian Sociology.* Toronto:
         University of Toronto Press.
Hollingsworth, Laura, and Vappu Tyyska
  1988   'The hidden producers: women's work in the 1930s'. *Critical
         Sociology* (15, 1).
Horan, Patrick M.
  1978   'Is status attainment research atheoretical?' *ASR* (43) 534-41.
Horn, Michiel
  1980   *The League for Social Reconstruction: Intellectual Origins of the
         Democratic Left in Canada, 1930-1942.* Toronto: University of
         Toronto Press.
Horowitz, Gad
  1968   *Canadian Labour in Politics.* Toronto: University of Toronto
         Press.
Horowitz, Gad
  1978   'Notes on 'Conservatism, Liberalism, and Socialism in
         Canada''. *CJPS* (11) 383-99.
Horowitz, Irving Louis
  1973   'The hemispheric connection: a critique and corrective to the
         entrepreneurial thesis of development with special emphasis
         on the Canadian case'. *Queen's Quarterly* (80) 327-59.
Houle, Gilles, ed.
  1987   Special Issue on Quebec Sociology, *CJS* (12) 1-149.

House, J.D.
1977    'The social organization of multinational corporations: Canadian subsidiaries in the oil industry'. *CRSA* (14) 1-14.
House, J.D.
1978    'A reply to Myles: power, decision-making, and entrepreneurship'. *CRSA* (15) 406-9.
Huber, Joan, ed.
1973    *Changing Women in a Changing Society*. Chicago: University of Chicago Press.
Hughes, Everett C.
1943    *French Canada in Transition*. Chicago: University of Chicago Press.
Hunter, Alfred A.
1982    'On class, status, and voting in Canada'. *CJS* (7) 19-39.
Innis, Harold A.
1956a    *The Fur Trade in Canada: An Introduction to Canadian Economic*
[1930]    *History*, rev. edn. Toronto: University of Toronto Press.
Innis, Harold A.
1956b    *Essays in Canadian Economic History*. M.Q. Innis, ed. Toronto: University of Toronto Press.
Irvine, William
1976    *The Farmers in Politics*. Toronto: McClelland and Stewart.
[1920]
Isajiw, W. Wsevolod
1978    'Olga in Wonderland: ethnicity in a technological society'. Pp. 29-39 in Driedger 1978.
Jain, H.C., J. Normand, and R.N. Kanungo
1979    'Job motivation of Canadian anglophone and francophone hospital employees'. *Canadian Journal of Behavioural Science* (11) 160-3.
Jansen, Clifford J.
1978    'Community organization of Italians in Toronto'. Pp. 310-26 in Driedger 1978.
Jarvie, I. C.
1976    'Nationalism and the social sciences'. *CJS* (1) 515-28.
Jensen, Joan
1980    'Cloth, butter and boarders: women's household production for the market'. *Review of Radical Political Economics* (12) 14-24.
Jensen, Joan
1986    *Loosening the Bonds: Mid-Atlantic Farm Women, 1750-1850*. New Haven: Yale University Press.
Johnson, Leo
1973    *History of the County of Ontario, 1615-1875*. Whitby Co.: The Corporation of the County of Ontario.

Johnston, William
1985 'Class and economic nationalism: attitudes toward foreign investment'. *CJS* (10) 23-36.
Johnston, William, and Michael D. Ornstein
1982 'Class, work, and politics'. *CRSA* (19) 196-214.
Jones, Elwood
1985 'The Loyalists and Canadian history'. *Journal of Canadian Studies* (20, 3) 149-56.
Kalbach, Warren E.
1970 *The Impact of Immigration on Canada's Population*. Ottawa: Queen's Printer.
Kalbach, Warren E., and Wayne W. McVey
1979 *The Demographic Bases of Canadian Society*, 2nd edn. Toronto:
[1971] McGraw-Hill Ryerson.
Kanungo, R.N, G.J. Gorn, and H.J. Dauderis
1976 'Motivational orientation of Canadian anglophone and francophone managers'. *Canadian Journal of Behavioural Science* (8) 107-21.
Kaufman, Michael
1987 'The construction of masculinity and the triad of men's violence'. Pp. 1-30 in M. Kaufman, ed. *Beyond Patriarchy*. Toronto: Oxford University Press.
Kay, Barry J.
1977 'An examination of class and left-right party images in Canadian voting'. *CJPS* (10) 127-43.
Kealey, Gregory
1980 *Toronto Workers Respond to Industrial Capitalism, 1867-1892*. Toronto: University of Toronto Press.
Kealey, Linda, ed.
1979 *A Not Unreasonable Claim: Women and Reform in Canada, 1880s-1920s*. Toronto: Women's Press.
Keyfitz, N.
1974 'Sociology and Canadian society'. Pp. 10-41 in Guinsburg and Reuber 1974.
King, William Lyon Mackenzie
1973 *Industry and Humanity: A Study in the Principles Underlying In-*
[1918] *dustrial Reconstruction*. Toronto: University of Toronto Press.
Kohl, Seena
1976 *Working Together: Women and Family in Southwestern Saskatchewan*. Toronto: Holt, Rinehart and Winston.
Kornberg, Allan, William Mishler, and Harold D. Clarke
1982 *Representative Democracy in the Canadian Provinces*. Scarborough, Ont.: Prentice-Hall of Canada.

Kornberg, Allan, and Alan Tharp
 1972 'The American impact on Canadian political science and sociology'. Pp. 55-98 in R. Preston, ed. *The Influence of the United States on Canadian Development*. Durham, North Carolina: Duke University Press.
Korpi, Walter
 1983 *The Democratic Class Struggle*. London: Routledge and Kegan Paul.
Lambert, Ronald, and James Curtis
 1973 'Nationality and professional activity correlates among social scientists'. *CRSA* (10) 62-80.
Lambert, Ronald, and Alfred Hunter
 1979 'Social stratification, voting behaviour, and the images of Canadian federal political parties'. *CRSA* (16) 287-304.
Lamy, Paul
 1976 'The globalization of American sociology: excellence or imperialism?' *American Sociologist* (11) 104-14.
Langille, David
 1987 'The Business Council on National Issues and the Canadian state'. *SPE* (24) 41-85.
Lanphier, C.M., and R.N. Morris
 1974 'Structural aspects of differences in income between anglophones and francophones'. *CRSA* (11) 53-66.
Lautard, E. Hugh
 1983 'Regional variation in Canada's cultural mosaic'. *Canadian Issues* (5) 59-65.
Lautard, E. Hugh, and Donald J. Loree
 1984 'Ethnic stratification in Canada, 1931-1971'. *CJS* (9) 333-44.
Lavigne, Marie, and Jennifer Stoddart
 1973 'Women's work in Montreal at the beginning of the century'.
 [1977] Pp. 129-48 in Stephenson 1973 [1977].
Laxer, Gordon
 1983 'Foreign ownership and myths about Canadian development'. Working Paper #50, Structural Analysis Program, Department of Sociology, University of Toronto.
Laxer, Gordon
 1985a 'Foreign ownership and myths about Canadian development'. *CRSA* (22) 311-45.
Laxer, Gordon
 1985b 'The political economy of aborted development: the Canadian case'. Pp. 66-102 in Brym 1985b.
Laxer, Jim
 1973 'Introduction to the political economy of Canada'. Pp. 26-41 in R. Laxer, ed. *(Canada) Ltd: The Political Economy of Dependency*. Toronto: McClelland and Stewart.

Laxer, Robert
   1976   *Canada's Unions*. Toronto: James Lorimer.
Leacock, Eleanor
   1981   *Myths of Male Dominance: Collected Articles on Women Cross-Culturally*. New York: Monthly Review.
Levitt, Kari
   1970   *Silent Surrender: The Multinational Corporation in Canada*. Toronto: Macmillan of Canada.
Li, Peter S.
   1978   'The stratification of ethnic immigrants: the case of Toronto'. *CRSA* (15) 31-40.
Li, Peter S.
   1979   'A historical approach to ethnic stratification: the case of the Chinese in Canada, 1858-1930'. *CRSA* (16) 320-32.
Light, Beth and Alison Prentice
   1980   *Pioneer and Gentlewomen of British North America*. Toronto: New Hogtown Press.
Lipset, Seymour Martin
   1963   'Value differences, absolute or relative: the English-speaking democracies'. Pp. 248-73 in *The First New Nation: The United States in Historical Perspective* (New York: Basic Books).
Lipset, Seymour Martin
   1967   'Values, education, and entrepreneurship'. Pp. 3-60 in S. Lipset and A. Solari, eds. *Elites in Latin America*. New York: Oxford University Press.
Lipset, Seymour Martin
   1968   *Agrarian Socialism: The Cooperative Commonwealth Federation in*
   [1950]   *Saskatchewan*. Berkeley: University of California Press.
Lipset, Seymour Martin
   1968   'Revolution and counterrevolution: the United States and Canada'. Pp. 31-63 in *Revolution and Counter-revolution*. New York: Basic Books.
Lipset, Seymour Martin
   1976   'Radicalism in North America: a comparative view of the party systems in Canada and the United States'. *Transactions of the Royal Society of Canada* (Series IV) (14) 19-55.
Lipset, Seymour Martin
   1985   'Canada and the United States: the cultural dimension'. Pp. 109-60 in C. Doran and J. Sigler, eds. *Canada and the United States*. Scarborough, Ont: Prentice-Hall of Canada.
Lipset, Seymour Martin and Stein Rokkan
   1967   'Cleavage structures, party systems, and voter alignments: an introduction'. Pp. 1-64 in *Party Systems and Voter Alignments: Cross-National Perspectives*. New York: Free Press.

Luxton, Meg
   1980    More Than a Labour of Love: Three Generations of Women's Work in
           the Home. Toronto: Women's Press.
Luxton, Meg
   n.d.    'Knowledge reconsidered: a feminist overview'. Ottawa: Ca-
           nadian Research Institute for the Advancement of Women.
McCallum, John
   1980    Unequal Beginnings: Agriculture and Economic Development in
           Quebec and Ontario until 1970. Toronto: University of Toronto
           Press.
McClelland, David C.
   1963    'The achievement motive in economic growth'. Pp. 74-96 in
           B.F. Hoselitz and W.E. Moore, eds. Industrialization and
           Society. The Hague: UNESCO - Mouton.
Macdonald, L. R.
   1975    'Merchants against industry: an idea and its origins'. Canadian
           Historical Review (56) 263-81.
MacDougall, John
   1973    Rural Life in Canada: Its Trend and Tasks. Toronto: University of
   [1913]  Toronto Press.
McKenna, Marian C.
   1969    'The melting pot: comparative observations on the United
           States and Canada'. Sociology and Social Research (53) 433-46.
McKie, Craig
   1977    'American managers in Canada: a comparative profile'. Pp.
           44-62 in Presthus 1977.
McNally, David
   1981    'Staple theory as commodity fetishism: Marx, Innis and Ca-
           nadian political economy'. SPE (6) 35-64.
McNaught, Kenneth
   1974    'Comment'. Pp. 409-20 in J. Laslett and S. Lipset, eds. Failure
           of a Dream? Essays in the History of American Socialism. Garden
           City, New Jersey: Anchor.
Macpherson, C. B.
   1962    Democracy in Alberta: Social Credit and the Party System, 2nd
   [1953]  edn. Toronto: University of Toronto Press.
McRae, Kenneth D.
   1964    'The structure of Canadian history'. Pp. 219-74 in Hartz 1964.
McRoberts, Hugh A., and Kevin Selbee
   1981    'Trends in occupational mobility in Canada and the United
           States: a comparison'. ASR (46) 406-21.
McRoberts, Hugh A., et al.
   1976    'Différences dans la mobilité professionelle des francophones
           et des anglophones'. Sociologie et Sociétés (8) 61-79.

McRoberts, Kenneth, and Dale Posgate
   1980    *Quebec: Social Change and Political Protest*, rev. edn. Toronto:
  [1976]  McClelland and Stewart.
Magill, Dennis William
   1980    'A Canadian Fabian: the intellectual work of Leonard Charles
          Marsh for the years 1930-1944'. Paper presented at a confer-
          ence on 'The League for Social Reconstruction: Its Economic,
          Political and Social Context'. Toronto.
Maheu, Louis, and Danielle Juteau
   1989    Special Issue on Quebec Sociology, *CRSA* (26, 5).
Makabe, Tomoko
   1978    'Ethnic identity and social mobility: the case of the second
          generation Japanese in metropolitan Toronto'. *Canadian
          Ethnic Studies* (10, 1) 106-23.
Makabe, Tomoko
   1979    'Ethnic identity scale and social mobility: the case of Nisei in
          Toronto'. *CRSA* (16) 136-46.
Makabe, Tomoko
   1981    'A theory of the split labor market: the Japanese experience in
          Canada and Brazil'. *Social Forces* (59) 786-809.
Mann, Michael
   1970    'The social cohesion of liberal democracy'. *ASR* (35) 423-39.
Mann, W.E.
   1955    *Sect, Cult and Church in Alberta*. Toronto: University of Toronto
          Press.
Maroney, Heather Jon, and Meg Luxton, eds.
   1987    *Feminism and Political Economy: Women's Work, Women's Strug-
          gles*. Toronto: Methuen.
Marsh, Leonard
   1940    *Canadians In and Out of Work: A Survey of Economic Classes and
          Their Relation to the Labour Market*. Toronto: Oxford University
          Press.
Marsh, Leonard
   1943    *Report on Social Security for Canada, Special Committee on Social
          Security, Advisory Committee on Reconstruction*. Ottawa: King's
          Printer.
Marston, Wilfred G.
   1969    'Social class segregation within ethnic groups in Toronto'.
          *CRSA* (6) 65-79.
Milner, Henry
   1978    *Politics in the New Quebec*. Toronto: McClelland and Stewart.
Marx, Karl
   1967    *Capital: a Critical Analysis of Capitalist Production*. Vol. 1. New
  [1887]  York: International Publishers.

Marx, Karl
1904 *A Contribution to the Critique of Political Economy*. N. Stone,
[1859] trans. Chicago: Charles H. Kerr.
Marx, Karl
1972 'The German ideology: part I'. Pp. 110-64 in Tucker 1972.
[1932]
Marx, Karl, and Friedrich Engels
1972 'Manifesto of the Communist Party'. Pp. 331-62 in Tucker
[1848] 1972.
Matthews, Ralph
1983 *The Creation of Regional Dependency*. Toronto: University of
Toronto Press.
Maxwell, Mary and James Maxwell
1971 'Boarding school: social control, space and identity' Pp. 157-
64 in D. Davies and K. Herman, eds. *Social Space: Canadian
Perspectives*. Toronto: New Press.
Medjuck, Sheva
1979 'Family and household composition in the nineteenth century: the case of Moncton, New Brunswick'. *CJS* (4) 275-86.
Meisel, John
1975 *Working Papers on Canadian Politics*. 2nd enlarged edn.
[1972] Montreal: McGill-Queen's University Press.
Meissner, Martin *et al.*
1975 'No exit for wives: sexual division of labour and the culmina-
tion of household demands'. *CRSA* (12) 424-39.
Middleton, Chris
1983 'Patriarchal exploitation and the rise of English capitalism'.
Pp. 11-28 in Gamarnikow *et al.* 1983.
Migus, Peter, ed.
1975 *Sounds Canadian: Languages and Cultures in Multi-Ethnic Society*.
Toronto: Peter Martin Associates.
Miles, Angela
1983 'Economism and feminism: a comment on the domestic labour debate'. *SPE* (11) 197-209.
Miliband, Ralph
1973 *The State in Capitalist Society*. London: Fontana.
[1969]
Millman, Marcia and Rosabeth Moss Kanter, eds.
1975 *Another Voice: Feminist Perspectives on Social Life and Social Science*. Garden City: Anchor.
Moore, Steve and Debi Wells
1975 *Imperialism and the National Question in Canada*. Toronto:
privately published.

Morgan, J. Graham
1969 'The development of sociology and the social gospel in America'. *Sociological Analysis* (30) 42-53.
Morgan, J. Graham
1970 'Contextual factors in the rise of academic sociology in the United States'. *CRSA* (7) 159-71.
Morris, Raymond N., and C. Michael Lanphier
1977 *Three Scales of Inequality: Perspectives on French-English Relations*. Toronto: Longman Canada.
Morton, Peggy
1971 'A woman's work is never done'. Pp. 211-29 in E. Altbach, ed. *From Feminism to Liberation*. Cambridge, Mass.: Schenkman.
Murphy, Raymond
1981 'Teachers and the evolving structural context of economic and political attitudes in Quebec society'. *CRSA* (18) 157-82.
Myles, John F.
1978 'Foreign direct investment and Canadian entrepreneurship'. *CRSA* (15) 402-5.
Myles, John F.
1979 'Differences in the Canadian and American class vote: fact or pseudofact?'. *AJS* (84) 1232-7.
Myles, John F., and Aage B. Sørenson
1975 'Elite and status attainment models of inequality of opportunity'. *CJS* (1) 75-88.
Naegele, Kaspar
1964 'Canadian society: further reflections'. Pp. 497-522 in B.
[1961] Blishen *et al.*, eds. *Canadian Society: Sociological Perspectives*, 2nd edn. Toronto: Macmillan of Canada.
*National Income and Expenditure Accounts: The Annual Estimates,*
1982 *1967-1981*. Ottawa: Statistics Canada.
Naylor, Tom
1972 'The rise and fall of the third commercial empire of the St Lawrence'. Pp. 1-41 in G. Teeple, ed. *Capitalism and the National Question in Canada*. Toronto: University of Toronto Press.
Naylor, Tom
1975 *The History of Canadian Business, 1867-1914*. 2 vols. Toronto: James Lorimer.
Neis, Barbara
1988 'Doin' time on the protest line: women's political culture, politics and collective action in outport Newfoundland'. In P. Sinclair, ed. *A Question of Survival: Newfoundland and Its Fisheries*. St. John's: Institute of Social and Economic Research, Memorial University.

Nightingale, D.V., and J.M. Toulouse
  1977   'Values, structure, process, and reactions/adjustments: a comparison of French and English Canadian industrial organization'. *Canadian Journal of Behavioural Science* (9) 37-48.
*1981 Census of Canada: Population: Religion.* Ottawa:
  1983   Statistics Canada.
*1981 Census of Canada: Ethnic Origin: Canada, Provinces, Urban*
  1984   *Size Groups, Rural Non-farm and Rural Farm.* Ottawa: Statistics Canada.
Niosi, Jorge
  1978   *The Economy of Canada: A Study of Ownership and Control.* P. Williams and H. Ballem, trans. Montreal: Black Rose Books.
Niosi, Jorge
  1981   *Canadian Capitalism: A Study of Power in the Canadian Business*
  [1980]  *Establishment.* R. Chodos, trans. Toronto: James Lorimer.
Niosi, Jorge
  1982   'The Canadian multinationals'. *Multinational Business* (2) 24-33.
Niosi, Jorge
  1983   'The Canadian bourgeoisie: towards a synthetical [*sic*] approach'. *Canadian Journal of Political and Social Theory* (7) 128-49.
Niosi, Jorge
  1985   *Canadian Multinationals.* R. Chodos, trans. Toronto:
  [1983]  Garamond.
Nisbet, Robert
  1943   'The French Revolution and the rise of sociology'. *AJS* (49) 156-64.
Nisbet, Robert
  1952   'Conservatism and sociology'. *AJS* (58) 167-75.
Noble, Joey
  1979   'Classifying' the poor: Toronto charities, 1850-1880' *SPE* (2) 109-28.
Nock, David
  1974   'History and evolution of French Canadian sociology'. *Insurgent Sociologist* (4, 4) 15-29.
Noel, Jan
  1984   'New France: Les femmes favorisees'. Pp. 18-41 in Prentice and Trofimenkoff 1984.
Oberschall, Anthony
  1973   *Social Conflict and Social Movements.* Englewood Cliffs, N.J.: Prentice-Hall.

O'Brien, Mary
  1981   *The Politics of Reproduction*. London: Routledge and Kegan Paul.
O'Connor, Julia S., and Robert J. Brym
  1988   'Public welfare expenditure in O.E.C.D. countries: towards a reconciliation of inconsistent findings'. *British Journal of Sociology* (39) 47-68.
Ogmundson, Rick
  1975a  'On the measurement of party class positions: the case of Canadian federal political parties'. *CRSA* (12) 565-76.
Ogmundson, Rick
  1975b  'On the use of party image variables to measure the poliical distinctiveness of a class vote: the Canadian case'. *CJS* (1) 169-77.
Ogmundson, Rick
  1975c  'Party class images and the class vote in Canada'. *ASR* (40) 506-12.
Ogmundson, Rick
  1976   'Mass-elite linkages and class issues in Canada'. *CRSA* (13) 1-12.
Ogmundson, Rick
  1977   'Two modes of interpretation of survey data: a comment on Schreiber'. *Social Forces* (55) 809-11.
Ogmundson, Rick
  1980   'Liberal ideology and the study of voting behaviour'. *CRSA* (17) 45-54.
Ogmundson, Rick, and M. Ng
  1982   'On the inference of voter motivation: a comparison of the subjective class vote in Canada and the United Kingdom'. *CJS* (7) 41-59.
Olsen, Dennis
  1980   *The State Elite*. Toronto: McClelland and Stewart.
O'Neil, Daniel J.
  1981   'American vs. Canadian policies toward their Japanese minorities during the Second World War'. *Comparative Social Research* (4) 111-34.
Ornstein, Michael D.
  1976   'The boards and executives of the largest Canadian corporations: size, composition, and interlocks'. *CJS* (1) 411-36.
Ornstein, Michael D.
  1981   'The occupational mobility of men in Ontario'. *CRSA* (18) 183-215.

Ornstein, Michael
   1983a 'Accounting for gender differentials in job income in Canada: results from a 1981 survey'. Ottawa: Women's Bureau, Labour Canada.
Ornstein, Michael D.
   1983b 'Class, gender, and job income in Canada'. *Research in Social Stratification and Mobility* (2) 41-75.
Ornstein, Michael
   1983c 'The development of class in Canada'. Pp. 216-60 in J. Grayson, ed. *Introduction to Sociology.* Toronto: Gage.
Ornstein, Michael D.
   1984 'Interlocking directorates in Canada: intercorporate or class alliance?'. *Administrative Science Quarterly* (29) 210-31.
Ornstein, Michael D.
   1985 'Canadian capital and the Canadian state: ideology in an era of crisis'. Pp. 129-66 in Brym 1985b.
Ornstein, Michael D.
   1986a 'The political ideology of the Canadian capitalist class'. *CRSA* (23) 182-209.
Ornstein, Michael D.
   1986b 'Regionalism and Canadian political ideology'. Pp. 47-87 in Brym 1986d.
Ornstein, Michael D.
   1989 'The social organization of the Canadian capitalist class in comparative perspective'. *CRSA* (26).
Ornstein, Michael D., H. Michael Stevenson, and A. Paul Williams
   1980 'Region, class and political culture in Canada'. *CJPS* (13) 227-71.
Ostow, Robin
   1984 'Everett Hughes: the McGill years'. *Society/Société* (8, 3) 12-16.
Ostow, Robin
   1985 'Everett Hughes: from Chicago to Boston'. *Society/Société* (9, 1) 8-12.
Palmer, Howard
   1976 'Mosaic versus melting pot?: immigration and ethnicity in Canada and the United States'. *International Journal* (31) 488-528.
Panitch, Leo, ed.
   1977a *The Canadian State: Political Economy and Political Power.* Toronto: University of Toronto Press.
Panitch, Leo
   1977b 'The role and nature of the Canadian state'. Pp. 3-27 in Panitch 1977.

Panitch, Leo
 1981   'Dependency and class in Canadian political economy'. *SPE*
        (6) 7-35.
Panitch, Leo
 1986   'The tripartite experience'. Pp. 37-119 in K. Banting, ed. *The
        State and Economic Interests*. Toronto: University of Toronto
        Press.
Panitch, Leo, and Donald Swartz
 1985   *From Consent to Coercion: The Assault on Trade Union Freedoms*.
        Toronto: Garamond.
Parkin, Frank
 1972   *Class Inequality and Political Order: Social Stratification in Capital-*
 [1971] *ist and Communist Societies*. London: Paladin.
Parsons, Talcott
 1951   *The Social System*. New York: Free Press.
Pentland, H. Clare
 1981   *Labour and Capital in Canada, 1650-1860*. Toronto: James
        Lorimer.
Phillips, Paul
 1982   *Regional Disparities*. 2nd edn. Toronto: James Lorimer.
 [1978]
Pinard, Maurice
 1973   'Working class politics: an interpretation of the Quebec case'.
        Pp. 253-70 in Curtis and Scott 1973.
Pinard, Maurice
 1971   *The Rise of a Third Party: A Study in Crisis Politics*. Englewood
        Cliffs, New Jersey: Prentice-Hall.
Pinard, Maurice
 1973   'Third parties in Canada revisited: a rejoinder and elabora-
        tion of the theory of one-party dominance'. *CJPS* (6) 439-60.
Pinard, Maurice, and Richard Hamilton
 1977   'The independence issue and the polarization of the elector-
        ate: the 1973 Quebec election'. *CJPS* (10) 215-59.
Pinchbeck, Ivy
 1930   *Women Workers and the Industrial Revolution, 1750-1850*.
        London: Frank Cass.
Pineo, Peter C.
 1976   'Social mobility in Canada: the current picture'. *Sociological
        Focus* (9) 109-23.
Pineo, Peter C.
 1977   'The social standing of ethnic and racial groupings'. *CRSA*
        (14) 147-57.

Pineo, Peter C.
  1981    'Prestige and mobility: the two national surveys'. *CRSA* (18)
          615-26.
Pineo, Peter C. and John Porter
  1973    'Occupational prestige in Canada'. Pp. 55-68 in Curtis and
          Scott 1973.
'Poll finds more favoring a socialist government'. *Toronto Star*
  1987    (29 July) A1.
Porter, John
  1965    *The Vertical Mosaic: An Analysis of Social Class and Power in
          Canada*. Toronto: University of Toronto Press.
Porter, John
  1979    *The Measure of Canadian Society: Education, Equality, and Oppor-
          tunity*. Toronto: Gage.
Porter, Marilyn
  1983    'Women and old boats: the sexual division of labour in a
          Newfoundland outport'. In Gamarnikow *et al.* 1983.
Porter, Marilyn
  1985a   'She was skipper of the shore crew'. Labour/Le Travail (15)
          105-23.
Porter, Marilyn
  1985b   '"The tangly bunch": outport women of the Avalon Penin-
          sula'. *Newfoundland Studies* (1)
Porter, Marilyn
  1987    'Peripheral women: towards a feminist analysis of the
          Atlantic region'. *SPE* (23) 41-73.
Poulantzas, Nicos
  1975    *Political Power and Social Classes*. T. O'Hagan, trans. London:
  [1968]  New Left Books.
Pratt, Larry, and Garth Stevenson, eds
  1981    *Western Separatism: The Myths, Realities and Dangers*.
          Edmonton: Hurtig.
Prentice, A., and S.M. Trofimenkoff, eds.
  1984    *The Neglected Majority: Essays in Canadian Women's History*. Vol.
          2. Toronto: McClelland and Stewart.
Presthus, Robert
  1974    *Elites in the Policy Process*. London: Cambridge University
          Press.
Presthus, Robert, ed.
  1977    *Cross-National Perspectives: Canada and the United States*. Lei-
          den, The Netherlands: E. J. Brill.
Presthus, Robert, and William Monopoli
  1977    'Bureaucracy in the United States and Canada: social, attitu-

dinal, and behavioural variables'. Pp. 176-90 in Presthus 1977.

Rasmussen, Linda
  1976   *A Harvest Yet to Reap*. Toronto: Women's Press.

Raynauld, André, Gerald Marion, and Richard Béland
  1975   'Structural aspects of differences in income between anglophones and francophones: a reply'. *CRSA* (12) 221-27.

Redekop, John H.
  1970   'Authors and publishers: an analysis of textbook selection in Canadian departments of political science and sociology'. *CJPS* (9) 107-20.

Regehr, T.D.
  1977   'Western Canada and the burden of national transportation policies'. Pp. 115-42 in Bercuson 1977.

Reitz, Jeffrey G.
  1980   *The Survival of Ethnic Groups*. Toronto: McGraw-Hill Ryerson.

Reitz, Jeffrey G.
  1981   'Analysis of changing group inequalities in a changing occupational structure'. Pp. 167-92 in P. Krishnan, ed. *Mathematical Models of Sociology*. Hanley, Eng.: J.H. Brooks.

Reitz, Jeffrey G., Liviana Calzavara, and Donna Dasko
  1981   'Ethnic inequality and segregation in jobs'. Research Paper No. 123, Centre for Urban and Community Studies, University of Toronto.

Research Committee of the League for Social Reconstruction
  1975   *Social Planning for Canada*. Toronto: University of Toronto
  [1935]   Press.

Reynolds, Lloyd
  1935   *The British Immigrant in Canada*. Toronto: Oxford University Press.

Rich, Harvey
  1976   'The Vertical Mosaic revisited: toward a macrosociology of Canada'. *Journal of Canadian Studies* (10, 1) 14-31.

Richards, John, and Larry Pratt
  1979   *Prairie Capitalism: Power and Influence in the New West*. Toronto: McClelland and Stewart.

Richardson, R.J.
  1982   '"Merchants against industry": an empirical study of the Canadian debate'. *CJS* (7) 279-95.

Richmond, Anthony H.
  1964   'Social mobility of immigrants in Canada'. *Population Studies* (18) 53-69.

Richmond, Anthony H.
  1967    *Post-War Immigrants in Canada*. Toronto: University of Toronto Press.
Richmond, Anthony H.
  1974    'Language, ethnicity and the problem of identity in a Canadian metropolis'. *Ethnicity* (1) 175-206.
Richmond, Anthony H.
  1976    'Immigration, population, and the Canadian future'. *Sociological Focus* (9) 125-36.
Richmond, Anthony H., and W.E. Kalbach
  1980    *Factors in the Adjustment of Immigrants and their Descendants*. Ottawa: Statistics Canada.
Richmond, Anthony H., and Jerzy Zubrzycki
  1981    'Occupational status in Australia and Canada: a comparative study of the native and the foreign born'. *Comparative Social Research* (4) 91-110.
Rinehart, James W., and Ishmael O. Okraku
  1974    'A study of class consciousness'. *CRSA* (11) 197-213.
Roberts, Barbara
  1979    '"A work of empire": Canadian reformers and British female immigration'. Pp. 185-201 in Kealey 1979.
Roberts, Wayne
  1979    '"Rocking the cradle for the world": the new woman and maternal feminism, Toronto 1877-1914'. Pp. 15-47 in Kealey 1979.
Rokeach, M.
  1974    'The place of values in Canadian social science'. Pp. 152-90 in Guinsburg and Reuber 1974.
Romalis, Coleman
  1972    'A man of his time and place: a selective appraisal of S. M. Lipset's comparative sociology'. *Sociological Inquiry* (42) 211-31.
Rosenbluth, G.
  1970    'The relation between foreign control and concentration in Canadian industry'. *Canadian Journal of Economics* (3) 14-38.
*Royal Commission on Bilingualism and Biculturalism, Report*
  1969    Book 3A, 'The Work World'. Ottawa: Minister of Supply and Services Canada.
Rubin, Lillian
  1983    *Intimate Strangers: Men and Women Together*. New York: Harper & Row.
Rueschemeyer, Dietrich, and Peter B. Evans
  1985    'The state and economic transformation: toward an analysis

of the conditions underlying effective intervention'. Pp. 44-77 in Evans, Rueschemeyer, and Skocpol 1985.

Russell, Susan
1987    'The hidden curriculum of school: reproducing gender and class hierarchies'. Pp. 229-47 in Maroney and Luxton 1987.

Ryerson, Stanley
1973    *Unequal Union: Roots of Crisis in the Canadas, 1815-1873.*
[1968]  Toronto: Progress Books.

Ryerson, Stanley
1976    'Who's looking after business?'. *This Magazine* (10, 5) 41-6.

Sachs, Carolyn
1983    *The Invisible Farmers: Women in Agricultural Production.* Totawa: Rowman and Allanheld.

Sales, Arnaud
1985    'La construction sociale de l'économie québécoise'. *Recherches Sociographiques* (26, 3) 319-60.

Sampson, William, and Peter Rossi
1975    'Race and family social standing' *ASR* (40) 201-14.

Samuelsson, Kurt
1961    *Religion and Economic Action.* E. French trans. Stockholm:
[1957]  Scandinavian University Books.

Saul, John Ralston
1987    'A gaping hole in free trade,' *GM* (25 Nov.) A7.

Saunders, S.A.
1936-7 'Maritime provinces and the national policy (comments upon economic regionalism in Canada)'. *Dalhousie Review* (16) 87-97.

Schmidt, Ray
1981    'Canadian political economy: a critique'. *SPE* (6) 65-92.

Schreiber, E.M.
1980    'Class awareness and class voting in Canada'. *CRSA* (17) 37-44.

Schwartz, Mildred
1974    *Politics and Territory: The Sociology of Regional Persistence in Canada.* Montreal: McGill-Queen's University Press.

Seccombe, Wally
1974    'The housewife and her labour under capitalism'. *New Left Review* (83) 3-24.

Seccombe, Wally
1975    'Domestic labour—reply to critics'. *New Left Review* (94) 85-96.

Shalev, Michael
1978    'Strikers and the state: a comment'. *British Journal of Political Science* (8) 479-92.

Shalev, Michael
  1983a 'Class politics and the Western welfare state'. Pp. 27-50 in S. Spiro and E. Yuchtman-Yaar, eds. *Evaluating the Welfare State: Social and Political Perspectives*. New York: Academic Press.
Shalev, Michael
  1983b 'The social democratic model and beyond: two generations of comparative research on the welfare state'. *Comparative Social Research* (6) 315-51.
Shalev, Michael, and Walter Korpi
  1980 'Working class mobilization and American exceptionalism'. *Economic and Industrial Democracy* (1) 31-61.
Shiry, John
  1976 'Mass values and system outputs: a critique of an assumption of socialization theory'. Pp. 36-58 in J. Pammett and M. Whittington, eds. *Foundations of Political Culture: Political Socialization in Canada*. Toronto: Macmillan of Canada.
Shore, Marlene
  1987 *The Science of Social Redemption: McGill, the Chicago School, and the Origins of Social Research in Canada*. Toronto: University of Toronto Press.
Silverman, Elaine
  1984 *The Last Best West: Women on the Alberta Frontier*. Montreal: Eden Press.
Simeon, Richard
  1977 'Regionalism and Canadian political institutions'. Pp. 292-304 in J. Meekison, ed. *Canadian Federalism: Myth or Reality*. 3rd edn. Toronto: Methuen.
Simeon, Richard, and David J. Elkins
  1974 'Regional political cultures in Canada'. *CJPS* (7) 397-437.
Skocpol, Theda
  1980 'Political response to capitalist crises: neo-Marxist theories of the state and the case of the New Deal'. *Politics and Society* (10) 155-201.
Smith, Dorothy
  1974 'Women's perspective as a radical critique of sociology'. *Sociological Inquiry* (44) 7-13.
Smith, Dorothy
  1975 'An analysis of ideological structures and how women are excluded: considerations for academic women'. *CRSA* (12) 353-70.
Smith, Dorothy
  1985 'Women, class and family'. Pp. 1-45 in Burstyn and Smith 1985.

Smith, Dorothy
 1987   *The Everyday World as Problematic: A Feminist Sociology.*
        Toronto: University of Toronto Press.
Smith, Michael R.
 1981   'Industrial conflict in post-war Ontario'. *CRSA* (18) 370-92.
Stasiulis, Daiva
 1980   'The political structuring of ethnic community action: a refor-
        mulation'. *Canadian Ethnic Studies* (12,3) 18-44.
Steedman, Mercedes
 1986   'Skill and gender in the Canadian clothing industry, 1890-
        1940'. Pp. 152-77 in C. Heron and R. Storey, eds. *On the Job:
        Confronting the Labour Process in Canada.* Montreal: McGill-
        Queen's University Press.
Stephens, John
 1979   *The Transition from Capitalism to Socialism.* London: Macmillan.
Stephenson, Marylee, ed.
 1977   *Women in Canada.* Don Mills: General Publishing Co.
 [1973]
Stevens, Gillian, and Monica Boyd
 1980   'The importance of mother: labour force participation and in-
        tergenerational mobility of women'. *Social Forces* (58) 186-99.
Stevenson, Garth
 1982   *Unfulfilled Union: Canadian Federalism and National Unity.* Rev.
 [1978]  edn. Toronto: Gage.
Stevenson, Paul
 1977a  'Class and left-wing radicalism'. *CRSA* (14) 269-84.
Stevenson, Paul
 1977b  'Frustration, structural blame, and left-wing radicalism'. *CJS*
        (2) 355-72.
Stevenson, Paul
 1980   'Accumulation in the world economy and the international
        division of labour'. *CRSA* (17) 214-31.
Stolzman, James, and Herbert Gamberg
 1975   'The national question and Canadian sociology'. *CJS* (1) 91-
        106.
Sundberg, Sara
 1986   'Farm women on the Canadian prairie frontier: the helpmate
        image'. Pp. 95-107 in V. Strong-Boag and A. Fellman, eds.
        *Rethinking Canada: the Promise of Women's History.* Toronto:
        Copp Clark Pitman.
Symons, T.H.B.
 1975   *To Know Ourselves: The Report of the Commission on Canadian
        Studies.* Ottawa: Association of Universities and Colleges in
        Canada.

Taylor, Barbara
   1983   *Eve and the New Jerusalem: Socialism and Feminism in the Nineteenth Century*. London: Virago.
Taylor, Norman W.
   1964   'The French-Canadian industrial entrepreneur and his social environment'. Pp. 271-95 in M. Rioux and Y. Martin, eds. *French-Canadian Society*. Vol. 1. Toronto: McClelland and Stewart.
Thompson, Paul
   1983   *Living the Fishing*. London: Routledge and Kegan Paul.
Tilly, Charles
   1979   'Collective violence in European perspective'. Pp. 83-118 in
   [1969]   H. Graham and T. Gurr, eds. *Violence in America: Historical and Comparative Perspectives*. Rev. edn. Beverly Hills: Sage.
Torrance, Judy M.
   1986   *Public Violence in Canada, 1867-1982*. Toronto: University of Toronto Press.
Traves, Tom
   1979   *The State and Enterprise: Canadian Manufacturers and the Federal Government, 1917-1931*. Toronto: University of Toronto Press.
Trofimenkoff, S.M., and A. Prentice, eds.
   1977   *The Neglected Majority: Essays in Canadian Women's History*. Toronto: McClelland and Stewart.
Truman, Tom
   1977   'A critique of Seymour Martin Lipset's article, "Value differences, absolute or relative: the English-speaking democracies"'. *CJPS* (4) 473-96.
Truman, Tom
   1977   'A scale for measuring a tory streak in Canada and the United States'. *CJPS* (10) 567-614.
Tucker, Robert, ed.
   1972   *The Marx-Engels Reader*. New York: Norton.
Turner, Frederick Jackson
   1970   'The significance of the frontier in American history'. Pp. 12-28 in M. Cross, ed. *The Frontier Thesis and the Canadas: The Debate on the Impact of the Canadian Environment*. Toronto: Copp Clark.
Turrittin, Anton H.
   1974   'Social mobility in Canada: a comparison of three provincial studies and some methodological questions'. *CRSA* (Special Issue) 163-86.
Tyree, Andrea, Moshe Semyonov, and Robert W. Hodge
   1979   'Gaps and glissandos: inequality, economic development, and social mobility in 24 countries'. *ASR* (44) 410-24.

Urquhart, John
   1984   'Canada's government proposes easing limits on foreigners' investment in nation'. *Wall Street Journal* (10 Dec.) 53.
U.S. Department of Commerce
   1986   *Statistical Abstract of the United States*. 107th edn. Washington.
Vallee, Frank G.
   1981   'The sociology of John Porter: ethnicity as anachronism'. *CRSA* (18) 639-50.
Vallee, Frank G., and Donald R. Whyte
   1968   'Canadian society: trends and perspectives'. Pp. 833-52 in
   [1961]   Blishen *et al.* 1968 [1961].
Valentine, Victor
   1980   'Native peoples and Canadian society: a profile of issues and trends'. Pp. 45-135 in Breton, Reitz, and Valentine 1980.
Valverde, Mariana
   1985   *Sex, Power and Pleasure*. Toronto: Women's Press.
Valverde, Mariana
   1988   '"Giving the female a domestic turn": the social, legal and moral regulation of women's work in British cotton mills, 1820-1850'. Unpublished paper.
Van den Berg, Axel, and Michael Smith
   1981   'The Marxist theory of the state in practice'. *CJS* (6) 505-19.
Van Kirk, Sylvia
   1980   *'Many Tender Ties': Women in the Fur-Trade Society in Western Canada, 1670-1870*. Winnipeg: Watson and Dwyer.
Vanneman, Reeve and Fred C. Pampel
   1977   'The American perception of class and status'. *ASR* (42) 422-37.
Veltmeyer, Henry
   1979   'The capitalist underdevelopment of Atlantic Canada'. Pp. 17-36 in Brym and Sacouman 1979.
Veltmeyer, Henry
   1980   'A central issue in dependency theory'. *CRSA* (17) 198-213.
Von Zur-Muehlen, Max
   1982   'Where have all the people gone? Graduate degrees in the social sciences from Canadian universities, 1970 to 1982'. *Social Sciences in Canada* (11,4) 12-13.
Ward, Bruce
   1981   'Coyote condition makes our strikes long, spiteful battles'. *Toronto Star* (5 Aug. 1981) A20.
Watkins, M.H.
   1967   'A staple theory of economic growth'. Pp. 49-73 in W. Easterbrook and M. Watkins, eds. *Approaches to Canadian Economic History*. Toronto: McClelland and Stewart.

Waxman, Chaim, ed.
   1968   *The End of Ideology Debate*. New York: Simon & Schuster.
Weber, Max
   1946   'Class, status, party,' Pp. 180-95 in *From Max Weber: Essays in*
   [1922]   *Sociology*. H. Gerth and C. Mills, eds. and trans. New York:
            Oxford University Press.
Weber, Max
   1947   *The Theory of Social and Economic Organization*. T. Parsons, ed.
   [1922]   New York: The Free Press.
Weber, Max
   1949   *The Methodology of the Social Sciences*. Glencoe, Ill.: Free Press.
Weber, Max
   1958   *The Protestant Ethic and the Spirit of Capitalism*. T. Parsons,
   [1904-5]   trans. New York: Charles Scribner's Sons.
Wellman, Barry
   1983   'Network analysis: some basic principles'. Pp. 155-200 in R.
          Collins, ed. *Sociological Theory 1983*. San Francisco: Jossey-
          Bass.
Wellman, Barry, and S.D. Berkowitz, eds.
   1988   *Social Structures: A Network Approach*. Cambridge: Cambridge
          University Press.
Wiley, N.
   1967   'The ethnic mobility trap and stratification theory'. *Social
          Problems* (15) 147-59.
Willcox-Magill, Dennis
   1983   'Paradigms and social science in English Canada'. Pp. 1-34 in
          Grayson 1983.
Williams, Glen
   1983   *Not for Export: Towards a Political Economy of Canada's Arrested
          Industrialization*. Toronto: McClelland and Stewart.
Wilson, John
   1974   'The Canadian political cultures: towards a redefinition of the
          Canadian political system'. *CJPS* (7) 438-83.
Winn, Conrad
   1988   'The socio-economic attainment of visible minorities: facts
          and policy implications'. Pp. 195-213 in Curtis *et al.* 1988.
Winn, Conrad, and John McMenemy, eds.
   1976   *Canadian Political Parties*. Toronto: McGraw-Hill Ryerson.
Winn, Conrad, and James Twiss
   1977   'The spatial analysis of political cleavages and the case of the
          Ontario legislature'. *CJPS* (10) 287-310.
Wise, S.F.
   1974   'Liberal consensus or ideological battleground: some reflec-
          tions on the Hartz thesis'. *CHAHP, 1974* (Ottawa) 1-13.

Wiseman, Nelson, and K.W. Taylor
  1974  'Ethnic vs. class voting: the case of Winnipeg, 1945'. *CJPS* (7) 314-28.
Woodsworth, J.S.
  1972  *Strangers Within Our Gates*. Toronto: University of Toronto
  [1909]  Press.
Wright, Erik Olin
  1979  'The class structure of advanced capitalist societies'. Pp. 30-110 in *Class, Crisis and the State*. London: Verso.
Wrong, Dennis
  1955  *American and Canadian Viewpoints*. Washington: American Council on Education.
Yancey, W.L., E.P. Ericksen, and R.N. Juliani
  1976  'Emergent ethnicity: a review and reformulation'. *ASR* (41) 391-402.
Younge, Eva R.
  1944  'Population movements and the assimilation of alien groups in Canada'. *Canadian Journal of Economics and Political Science* (10) 372-80.
Zakuta, Leo
  1964  *A Protest Movement Becalmed: A Study of Change in the CCF*. Toronto: University of Toronto Press.
Zeitlin, Irving M.
  1987  *Ideology and the Development of Sociological Theory*, 3rd edn. En-
  [1968]  glewood Cliffs, N.J.: Prentice-Hall.
Zipp, John F.
  1978  'Left-right dimensions of Canadian federal party identification: a discriminant analysis'. *CJPS* (11) 251-77.
Zipp, John F., and Joel Smith
  1982  'A structural analysis of class voting'. *Social Forces* (60) 738-59.

# Author Index